Arnulfo L. Oliveira Memorial Library

Manitou and God

MANITOU AND GOD

North-American Indian Religions and
Christian Culture

R. Murray Thomas

PRAEGER

Westport, Connecticut
London

Library of Congress Cataloging-in-Publication Data

Thomas, R. Murray (Robert Murray), 1921–
   Manitou and God : North-American Indian religions and Christian culture /
   R. Murray Thomas.
     p. cm.
   Includes bibliographical references and index.
   ISBN-13: 978–0–313–34779–5 (alk. paper)
1. Indians of North America—Religion. 2. Indian mythology. 3. Manitou (Algonquian deity).
4. Christianity and culture—North America. 5. Christianity and other religions—North
America, I. Title.
   E98.R3T46 2007
   299.7—dc22   2007027856

British Library Cataloguing in Publication Data is available.

Library of Congress Catalog Card Number: 2007027856
ISBN-13: 978–0–313–34779–5

First published in 2007

Praeger Publishers, 88 Post Road West, Westport, CT 06881
An imprint of Greenwood Publishing Group, Inc.
www.praeger.com

Printed in the United States of America

The paper used in this book complies with the
Permanent Paper Standard issued by the National
Information Standards Organization (Z39.48–1984).

10 9 8 7 6 5 4 3 2 1

CONTENTS

PREFACE

In Algonquin Indian lore, *Manitou* is a supernatural power that permeates the world, a power that can assume the form of a deity referred to as The Great Manitou or The Great Spirit (*Gitche Manitou*), creator of all things and giver of life. In that sense, *Manitou* can be considered the counterpart of the Christians' God. Since early times, the belief in *Manitou* has extended from the Algonquins in Eastern Canada to other tribal nations—the Odawa, Ojibwa, Oglala, and even the Cheyenne in the western plains. Thus, the title of this book, *Manitou and God,* symbolizes the confrontation between American Indian religions and Christian beliefs that first occurred when European settlers arrived in North America, a confrontation that continues even today.

This book has three main purposes:

- To describe in considerable detail the contents of North-American Indian religions as they compare with principal features of Christian doctrine and practice.

- To trace the development of sociopolitical and religious relations between American Indians and the population of European immigrants who, over the centuries, spread across the continent, capturing Indian lands and, to a marked degree, decimating Indian culture in general and religion in particular.

- To identify the modern-day status of North-American Indians and their religions, including (a) progress Indians have made toward improving their political power, socioeconomic condition, and cultural-religious recovery and (b) difficulties they continue to face in their attempts to better their lot.

Now, an explanation is in order about my use of the term *Indians* through-out this book. As history explains, the original inhabitants of the Western Hemisphere were dubbed *Indians* because when Christopher Columbus in 1492 encountered the islands of the Caribbean, he mistakenly thought he had arrived in India—or, more precisely, in what we know today as the Indone-sian islands. So he applied the name *Indians* to the inhabitants of this region that he had chanced upon, the region that Europeans would soon refer to as The New World.

In those early times, Indians themselves had no label that would embrace all original residents of the West Hemisphere and distinguish them from people from other lands, such as the Europeans who now appeared on their shores. Instead, the hemisphere's inhabitants were accustomed to identify themselves by their more specific tribal-nation titles—Bannock, Sioux, Zuñi, Iroquois, Cree, Cherokee, Chumash, Ute, and the like. Therefore, the word *Indians* served as the term European settlers found convenient for referring to the entire collection of original occupants of the land. And *Indian* has continued to be used across the centuries by immigrants to North America and by the descendents of the original inhabitants.

Over recent decades, critics of the term *American Indians* have charged that such an expression is not only historically inaccurate but it offends the people to whom it refers. The alternative term most often substituted has been *Native Americans*. Other options have included *original Americans, original peoples, aboriginal Americans, native inhabitants, First Nations,* and *the first Americans.* However, among the descendents of the continent's earliest resi-dents, these recent identifiers—proposed as politically correct substitutes—have not been universally approved and adopted. Some present-day progeny of the original peoples contend that such expressions as *Native Americans* have not been created by offspring of the earliest inhabitants but, rather, by U.S. Americans and Canadians of Caucasian extraction who have sought to assuage their own guilt feelings that were caused by their ancestors' stealing the earliest inhabitants' lands and defiling their culture. It is apparent that most descend-ants of the original occupants of the continent continue to identify themselves as *American Indians* in their writings and in the titles of their organizations, while also classifying themselves by their traditional tribal-nation names.

Therefore, because *American Indians* continues to be the most common self-designator used by the descendents of the continent's earliest inhabitants, throughout this book I use *Indians* and *American Indians* as the principal iden-tifiers of people from those ancestral lines. Other terms, such as *Native Amer-icans* and *the original peoples,* are used in the book far less frequently.

In addition to the disagreement over what to call the western hemisphere's first humans, a debate continues about how best to label their groups. Should collectivities of Indians be referred to as *tribes, nations, bands, communities,* or what? It is apparent that people who speak and write about such matters often disagree. But in this book, rather than distinguish among them or favor one term over another, I treat them all as synonyms.

· 1 ·

In the Beginning

Before Europeans arrived in North America to establish colonies around the beginning of the seventeenth century, the continent for untold millennia had been inhabited by hundreds of tribal nations that bore such names as Delaware, Choctaw, Mohawk, Seminole, Huron, Hopi, Cheyenne, Apache, Lakota, Winnebago, and more. Where and when those early residents had originated is a matter of continuing debate. Paleontologists, anthropologists, and linguists who study such matters continue to disagree. Most of them suggest that the western hemisphere's initial arrivals came from East Asia, traveling across the Bering Strait in the far-north Pacific when that region was a frozen land mass rather than a string of islands as it is today. However, experts still argue about when the newcomers came, their mode of travel, and the routes they followed to populate the entire western hemisphere, from far-north Canada to the southern tip of South America.

During the opening decade of the twenty-first century, recent geological and genetic findings, along with their diverse interpretations, confronted scientists with an abundance of puzzles to ponder. Did the initial occupants of the Americas appear 10,000 years ago, as many scholars had thought, or did the first one's arrive even 10,000 or 20,000 years earlier? Had those travelers walked all the way from Northeast Asia to what is now Alaska and Northern Canada, then trudged south through valleys on the eastern side of the coastal mountains to eventually—after many centuries—disperse across North America, into Central America, and throughout South America? Or, instead of coming by land, had the migrants fashioned boats of stretched animal skins to sail along the coast of the Bering Sea and down the western shores of North America? Or might some have come by land and others by sea? And did the

Asian travelers arrive during only a few time periods or were there many migrations? (Mann 2005)

Although such matters are still unsettled, there is no question that millions of Native Americans occupied the western hemisphere and, in North America, spoke more than 1,000 languages and dialects by the time Europeans began colonizing the continent (Nagel 1996, 4).

Europeans who had landed before 1600 in what would eventually become Canada, the United States, and the northernmost part of Mexico had not settled down as permanent residents. Leif Erikson, a Norseman sailing from Greenland, had arrived in Eastern Canada during the eleventh century CE and is thus credited with being the first European to visit North America. However, Erikson's followers who attempted to settle permanently in Canada's Newfoundland were forced to abandon their plan when attacked by Indians. Nearly 500 years later, Spanish attempts between 1513 and 1560 to establish a colony in Florida failed, so the successful efforts of Europeans to settle in North America awaited the founding of the British colonies of Jamestown (Virginia) in 1607 and Plymouth (Massachusetts) in 1620, the French colony of Quebec in 1608, and the Spanish venturing north from Mexico in 1598 to settle in what is now the U.S. Southwest.

Apparently most settlers came to America with two motives—one secular, the other religious. The secular motive was to earn a good living—to "get ahead in the world." The religious mission was not only to perpetuate Christianity among the colonists' own descendents but also to bring "heathens"—the American Indians—into the Christian fold. In effect, religious leaders and much of the populace sought to obey Jesus's biblical command to "Go ye into all the world and preach the gospel to every creature" (St. Mark 16:15).[1]

Thus, continuing interaction between American Indian religions and Christian culture began only in the early seventeenth century. Over the following four centuries those interactions would favor the immigrants to the disadvantage of the native peoples and their traditional belief systems. Not until the latter decades of the twentieth century and into the twenty-first century would serious efforts be mounted to repair the damage suffered by Indians in the past.

As explained earlier in the preface, the purpose of this book is to analyze Indians' and Europeans' religious interactions by answering three questions:

1. In the past and at present, how have the contents of American Indian religions compared with Christian beliefs and practices?

2. Over the past four centuries, how did sociopolitical and religious relations develop between American Indians and the European immigrants who, as the centuries advanced, spread across the continent, capturing Indian lands and, to a significant degree, decimating Indian culture in general and religion in particular?

3. What is the modern-day status of American Indians and their religions, including (a) progress Indians have made toward promoting

their political power, socioeconomic condition, and cultural/religious recovery and (b) difficulties they continue to face in their attempts to better their lot?

In the following chapters, the first of those questions is addressed in Part I —The Religions' Components. The second is answered in Part II—History's Path. The third is answered in Part III—Modern Times. To prepare readers for those chapters, the remainder of this introduction explains what is intended by four key terms—*North-American Indian religions, Christian culture, North-American Indians,* and *Indian tribes.*

NORTH-AMERICAN INDIAN RELIGIONS

Indian religions are ways of interpreting life that assign many kinds of invisible spirits a central role for explaining why things happen as they do. There have been, and continue to be, multiple varieties of Indian religions, partly because over the centuries groups of North America's indigenous peoples have been dispersed into different regions of the vast continent and because all religious lore has been transmitted orally from one generation to the next, rather than communicated in a permanent written form.

CHRISTIAN CULTURE

Christianity is a set of ideas and practices based on belief in the Christian Bible as the dominant source of truth about the nature of the universe, about causes of events, and about how people should conduct their lives. Although Christian groups may differ from each other in details of belief or forms of organization, virtually all subscribe to certain fundamental convictions, such as (a) the universe was created by an all-powerful, all-knowing God, (b) Jesus was divine and died to atone for Christians' sins, and (c) the Ten Commandments and Golden Rule are proper guides to moral behavior. Because Christian culture is founded on a long-standing written document—the Bible— rather than on oral tradition, Christian religion has displayed less diversity than have American Indian religions.

NORTH-AMERICAN INDIANS

The question of who qualifies as an American Indian was easy to answer in 1600. Nearly everyone who lived in the Western Hemisphere was at that time a full-blooded Indian. And the relatively few offspring of European explorers, fur trappers, and frontiersmen who mated with Indian women were considered to be only part Indian, often referred to as half-breeds. But by the twenty-first century, the continuing intermixture of ethnicities that had occurred across four centuries made the question of who qualifies as an Indian a highly debatable issue. For example, among U.S. government agencies that provide services to Indians, at least 30 different definitions of *Indian* have been used to identify who deserves such services (Wilkins 2002, 26).

Today, three different definitions of *Indian* are provided by the three most popular methods of identifying Indianness. The *blood-quantum* method focuses on ancestry, the *self-identification* method uses people's claims that they are Indians, and the *tribal-acceptance* method depends on individuals meeting a particular band's criteria for membership.

The blood-quantum standard has been used by the U.S. government for certain legal decisions, with claimants needing to show at least one quarter Native-American ancestry to qualify as an Indian. Thus, a person with one grandparent who was a full-blooded Native American would be considered an Indian, as would an individual with two great-grandparents who were full-blooded Native Americans.

The self-identification criterion has been used in the U.S. national census since 1960. When asked their ethnic background, respondents to census questions could identify themselves as Indians, regardless of the actual ethnic composition of their ancestry.

The tribal-acceptance method requires that an individual meet the membership requirements set by a particular tribe. Therefore, who qualifies as an Indian can differ between one tribe and another.

Because there is no single definition of *American Indian,* and data have often been difficult to collect, there is no agreement about how many Indians have been in North America at any given time. Scholars' estimates of the size of the sixteenth century's indigenous population in the Western Hemisphere range from a low of 8.4 million people to a high of 112.5 million, with the most frequent figure calculated by geographer William Denevan at around 54 million. Denevan estimated that 3.8 million of that total lived north of the Rio Grande River that separates Texas from Mexico (Lord 1997). As another figure, Nagel (1996, 4) speculated that there were between 2 million and 5 million indigenous peoples in North America by 1600. But, of course, no one really knows.

It is apparent, however, that the Indian population was decimated from the seventeenth through the nineteenth centuries, with much of the damage from diseases carried by the Europeans—smallpox, typhus, measles, influenza, bubonic plague, mumps, yellow fever, and whooping cough. The colonists also destroyed Indians' food sources (killing buffalo, trapping beaver), confiscated Indian lands, and waged war, so that by 1900 the U.S. Census reported an Indian population of only 237,196. Historian David Stannard described the slaughter of the hemisphere's native peoples as "far and away the most massive act of genocide in the history of the world" (Lord 1997).

However, the indigenous population decline reversed in the twentieth century when the number of people reported as being Indians in the United States rose at an accelerating pace—from 244,437 in 1920, to 337,499 in 1950, to nearly 2 million in 1990. In 2000, almost 2.5 million U.S. residents identified themselves as Indians. An additional 1,643,345 claimed to be of Indian ancestry mixed with another ethnic line, bringing the total of full-blooded and partially-blooded individuals to over 4 million (Nagel 1996, 5; Ogunwole 2002, 2).

The native peoples of Canada form three classifications—Indians (whose bands are referred to as First Nations), Inuit (also known as Eskimos) and Métis (a French word for Indian/non-Indian mixed ancestry and pronounced MAY-tee). Whereas the First Nations are generally distributed in the lower subarctic region, the Inuit are the original residents of Arctic Canada and Alaska. The history of the native peoples of Canada has been similar to that of the United States, although apparently with less bloodshed. Whereas the number of Canada's aboriginal people declined markedly after the arrival of the European settlers, during the twentieth century population growth renewed. In the 2001 census, 931,235 people identified themselves as Indian and 45,070 as Inuit. The Inuit population increased by 12 percent during the 1996–2001 period, due primarily to high birth rates (twice that of the general population) and longer life expectancy (Inuit 2001).

In summary, the original residents of North America are known as Indians and Inuits. Today, many individuals who identify themselves as Indian or Inuit are of mixed ancestry, with more than one ethnic or racial line represented in their genetic and cultural composition. But knowing that a person is an Indian or Inuit tells us nothing about the person's religious affiliation or worldview, which could be one of many traditional Indian faiths or else of a Protestant, Catholic, Jewish, Muslim, Wicca, humanist, agnostic, atheist, or other persuasion. Many Indians' faith may well be a synthesis of traditional Indian and Christian beliefs, because over the centuries Christian missionaries continually noted—usually with distress—how easily Native Americans adopted portions of Christian doctrine without abandoning tribal practices.

INDIAN TRIBES

Groups of Indians who share the same culture—and, in particular, share the same language—have been variously referred to as tribes, bands, nations, and communities. Questions can then be asked about (a) what qualifies a group to call itself a *tribe* or *band* and (b) how many tribes there are in North America.

In modern times, collectivities of North American Indians also have been identified by a wide range of labels other than *tribe* and *band*. Additional titles have included *Amerindians, native peoples, aboriginal peoples, fourth-world peoples, native-American peoples,* and *first nations.* Those in northernmost Canada and Alaska have been called Inuits, Aleuts, and Eskimos. Tribes usually identify themselves by their traditional names—Algonquin, Arikara, Comanche, Delaware, Huron, Kansa, Osage, Seminole, Shoshone, Sioux, Ute, and the like.

The Canadian and U.S. governments categorize tribes under two types—recognized and unrecognized (nonrecognized). A tribe becomes recognized by meeting government standards and thereby qualifying for privileges and services. By 2006, there were 615 recognized bands in Canada and 562 in the United States (333 in the lower 48 states and 229 in Alaska) (Wilkins 2002, 17; McGregor 2006, ix). The precise number of nonrecognized U.S. tribes is unknown. Giese (1997) identified 245 of them in 1997; most were currently applying for government recognition. Greaves in 2002 (146) estimated the total to be around 200. The Mashpee Wampanoag tribe, which is commonly believed to have celebrated the first Thanksgiving with the Pilgrims in 1621, did not achieve U.S. Government recognition until February 2007.

A 12-regions system of classification is often used for identifying the locations of Indian tribes at the time of the European settlers' arrival (Map 1.1). However, in many cases, tribes and bands today live mainly in other sections

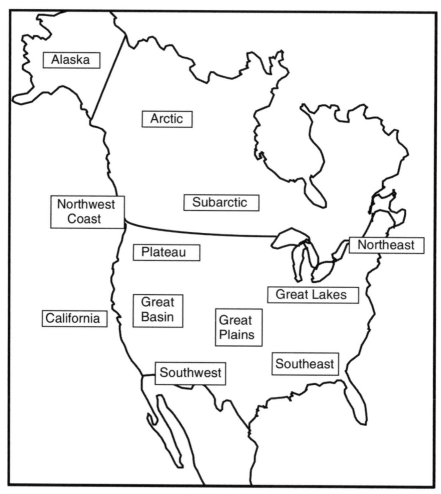

Map 1.1   Regions of North American Indian Tribes' Original Locations

of the continent, chiefly because they were driven out of their homelands by the European colonists over the 1600–1900 era. In this book's later chapters, one of the 12 region designators from Map 1.1 is placed in brackets [ ] following a tribe's name to indicate that group's principal present-day location. If the tribe or band was moved far from its original homeland and now is primarily in a different region, the name of the state or province in which the band now lives will be indicated in brackets following the tribe's title. For example, the Hopi have always lived in the territory they now occupy, so they are designated as "Hopi [Southwest]." In contrast, most of the Choctaw who originally lived in the Southeast (Alabama, Mississippi, Louisiana) were forced by the U.S. Government in the 1830s to relocate in what is now Oklahoma, so references to that tribe appear as "Choctaw [Oklahoma]."

So, with the beginnings of the confrontation between Indians and European settlers now in mind, we move to Part I and its detailed description of traditional Indian religions and Christian culture.

NOTE

1. Biblical quotations throughout are from the King James Bible, first published in 1611.

PART 1

THE RELIGIONS' COMPONENTS

As noted in Chapter 1, this book is much concerned with people's belief systems or worldviews. The term *belief system* refers to a collection of convictions a person uses for interpreting life's events. Such a system typically concerns matters of:

- The purpose of life (teleology);
- The nature of existence and reality (ontology);
- The nature of knowledge and how to distinguish fact from fantasy, truth from falsehood (epistemology);
- The origin of the world and of life forms (cosmology);
- Why things happen as they do (causality);
- Rules governing people's treatment of other beings and the physical environment (morality, ethics); and
- People's rights and obligations (privileges, responsibilities).

An important distinction can be drawn between (a) secular or nonreligious belief systems and (b) religious belief systems. For people who subscribe to a secular worldview, *reality*—in the sense of what actually exists in the universe —is confined to things that can be directly perceived (seen, heard, touched, smelled), including things perceived with the aid of such sensory-extending tools as telescopes, microscopes, radar, x-rays, ultrasound scanning, and the like.

In contrast, for people who subscribe to a religious worldview, *reality* not only includes things directly perceived but also (a) invisible beings (spirits, deities), (b) invisible places (heaven, hell, limbo, nirvana), (c) the invisible continuation of a person's spiritual life after the person's earthly death, (d) ways that spirits and deities influence events in the universe (earthquakes, floods, droughts, individual people's good and bad fortune), and (e) methods by which humans can contact spirit beings (prayer, ceremonies, offerings) to solicit their aid or to express thanks for favors received.

Because this book is about religious belief systems, secular views will rarely be mentioned. The religions of interest throughout the book are those of North American Indians and of the North American Christians who today make up the great majority of the continent's population. The dominant role played by Christian belief in the lives of North America's peoples is reflected in census reports for Canada, Mexico, and the United States. Within those nations' populations during the first decade of the twenty-first century, the proportion of people identifying themselves as Christians was 77 percent in Canada, 96 percent in Mexico, and 85 percent in the United States (Sparks 2006).

The purpose of this introduction to Part I is to set the stage for Chapters 2 through 9 by identifying general likenesses and differences between Indian religions and Christian doctrine. Then, in the following eight chapters, specific examples of such similarities and differences are described in considerable detail under the headings: (a) sources of belief (b) spirits, (c) places, (d) creating the universe, (e) causes and ceremonies, (f) maxims and tales, (g) symbols and sacred objects, and (h) religious societies.

Now consider ways in which American Indian religions and Christianity are alike. Both of those worldviews share the following convictions.

- Reality is not limited to what everyone who has intact sense organs can see, hear, or feel in this world. Reality also includes invisible beings, places, and events that are revealed only to special individuals and, perhaps, only when those individuals are in an altered state of mind.

- Sources of knowledge include trusted authorities, traditions, dreams, and visions.

- Invisible spirits, gods, or deities that created the universe continue to influence natural phenomena (crop yields, epidemics, floods, earthquakes) and affect individuals' lives (health, personal relationships, occupational success).

- People must abide by the spirits' rules of conduct or else suffer unpleasant consequences. Not only is it important to know and obey the rules, but people are also wise to show that they honor and respect the spirits.

- When a personal or general disaster strikes, it is necessary to placate the spirits that have caused the catastrophe. Methods of mollifying the deities include admitting one's wrongdoing, asking to be forgiven, performing acts of penance, promising to reform, and presenting offerings to the spirits.

- One's life span does not end with the death of the body. Rather, an essence of the individual's personality—often called the *soul*—can continue to exist in some form, perhaps as an invisible spirit.

Next, consider ways that American Indian worldviews differ from those of European Christians. When colonists first came to North America, and for centuries thereafter, Indians were seen by the arrivals as ignorant heathen and pagan savages—not because Indians failed to believe in spirits, divine influences on events, and life after death, but because (in the Europeans' opinion) Indians revered the wrong spirits, mistook the nature of divine influence, and held an erroneous idea of humans' after-death destiny. In effect, Indians and Christians agreed on the general contours of religion but disagreed on the details. Yet those details were of sufficient import to alienate the continent's original inhabitants from the European immigrants.

Furthermore, a particularly important way that Indians' and Christians' religions differed was in their form of communication. The European immigrants brought a sophisticated variety of written language in which their religious doctrine was cast. That is, they brought the Bible and its accompanying exegeses and hymns. In contrast, the Indians lacked any mature version of written language, so their beliefs were passed orally from one generation to the next. As a result, the worldview of the immigrant colonists was in a stable form. As time passed, that form was altered in no more than minor ways by such interpreters as ministers and theological scholars. Even today, the most popular Protestant edition of the Bible continues to be the one authorized by King James I of England in 1611. On the other hand, Indian religions, when conveyed orally over the centuries, would often be modified and embellished by each teller of tales who instructed the young in their clan's lore. Consequently, the versions of American Indian worldviews described in Chapters 2 through 9 should be seen as only partially authentic renditions of the beliefs and practices in vogue when Christians settled in North America during the seventeenth and eighteenth centuries. The versions in Chapters 2 through 9 are ones recorded in writing or as audiotapes by Indian and non-Indian researchers from the seventeenth century until the present day.

The varieties of Indian beliefs are so numerous that the examples in Chapters 2–9 represent only a small part of the entire collection. The examples in those chapters were chosen to illustrate the marked diversity that Indian worldviews assumed and not to reveal all available information about those belief systems.

All chapters in Part I are cast in the same pattern. Each opens with a brief definition of the chapter's central topic. Then a Christian version of that topic is described, with the contents of the description drawn from the King James I authorized edition of the Bible, occasionally supplemented with material from a Roman Catholic Bible. The chapter continues with multiple examples of

American Indian religious beliefs and practices that are related to the chapter's central topic. The portrayal of Indian religions is based on depictions of those belief systems in a variety of books and Internet web sites. Each chapter closes with observations about the relationship between Christian and Indian versions of the chapter's main theme.

· 2 ·

Sources of Belief

The attempt to understand American Indian and Christian belief systems can usefully begin with our inspecting the origins of a religion's beliefs and the reasons that a religion's adherents accept those beliefs as true. The following discussion opens with a scheme for interpreting the sources of religious beliefs. The discussion continues with reasons people adopt such beliefs and finishes with applying the interpretive scheme to Christianity and American Indian religions.

THE ORIGINS OF BELIEFS

In addressing the question of how a religion's ideas and practices originate, I propose a set of concepts which, in my estimation, are assumptions on which religious beliefs are founded. It should be recognized that the following interpretation of the sources of beliefs applies only to religious people, that is, to those who are convinced that spirits influence events in the world. Consequently, this proposal does not apply to people who are not religious, such as agnostics, secular humanists, materialists, realists, and atheists.

The central concept in the scheme is that religious convictions are products of a human thought process called *spirit personification*. The word *spirit* means an unseen power that gets things done in the world. *Personification* means attributing human traits to that power. Thus, when accounting for happenings, religious people explain that the world's objects and events are caused by spirits (gods, angels, genies). Those spirits are *personified*, meaning they are invested with human or "person" characteristics—intelligence, motives, desires, ambitions, preferences, and such emotions as joy, anger, love, hate, jealousy, vengeance, envy, guilt, and fear. Spirits also have domains of influence. A spirit whose domain is the entire universe can influence events everywhere and thus deserves such titles as The Great Spirit or Universal God. The domains of other spirits are limited, so those spirits can affect only certain kinds of events—protect people from illness, ensure the safety of travelers, promote success in fishing or hunting, foster the happiness of lovers, control the fate of warriors, cause crop failure, produce earthquakes, and more. In addition, spirits vary in strength. The most powerful can accomplish any feat and can vanquish any rival, so they deserve the label *omnipotent.* Strength is particularly important when spirits compete against each other, as when a virtuous spirit battles a malevolent one. Although spirits are generally invisible, under certain conditions they can inhabit—or can assume the form of—such mundane, visible entities as humans, animals, or inanimate objects (trees, lakes, mountains, rocks, and more).

Within such a spirit-personification worldview, religious beliefs are created by the spirits who then convey those beliefs to selected humans who may either keep the beliefs to themselves or share the beliefs with others.

The spirits transmit the beliefs to humans via five channels of thought or action—prayer, inspiration, dreams, visions, and instruction.

Prayer consists of an individual or group intentionally communicating with a spirit—sending messages to the spirit and, if fortunate, receiving messages from the spirit. Prayers take the form of spoken words, silent thoughts, actions, or ceremonies directed to a spirit in order to offer thanks for blessings already received, to solicit help with problems, or to honor the spirit. The spirit's reply can be either an immediately returned message or a subsequent event—such an event as a bountiful harvest, the supplicant's recovery from an illness, the return home of a loved one, success in battle, or the like. The supplicant's belief in the spirit is strengthened when an expected response to the prayer occurs. The less frequently that prayers appear to be answered, the weaker a supplicant's trust in the spirit is likely to become.

Another communication channel is *inspiration.* For instance, at the time a person is consciously trying to find the answer to a question or trying to solve a problem, a convincing answer comes to mind. In effect, the process of pondering the problem has produced a persuasive insight—a belief that is accepted as true. That insight can be attributed to the miraculous power of an inspiring spirit.

Neither *dreams* nor *visions* are within a person's intentional control but, instead, they operate during altered states of consciousness. Dreams consist of images and messages people receive when they are asleep. Visions are extraordinary sights and sounds that appear to a person in a waking state. Religious beliefs derived from dreams and visions can be either *explicit revelations* of a spirit's words, sounds, and images or can be *symbolic revelations.* A person who receives an explicit revelation need only report precisely what the spirit said or displayed in order to divulge that belief to other people. In contrast, a symbolic revelation disguises its true meaning in garb that must be interpreted if the message—the belief—is to be understood.

Instruction results from a spirit speaking from afar or even assuming a visible worldly form (human or animal) in order to tell people truths they should accept. Instruction is sometimes referred to as *revelation.* In American Indian religions, such instruction has often been offered by spirits disguised as animals—coyotes, foxes, blue jays, bears, and more.

Religions are not all alike in the kinds of people considered capable of receiving messages from spirits or of interpreting messages that appear in symbolic form. Some faiths attribute interpretive power to a limited number of seers. Others extend the power to all members of the faith. Most sects identify conditions that are either necessary for—or conducive to—spirit messages being transmitted to humans. Such conditions can include (a) environmental settings (holy places, ceremonies), (b) physical/mental states (meditation, trance, deprivation) of the individuals who receive spirit visitations, and (c) particular seasons, days, or times of day (harvest season, the summer solstice, December 25, New Year's Day, dawn, midday, sunset).

In summary, this scheme for analyzing the origins of religious beliefs proposes that personified spirits create religious wisdom that is conveyed to selected humans via both conscious channels (prayer, inspiration, instruction) and subconscious channels (dreams, visions).

ACCEPTING BELIEFS AS TRUE

Why do people accept religious beliefs as true and use those beliefs to guide their lives?

I estimate that there are various reasons for such acceptance and that the reasons can differ from one person to another. Consider, for example, the potential influence of such factors as tradition, a line of logic, authority, social pressure, lack of alternatives, and tolerance of ambiguity.

First, when a religious faith has thrived across the centuries, such success can be accepted as evidence that the faith's beliefs and practices are authentic—that the religion's tenets are true and everlasting. A long-standing, unchanging tradition can offer people a sense of security as they attempt to cope with a turbulent, puzzling world.

Second, proponents of a religion may present a line of logic that listeners find so persuasive that they agree with the tenets and practices of the faith.

Third, people who hold positions of authority in a religion's hierarchy—ministers, bishops, priests, shamans—are expected to have intimate knowledge of the religion's beliefs and of the consequences to be expected by individuals who abide by or who violate the faith's doctrine. Therefore, followers of the faith are well advised to accept what the authorities tell them.

Fourth, when all—or at least most—people in a society share the same beliefs about life, there is reason to expect those beliefs to be true, particularly if the majority conduct their daily affairs in a reasonable manner so they apparently are neither stupid nor mad. And even if a person feels that the majority of people have been misled and that their beliefs are no more than illusions, prudence suggests that it would be unwise to question their viewpoints and thereby attract their ire and repercussions. In other words, it would be well not to challenge the majority's convictions and then suffer the widespread disapproval resulting from the challenge.

Fifth, people are prone to accept a religion's explanations about life when those people are unaware of alternative explanations. Consequently, limiting people's access to competing doctrines helps ensure that adherents subscribe to the beliefs of a particular faith.

Sixth, individuals can differ in the extent to which they can bear uncertainty. Some people have a low degree of tolerance for ambiguity about the purpose of life and the nature of the universe and its origins. They become distressed by such answers as "We really don't know the goal of life" or "This is one possibility, but it's just tentative" or "As yet, we can only estimate; we need to learn more." Such individuals find security in beliefs portrayed as universal, unquestionable, everlasting truths. Religions offer such beliefs.

Now, with the foregoing introduction to the origins of belief and to reasons people may subscribe to a particular religion, we consider the sources of the beliefs described throughout Part I, beginning with Christianity and continuing with North-American Indian worldviews.

SOURCES OF CHRISTIAN BELIEFS

Christian beliefs are those found in the Bible, along with subsequent embellishments and interpretations by theologians, pundits, priests, ministers, and evangelists. Christian denominations can vary in their conceptions of who is qualified to receive and explain the religion's beliefs and practices. The Roman Catholic Church is perhaps the clearest example of a hierarchy of belief analysts, with the analysts on the upper rungs of the ecclesiastical ladder regarded as closer to God and thus capable of rendering more authentic versions of belief than do clerics on lower rungs. The pope is at the pinnacle of the hierarchy and thus the most trusted authority about God's intentions. Then the authenticity of belief interpretations descends by degrees through cardinals, archbishops, bishops, priests, and nuns. In contrast, Protestant tradition teaches that each member of the faith is capable of communicating directly with God through prayer, inspiration, dreams, or visions. However, some Protestants—mainly ministers, pastors, and evangelists—are credited with deeper knowledge of the Bible and more accurate skills of analysis. Hence, through sermons, prayer meetings, and revival sessions such experts guide parishioners in understanding their faith's doctrine and how to apply the doctrine in everyday living.

Consider, now, examples of beliefs in the Bible that Christians assume were received from God through prayer, inspiration, dreams, visions, and instruction.

Prayer

Praying in Christian culture assumes many forms. Individuals can engage in silent moments of meditation, in spoken pleas for help or expressions of thanks at mealtime and bedtime, and in such acts as fingering prayer beads, lighting candles, or gesturing (making the sign of the cross). A group, during a church service or special prayer meeting, may recite in unison a prayer from the Bible, sing a prayerful hymn or anthem, or listen to an individual—a pastor or evangelist—voice a supplication, with the audience at the close of the prayer endorsing the appeal by uttering "Amen." (See Chapter 6 for examples of prayer.)

Inspiration

The thought process of inspiration can be credited for many of the detailed beliefs in Christian culture. The contents of the Bible that are not attributed to direct revelations from God are generally considered the result of divine inspiration. Such is also the case of many writings about Christianity over the past two millennia—St. Augustine's *Immortality of the Soul,* Dante's *Inferno* and *Purgatorio,* Jonathan Edwards' *The Justice of God in the Damnation of Sinners,* C.S. Lewis' *Mere Christianity,* and many thousands more. Likewise, parishioners often regard the content of weekly sermons in Christian churches as inspired truths. Thus, inspiration, as a source of belief, is apparently responsible for a large portion of most Christians' worldview.

Dreams

Not only has dreaming been reported in the Bible, but Christians over the centuries have experienced dreams of a religious nature. Five functions of dreams in Christian culture have been those of providing information, giving advice, prophesying future events, promoting God-and-person dialogue, and frightening people.

As a prime New Testament example of dreams' information function, prior to Jesus's birth God sent an angel to inform Joseph in a dream that Joseph could properly wed the pregnant Mary, because the infant Jesus whom Mary carried in her womb was not the result of an illicit sexual affair. Instead, the pregnancy was divine, conceived in Mary by the Holy Ghost (Matthew 1:20).

Three examples of advice are (a) God commanding Abemelech in a dream to return Sarah to her husband (Genesis 20:3–7), (b) God ordering Jacob in a dream to return to his own homeland (Genesis 31:10–13), and (c) God sending an angel in a dream to advise Joseph to take his wife Mary and infant Jesus to Egypt so as to prevent King Herod from slaying the child (Matthew 2:13).

The prophecy role of dreams is illustrated in God's telling Moses, Aaron, and Miriam, "If there be a prophet among you, I the Lord will make myself known unto him...and will speak to him in a dream" (Numbers 12:6). Thereafter, prophets' predictions would often come to them in dreams.

The manner in which God promotes dialogue with humans is shown by the Bible passage: "In Gideon the Lord appeared to Solomon in a dream by night, and the Lord said, 'Ask what I shall give thee.'" And Solomon replied, "'Give [me] an understanding heart to judge thy people, that I may discern between good and bad'" (1 Kings 3:5, 9).

The frightening function of dreams was referred to by Job when he complained to the Lord, "Thou scarest me with dreams" (Job 7:14).

The content of dreams in Judeo-Christian tradition can be either explicit or symbolic. As noted earlier, dreams are explicit whenever their images tell exactly what they mean. Dreams are symbolic whenever their meaning is cloaked in imagery or in events that must be interpreted to reveal their intent.

When God spoke to Laban in a dream, the meaning was explicit: "Take heed that thou speak not to Jacob either good or bad" (Genesis 31:24). In contrast, the images in a dream of the prophet Daniel were symbolic—four great beasts coming from the sea. They included a lion, a bear, a leopard, and a fantastic ten-horned creature with iron teeth, brass claws, and human eyes. In Daniel's interpretation, the beasts symbolized a sequence of four kingdoms that would rule in the Middle East, with the fourth kingdom destroying the other three (Daniel, 7:1–28).

Sometimes a dreamer is able to explain the meaning of symbolic images, as did Daniel. But in many cases, individuals with special insight are needed to interpret the codes and signs. Such was the case when the Jewish slave Joseph in the book of Genesis revealed what Pharaoh's dreams foretold. Pharaoh had dreamt of seven well-fed cows followed by seven starving cows, and then of seven healthy ears of corn on a stalk along with seven dried-out, shrunken ears. Pharaoh was distressed about what his dream might portend until Joseph solved the puzzle by explaining that seven years of good harvests would be followed by seven of drought, so the Egyptians would be wise to store up foodstuffs during the seven years of plenty for use during the seven years of famine (Genesis 41:1–31).

Visions

Visions—as extraordinary sights and sounds that appear to people in their waking state—can achieve for Christians the same range of functions as do dreams. Visions are able to inform, advise, prophesy, foster God-and-humans dialogue, and frighten.

Perhaps the best-known biblical vision involved a Jewish tentmaker named Saul, born in the city of Tarsus, whose life was transformed in his early adulthood by a blinding, miraculous appearance of Jesus while Saul traveled on the road to Damascus. Jesus's words to Saul converted the tentmaker to Christianity, so that Saul changed his name to Paul and thereafter served as the missionary mainly responsible for bringing non-Jews into the Christian fold during the first century CE. The vision not only informed and advised Saul, but also astonished and frightened him (Acts 9:1–22; 13; 9).

An instance of a prophesy was Daniel's vision in the Old Testament that enabled him to predict the succession of kingdoms that would rule (Daniel 12:1–45).

Across the centuries and up to the present day, dreams and visions have conveyed religious meanings to many Christians, both to leaders—popes, priests, ministers, evangelists—and to ordinary parishioners who accept the messages as guides to their beliefs and behavior.

Instruction

Instruction can be divided into two major types—direct and mediated. It is direct when it involves God revealing a truth or issuing a command to a selected person or group. Instruction is mediated when the person to whom God has spoken then serves as an intermediary who conveys God's message to others. For example, in the biblical book of Exodus (20:2–17), God dictated to Moses ("mouth to mouth...and not in dark speeches" [Numbers 12:8]) ten commandments embossed on stone; then Moses became the mediator who passed the commandments on to the people of Israel. Throughout the Bible's Old Testament, God is also reported to have spoken directly to a variety of other Jewish leaders—Abraham, Joshua, David, Solomon, and more—who then told their followers the content of such messages.

A further example of a mediator is St. Paul whose letters to members of churches in Rome, Corinth, and Ephesus appear in the Bible's New Testament. In his epistle to the Ephesians, he contended that what he was telling them were truths he had received directly from God "by revelation" (Ephesians 3:3).

The four gospels in the Bible's New Testament (Matthew, Mark, Luke, John) tell of Jesus—in his earthly guise as the Son of God—issuing truths and advice to his disciples and to audiences that attended his sermons. Hence, his lectures might be viewed as a combination of direct and indirect instruction, since he is depicted in the gospels as both divine (the originator of truths) and human (the teller of truths to ordinary earthlings).

Mediated instruction can become a two-stage process. At the first stage, a person who receives a communication directly from God can transmit its content to others (as through the Bible); those others then convey the message to additional people. Such is the case with the preaching of today's ministers and priests and the lessons taught by missionaries and Sunday school teachers. In delivering homilies, pastors typically use the Bible in two ways. The first involves the pastor quoting a passage of biblical scripture, then interpreting the passage (offering an exegesis) to show what the passage means in relation to historical events and people's daily lives. Here are three examples of verses that provide themes for such sermons.

Functions of mercy, truth, and fear. By mercy and truth iniquity is purged, and by fear of the Lord men depart from evil. (Proverbs 16:6).

Steadfast faith in Jesus. Blessed are ye, when men shall hate you, and when they shall separate you from their company, and shall reproach you, and cast out your name as evil, for the Son of man's [Jesus's] sake. Rejoice ye in that day, and leap for joy, for, behold, your reward is great in heaven. (St. Luke, 6:22)

The end of the world. But the day of the Lord will come as a thief in the night, in which the heavens shall pass away with a great noise, and the elements shall melt with fervent heat, the earth also and the works therein shall be burned up. (2 Peter 3:10)

A second way of using the Bible consists of a minister or priest selecting a topic as the focus of discourse, then drawing on relevant passages of scripture to illustrate the Bible's pertinence for that topic. Over the centuries, typical themes of such instruction have been:

What It Means to Obey the Lord

The Wages of Sin

The Nature of Charity

That Old Deluder Satan

Men's and Women's Roles

Sacrifice as a Virtue

The Rewards of Chastity.

Summary

In the foregoing discussion, God was identified as the originator of Christian beliefs, with the beliefs then communicated to humans through prayer, inspiration, dreams, visions, and instruction. Christians can differ among themselves in how much faith they invest in each of those sources. Some people accept all five as persuasive bases of conviction. Others would trust prayer and inspiration but not dreams and visions. Still others would place their confidence in the interpretations of particular mediators, such as specific priests or evangelists.

SOURCES OF INDIAN BELIEFS

Who deserves credit for creating the beliefs and practices of Indian faiths and disseminating them throughout the populace?

Like Christianity, Indian religions identify spirits as the originators of their beliefs, with the beliefs then conveyed from the spirits to humans via prayer, dreams, visions, inspiration, and instruction. In Christian tradition, a single all-knowing and all-powerful God is the creator of all truths. Among Indian religions, as in Christian doctrine, there are monotheistic varieties of faith that identify a single Great Spirit as the source of beliefs. But there are also polytheistic Indian religions that have various spirits as the creators of beliefs and practices bearing on particular aspects of life—personal health, weather conditions, warfare, and more.

Although Indian religious beliefs have been conveyed to recipients through the same channels as have Christianity's beliefs—prayer, inspiration, dreams, visions, and instruction—the proportion of each source and the manner of using each has differed between Indian and Christian traditions. For example, Indian religions have accorded dreams and visions a far larger role in conveying beliefs to people than has Christianity; and Indian lore has placed prayer at the core of a greater variety of ceremonies than has Christian dogma.

It is also important to recognize that Indians' religious ideas have been far more diverse than have Christians'. As noted in Chapter 1, an especially influential factor behind such diversity has been Native Americans' lack of a written language. True, a few tribes invented pictographs to communicate ideas, but the drawings have been too crude to convey more than the simplest of meanings. As a result, until modern times, oral language was the medium through which religious notions were spread, and that mode required face-to-face contact between members of Indian communities. Christians, in contrast, could spread the gospel by sending printed accounts—especially the Bible—to recipients near and far, thereby maintaining a considerable consistency of belief from one place to another and one era to another.

Now consider how Indian faiths have transmitted beliefs from spirits to humans.

Prayer

A host of rituals in Indian cultures have served such purposes of prayer as those of thanking spirits for their beneficence, pleading for aid in times of trouble, and honoring the spirits. Some ceremonies have been shared among numerous tribes, whereas others have been limited to a few bands. For instance, the annual Sun Dance—whose intent included renewing nature (sun, sky, earth), bringing victory in battle, healing the sick, and testing warriors' courage—has been practiced by a wide range of tribes, particularly those of the Great Plains (Waldman 1999, 195). In contrast, kachina ceremonies have been limited to the Hopi, Navajo, and Zuñi [Southwest]. (See Chapter 6 for descriptions of rituals.)

Dreams

In virtually all American Indian communities over the centuries, dreams have served as principal media through which people receive messages from spirits. As early as 1611, French missionaries (Gabriel Sagard and Jean de Brébeuf) described the role of dreaming among the Huron and Iroquois [Northeast, Great Lakes]. Like members of most other tribes, young Huron and Iroquois men would fast for weeks in order to experience dreams in which spirits would bless them with special powers and teach them sacred chants and rituals.

The dream spirit would then become a lifelong protector and helper whose aid and abilities could be solicited through prayers and tobacco offerings. In dreams, the dreaming soul—an aspect of self that travels in visions away from the body—could contact the dream spirit and receive instructions. Dreams were considered by many native groups to be the most valid means for communicating with the spiritual powers and the primary basis of religious knowledge (Irwin 1996).

Dreams can be either spontaneous (occurring during sleep without the dreamer's effort) or intentionally induced through fasting and magic formulas. An example of a person's extraordinary physical state that stimulated a prophetic dream was the experience of the Oglala Sioux [Great Plains] holy man Black Elk (1863–1950) during an illness at age nine.

> Then I was standing on the highest mountain of them all, and round about beneath me was the whole hoop of the world...and I saw that the sacred hoop of my people was one of many hoops that made one circle, wide as daylight and as starlight, and in the center grew one mighty flowering tree to shelter all the children.
>
> (Neihardt 1932/1979)

As already mentioned, the content of dreams can be either explicit or symbolic. The meaning of explicit content is quite obvious to the dreamer, such as a name to adopt (Bold Bear, Swift Deer, Morning Star), an action to take (erect a teepee, trap beaver, seek a bride), or a place to visit (sacred mountain, nearby tribe). However, dreams' meanings can also be hidden in symbols. In that case, an interpreter is needed to reveal the concealed intent. The interpreter is usually a shaman—a respected seer skilled in diagnosing illness and foretelling such future events as a dreamer's vocational destiny, marital fate, success in warfare, death, or reincarnation.

Many religious innovations in the past were attributed to dreams, such as the designs of the Ghost Dance shirts in the 1890s (Irwin 1996, 170). Images received in dreams often became the source of new rituals, with the portrayed rite then becoming a possession of the dreamer's family and thereafter enacted in the manner determined by the family.

Among the Sioux [Great Plains], villagers were particularly impressed by individuals whose dream revelations were frequent and persuasive. Such individuals were known as Dreamers, who sought to maintain their prestige by occasionally scheduling public tests of their powers. Hassrick (1964) described a typical demonstration in which a Dreamer named Brave Buffalo dressed himself in a buffalo hide, complete with head and horns, and painted a circle on his back to serve as a target. Then competing Dreamers would shoot arrows at the target.

> But a Dreamer who was strong could deflect the missiles. These exhibitions were apparently required of all neophytes to prove their power, as

a kind of final examination. [Such] displays were also given to reestablish in the minds of the people the mystical potency of [a Dreamer's] abilities.

(Hassrick 1964, 279)

Typical kinds of Indian dreams are illustrated in the following three examples. The first was reported by Henry Rowe Schoolcraft (1793–1864) when he was in charge of several U.S. Government Indian agencies during the early decades of the nineteenth century. In his official capacity, Schoolcraft mastered the Chippewa [Northeast] language and spent much time in Indian villages, where he recorded traditional stories told by residents. A tale entitled *Iosco—A Visit to the Sun and Moon* concerned six youths who set out to reach the sun. During their adventure they were guided by messages that came in dreams to the eldest youth, Iosco.

Last night my [guardian] spirit appeared to me, and told me to go south, and that but a short distance beyond the spot we left yesterday, we should come to a river with high banks. By looking off in its mouth, we should see an island, which would approach to us....He then informed me that we must return south and wait at the river until the day after tomorrow. I believe all that was revealed to me in this dream, and that we shall do well to follow it.

(Williams 1956, 140)

Next is the second dream example. At the close of the American Civil War, the Union leader who drafted the terms of the Confederacy's surrender was Ely Parker, an Iroquois chief whom the South's General Robert E. Lee described as "the one real American" involved in the affair. Historical accounts of Parker's life tell that in 1828, four months before his birth at the Tonawanda Seneca reservation in Indian Falls (New York), Parker's mother dreamed that she saw a broken rainbow stretching from the reservation to the home of Indian agent Erastus Granger in the city of Buffalo. Distressed at this vision, she visited a Seneca dream interpreter to learn its meaning. The Seneca shaman told her:

A son will be born to you who will be distinguished among his nation as a peacemaker; he will become a white man as well as an Indian, with great learning; he will be a warrior for the palefaces; he will be a wise white man, but will never desert his Indian people or "lay down his horns as a great Iroquois chief"; his name will reach from the East to the West, the North to the South, as great among his Indian family and the palefaces. His sun will rise on Indian land and set on the white man's land. Yet the land of his ancestors will fold him in death.

(Yupanqui 1998)

As the decades advanced, the interpreter's prophecy came true.

Now to the third dream. As a young adult, an Indian named White Loon recalled that at age 10 his grandparents prepared a small wigwam in which he would sleep as he engaged in his tribe's puberty rite. To prepare for the event, he fasted, and then his grandmother told him that in his sleep he would be visited by spirits offering gifts. But he should not accept the gifts of the first visitor, because that one would be a deceiver and lead him to destruction. The boy's first four nights in the wigwam were without dreams. However, on the fifth night, a large, beautiful bird appeared in a dream, offering the lad attractive presents. In keeping with his grandmother's advice, he refused the gifts, and immediately the large bird sank into the form of a chickadee. The next two nights were dreamless, but on the eighth night another great bird appeared "and I determined to accept its gift, for I was tired of waiting and of being confined in my little fasting wigwam" (Crisp 2006).

> [The bird] took me far to the north where everything was covered with ice. There I saw many of the same kind of birds. Some were very old. They offered me long life and immunity from disease. It was quite a different blessing from that which the chickadee had offered, so I accepted. Then the bird brought me to my fasting wigwam again. When he left me, he told me to watch him before he was out of sight. I did so and saw that he was a white loon. In the morning when my grandmother came to me, I told her of my experience with the white loons and she was very happy about it, for the white loons are supposed to bless very few people. Since then, I have been called White Loon.
>
> (Crisp 2006)

Visions

Dreams and visions are so intimately linked in Indian cultures that it is often difficult to determine if a message or image from the spirits has come during a person's sleep or during a trance when the recipient was awake.

Sometimes a vision would suddenly appear as an unexpected, spontaneous event, not sought by its receiver. However, most Indian visions have been the products of intentional *vision quests*. A great many of Native North Americans' most significant religious convictions are ones acquired during quests. The search for knowledge and power has typically been attempted around the age of puberty, during the mid-teens, or in early adulthood as a means of charting the quester's future—identifying a guardian spirit, adopting a propitious name, and furnishing power.

Potential questers could not hope for success if they were not pure in body and spirit. Thus, a typical search began—and still begins today—with a purification rite in a *sweat lodge,* which is the Indian counterpart of a Scandinavian sauna. During a sweat bath, physical and spiritual impurities are expected to ooze from the body in globules of perspiration.

A typical sweat lodge (*inipi*) consists of a framework of 12 to 16 willow poles stuck into the ground and covered with hides or blankets. The lodge opens to the west from whence storms come (Figures 2.1 and 2.2). The Sioux [Great Plains] believe the deity *Wakinyan*—the Thunderer—lives in the west. The sweat lodge symbolizes the universe, with a round hole (fire pit) in the middle of its sage-covered earthen floor. The pit symbolizes the center of the universe where the supreme spirit, *Wakan Tanka,* lives.

A sweat-bath ceremony usually begins with the naked participants—perhaps five or six—entering through the doorway and saying a prayer to *Wakan Tanka,* whom the group's leader asks to purify the members during the ritual. The members sit in a circle around the fire pit. To assist with the ceremony, a young woman periodically brings red-hot stones on forked sticks from a fire outside and places the stones in the pit. Or the leader accepts the stick at the doorway and gingerly carries the stone to the fire pit. When the pit has been filled, the leader points a sacred tobacco pipe to the four directions, to heaven, and to the earth. He lights the pipe, smokes it, and passes it around the group, with each member smoking it briefly.

Next, a flap is pulled down to cover the door opening, casting the interior of the lodge into complete darkness except for the glow of the stones. When the leader pours water on the scorching rocks, clouds of steam fill the lodge, causing the occupants to sweat profusely.

During the sweat bath, the participants pray in the four directions, occasionally drink water, have newly heated stones replace the original ones, and smoke the sacred pipe. At the end, the door flap is opened, the group exists, and a final prayer is offered to the Great Spirit. Now purified, those among the participants who are seeking a spiritual revelation are ready to begin their vision quest. (Hassrick 1964, 266–295; Kehoe 1981, 360; Inipi lodge 2006).

The seeker of a vision starts by traveling away from the village to a mountain, grove, lake, or rock formation that seems to be an auspicious site for

Figure 2.1   Sweat Lodge Frame.

Figure 2.2   Hide-Covered Sweat Lodge.

encountering a beneficent apparition. Over the coming days and nights, the seeker engages in austerities and self torture—fasting, braving the cold, lying exposed to the burning sun, praying, and perhaps lashing or cutting his flesh. Such self-torment is intended to elicit the sympathy of a powerful supernatural spirit that pities the quester enough to reveal itself in a visible form—typically that of an animal—and to confer its sacred symbol on the supplicant, teach the seeker the spirit's song, and promise lifelong aid and power at times of the seeker's need.

As with dreams, the content of a vision can be either explicit or symbolic. If symbolic, then the quester must find an interpreter—usually a shaman—to solve the vision's puzzle.

Sweat baths have been used on numerous occasions other than that of preparing for a vision quest. The intent of the bath can be to purify oneself before any religious festival, to generate hints about the future, to seek good fortune during an intended venture (warfare, a trip, a love affair), or to guide a critical decision, such as about an occupational opportunity (becoming a shaman or artist) or about joining one of the tribe's secret societies.

Many features of Indian cultures are said to have originated from visions. For example, consider the tale of how fire came to the six Iroquois Confederacy nations—Cayuga, Mohawk, Oneida, Onondaga, Seneca, Tuscarora [Northeast].

According to legend, a 13-year-old Mohawk lad—who was named Three Arrows because of his archery skill and stealth in hunting—went to a sacred mountain cave where he fasted for days in the hope of being blessed with a prophetic vision. During his vigil, Three Arrows prayed to the Great Spirit, begging that his clan's spirit would appear and reveal what the boy's lifetime guardian animal or bird would be. Five days and nights passed without a vision. But on the sixth night, when Three Arrows was desperately weary from hunger and anxiety, he cried out to the Great Spirit, "Have pity on he who stands humbly before thee. Let a spirit or a sign from beyond the Thunderbird come before tomorrow's sunrise."

Suddenly, a great clap of thunder sounded, lightning flashed across the sky in the form of a flaming arrow, and the vision of a giant bear rose beside the boy. The bear told the lad, "Your clan has heard your prayer. Tonight you will learn a great mystery which will bring help and gladness to all your people." Then the bear disappeared in blaze of lightning. Three Arrows was next startled by a scratching sound. As he squinted into the distance to find the cause, he saw a fierce wind scraping two young balsam trees against each other until the trees began to smoke and then burst into flame.

> Three Arrows had never seen fire of any kind at close range, nor had any of his people. . . . Then he thought of his vision, his clan spirit, the bear, and its message. This was the mystery which he was to reveal to his people. The blazing arrow in the sky was to be his totem and his new name— Blazing Arrow.
>
> At daybreak, Blazing Arrow broke two dried sticks from what remained of one of the balsams. He rubbed them violently together, but nothing happened. "The magic is too powerful for me," he thought. Then a picture of his clan and village formed in his mind, and he patiently rubbed the hot sticks together again. His willpower took the place of his tired muscles. Soon a little wisp of smoke greeted his renewed efforts, then came a bright spark on one of the sticks. Blazing Arrow waved it as he had seen the fiery arrow wave in the night sky. A resinous blister on the stick glowed, then flamed.
>
> Fire had come to the Six Nations!
>
> (Iroquois 2006)

Inspiration

Perhaps the largest number of Indian religious beliefs that can be attributed to inspiration are those imbedded in the thousands of stories told over the centuries around campfires and in longhouses, wigwams, and teepees. Although some creators of tales might claim that the stories they tell had been dictated to them literally by deities, I suspect that many would accept the proposal that they themselves created their accounts by dint of spirit-induced inspiration. Then those accounts would be retold from one generation to the next, with successive narrators feeling free to revise plots and settings through their own spirit-generated inspirations. (See Chapter 7: Maxims and Tales.)

Instruction

As in Christian culture, Indian religious beliefs have been passed from spirits to people by both direct and mediated methods. Prayer, dreams, and visions have often provided the occasions for spirits to give direct instruction, as when the Indian youth Three Arrows received a message from the bear spirit during a vision session. However, Indians have acquired most of their instruction in religious beliefs from such intermediaries as shamans, parents, and storytellers.

The position of shaman in Indian cultures can be filled by either men or women and can involve several roles. Some shamans specialize in a single role. Others perform multiple functions. One key role is that of receiving messages directly from spirits via rituals, dreams, or visions, then explaining those messages to ordinary people.

Some shamans also induce dreams and visions for patrons by means of rites and potions. For example, shamans among the Chumash [California] traditionally served their clients *toloache,* a brew made from jimson weed that cast drinkers into a hallucinatory coma during which they met spirits who were thought to be "dream helpers" capable of conferring special power on dreamers (Miller 1988, 125).

Another shaman role involves interpreting symbols and signs, including the meaning of (a) events in nature (earthquakes, droughts, rainstorms, eclipse of the sun, the appearance or disappearance of certain birds or animals), (b) dreams and visions, (c) death, and (d) success or failure in such ventures as warfare, love, travel, and occupations. A subtype of the interpretive role is that of prophesying the future and sensing events beyond those known to most people. As a consequence, a shaman can be asked to find lost objects, identify when and where deer or elk can be found, locate the whereabouts of an enemy force, and recognize a storm in the offing.

A fourth role is that of healer, with healers often referred to as *medicine men* or *medicine women.* Principal means of treating both physical and mental ailments have been herbs, incantations, and rituals. Ailments are frequently assumed to be caused by a person or group offending a spirit, with the spirit retaliating by striking the offender with illness or accident. In such cases, curing the sufferer requires that the displeased spirit be placated with prayers, chants, and sacrifices in the hope that the spirit will then relieve the victim of pain and debility.

Two other presumed causes of disease are (a) a foreign substance has invaded the patient's body or (b) the patient's soul has wandered away.

> It is [the shamans'] duty to discover the [harmful substance] which is located in the patient's body, and which they extract by sucking or pulling

with the hands; or to go in pursuit of the absent soul, to recover it, and to restore it to the patient. Both of these forms of shamanism are found practically all over [North America].

(Blair 1911, 268)

Shamans have also served as experts in cosmic analysis and as keepers of tribal lore. For instance, shamans among the Sioux [Great Plains] could explain that the universe began when the deity *Skan* (the sky) decreed that the world should be created in fours—with four levels of gods, four directions (west, north, east, south), four divisions of time (day, night, month, year), four classes of animals (crawling, flying, two-legged, four-legged), and four stages of life (infancy, childhood, maturity, old age) (Hassrick 1964, 256).

In fulfilling their assignment of maintaining tribal lore, shamans guide the conduct of public religious ceremonies by supervising songs, poetry, dances, decorations, costumes, and styles of presentation. (See Chapter 6: Causes and Ceremonies.)

Shamans have typically learned their vocation under the tutelage of a respected prophet or magician—"a great master of legerdemain surrounded by a number of disciples" (Lowie 1954, 161). In some tribes—such as the Wahpeton Dakota [Great Plains]—shamans were thought to have lived their prenatal existence among the Thunders and thus, prior to birth, already knew what would happen to themselves as mortals.

To maintain their reputation for extraordinary knowledge and power, shamans have often gathered audiences to observe wondrous feats.

The most elaborate organization for such miraculous performances appeared among the Pawnee [Great Plains]....In the late summer or early fall, all the accepted masters at sleight-of-hand gathered in one of two earthlodges reserved in the village for that purpose; and with the aid of pupils they erected their several booths....After a dedication ceremony there was an impressive procession through the village, each shaman wearing a costume in mimicry of his animal protector.

(Lowie 1954, 161–162)

Upon their return to the earthlodge, the shamans displayed their skills—"handled burning corn husks with their bare hands, took meat out of a kettle of boiling soup, and stood on red-hot rocks." Shamans among the Mandan and Hidatsa [Great Plains] could be seen harboring "some animal or plant inside [their] body and have it emerge to the amazement of the spectators" (Lowie 1954, 162).

Summary

The foregoing discussion has illustrated ways that prayers, dreams, visions, inspiration, and instruction have served as channels through which

Amerindians have acquired religious beliefs from the world of spirits. Across the centuries, supernaturalism has pervaded every sphere of tribal life—occupational, marital, economic, spiritual, social, and recreational. Shamans have been—and continue to be—essential to the conduct of religion and to the transmission of religious lore from one generation to the next.

TRADITIONS COMPARED

Now consider a comparison of American Indian and Christian religious traditions. First are the traditions' similarities, then their differences.

Similarities

Indians and Christians alike are convinced that invisible spirits profoundly influence daily events and people's destinies. According to members of each faith, their beliefs and practices have been created by spirits and transmitted to humans via prayer, dreams, visions, inspiration, and instruction. Both Indian and Christian traditions have depended on religious specialists to guard, interpret, and teach their doctrine. Such specialists—priests, shamans, healers, ministers, evangelists—occupy respected positions in Indian and Christian societies.

Differences

Indian and Christian beliefs differ dramatically in the form in which they have been disseminated. From Christianity's earliest days, its teachings have been cast in print, both as the Bible and as interpretations by clerics across the past two millennia. But until recent times, Indian beliefs were transmitted exclusively in oral form. Only after colonists from Europe settled in North America did academically trained and curious authors—mostly non-Indians —compile written reports of Amerindian religious wisdom. The greater inconsistency of oral versions of beliefs across time and place, in contrast to written versions, helps account for the content of Indian religions being far more diverse than Christianity's content. Oral versions not only must depend for their stability on the accuracy of individuals' memories, but they are more vulnerable to different shamans' whims and motives than are written accounts.

The two religious traditions also differ in the emphasis they place on the several modes of conveying beliefs from spirits to persons. Christianity depends (a) less than Indian religions on dreams and visions and (b) more on the written word—primarily the Bible—to disseminate doctrine.

Indian religions feature a greater variety of rituals for communicating with the spirits than does Christianity. Christian ceremonies (Christmas, Easter, Lent) are likely to be universal, celebrated much the same way everywhere, whereas Indian rituals are apt to be influenced by tribes' locations and lifestyles. As a consequence, bands in the Northwest that hold potlatches do not perform the rain dances of the Southwest, and ones in the northeast woodlands cannot be expected to celebrate the buffalo dance of the Great Plains. The gourd dance of Oklahoma's Comanche and Kiowa would not be found among Canada's Algonquin.

In summary, the differences between Indian and Christian methods of transmitting beliefs from spirits to people seem greater in number than the similarities.

· 3 ·

Spirits

The word *spirits,* as intended throughout this book, refers to invisible beings that are described in religious lore. Spirits' role in the universe is that of hovering about and influencing events, including what happens to each of the world's inhabitants. Spirits do not always remain invisible. On occasion, some adopt a perceptible form, such as that of a human (Christianity's Jesus), an animal (the coyote among the Karok Indians [California]), or an inanimate object (the sun, a sacred tree, lightning, clouds).

Spirits differ from each other in the amount of power they wield and in the aspects of life they affect. For Algonquin peoples [Northeast, Great Lakes, Subarctic Canada], Manitou is the supreme power controlling the entire universe, just as God is the ultimate, all-encompassing power for Christians. More limited in influence are spirits whose domain is a particular location or facet of life. Christian tradition recognizes St. Christopher's spirit as the guardian of travelers and St. Andrew's spirit as the protector of fishermen. The Cheyenne [Great Plains] Indians have identified a spirit named Cold Maker as the cause of winter and Thunderbird as both the source of rain and the nemesis of the bogey-like Horned Hairy Water Spirits (Mails 2002, 12; Hoebel 1960, 86).

Spirits also are credited with personality traits. The biblical book of Deuteronomy portrays the Judeo-Christian God as merciful, compassionate, angry, vengeful, and jealous (13:17; 32:15, 35). For the Sioux [Great Plains] Indians, the bear spirit represents *wisdom,* the wolf *craftiness* in war, the eagle and hawk *courage,* and the spider *intelligence.* To the Blackfeet [Great Plains], the butterfly spirit is a bringer of dreams (Mails 2002, 13–14).

The following discussion focuses first on Christian spirits, then turns to the gods and apparitions of American Indian religions.

CHRISTIAN SPIRITS

The collection of Christian spirits can be depicted as a three-tier hierarchy that involves different levels of power and responsibility.

God, also known as The Lord, is male and occupies the top tier. He is said to be all-powerful (omnipotent), all-knowing (omniscient), and existing everywhere at once (omnipresent). The biblical Old Testament's pre-Christian Judaic doctrine describes God as a single being. But in the New Testament's gospels according to Jesus, God takes the form of a trinity—a tripartite entity consisting of God the Father, Jesus the Son, and the Holy Ghost or Holy Spirit. God created the universe and all of its contents. Since that early time, he has continued to monitor events and influence them.

The second level of the hierarchy is populated by angels, all created by God. Angels are invisible, occupy no space, and are indeterminate in number. On extremely rare occasions an angel may assume a temporary human form in order to deliver messages to selected persons on earth. Three important archangels are Gabriel, Michael, and Raphael. Most angels are beneficent, serving as God's aides, messengers, and heralds of God's glory. But one especially powerful archangel is a devious, malevolent enemy of God, of righteousness, and of humankind. He is identified in biblical texts by various names—Satan, the Devil, Lucifer, Belial, Beelzebul, the Serpent, the Evil One, and Prince of Demons. Satan was one of God's creations who—when overcome with pride and ambition—disobeyed the Lord and was no longer worthy of God's blessing and support. Ever since Satan's fall from grace, his mission has been to lure humans into evil deeds. Satan's own angels help him pursue that goal.

The third tier is inhabited by the spirits of Christian saints. Those spirits are the souls of humans who, when alive on earth, led such blessed, miraculous lives that, upon their death, they deserved special recognition, power, and assignments in their afterlife. Whereas all Christian denominations recognize as saintly such early luminaries as Jesus's disciples and Paul of Tarsus, only the Roman Catholic Church has assumed the task of systematically conferring postmortem sainthood on individuals during more recent centuries. The process of verifying that a deceased human deserves to be a saint is called *canonization*, a procedure introduced in the tenth century CE. Prior to that time, saints were chosen by public acclaim.

The process begins after the death of a Catholic whom people regard as holy. Often, the process starts many years after death in order give perspective on the candidate. The local bishop investigates the candidate's life and writings for heroic virtue (or martyrdom) and orthodoxy of doctrine. Then a panel of theologians at the Vatican evaluates the candidate. After approval by the panel and cardinals of the Congregation for the Causes of Saints, the pope proclaims the candidate "venerable."

The next step, beatification, requires evidence of one miracle (except in the case of martyrs [who died for the Christian cause]). Since miracles are considered proof that the person is in heaven and can intercede for us, the miracle must take place after the candidate's death and as a result of a specific petition to the candidate. When the pope proclaims the candidate beatified or "blessed," the person can be venerated by a particular region or group of people with whom the person holds special importance.

Only after one more miracle will the pope canonize the saint (this includes martyrs as well). The title of saint tells us that the person lived a holy life, is in heaven, and is to be honored by the universal Church. Canonization does not "make" a person a saint; it recognizes what God has already done.

(All About Saints 2006)

Some canonized souls are designated *patron saints,* since they are thought to protect and promote particular groups or places. St. John-Baptist de la Salle is the patron of teachers, St. Joan of Arc is the patron of rape victims, St. Hubert is the patron of dogs and hunters, and St. Genevieve the patron of the city of Paris. Dozens of other guardian saints are assigned their own groups and places.

The total number of saints and beati, as listed in historical sources and Catholic archives, exceeds 10,000.

It is useful to recognize that, according to Christian doctrine, an invisible ethereal essence of each human continues to exist following the person's death. That essence is the *soul,* which, upon departing from the inert body at the time of death, will dwell eternally in heaven, hell, or limbo. However, souls of the non-saintly are not considered spirits (as the concept *spirits* is intended in this chapter), because Christian culture does not portray those souls as influencing events in the world as God, angels, and saints do.

An important feature of Christian spirits is their set of personality traits. For example, as noted earlier, the Bible describes God as powerful, wise, merciful, jealous, fearsome, vengeful, angry, and loving.

Behold, God is mighty...in strength and wisdom. (Job 36:5)

For the Lord thy God is a merciful God. He will not forsake thee. (Deuteronomy 4:31).

For thou shalt worship no other god; for the Lord...is a jealous God. (Exodus 34:14)

God is greatly to be feared in the assembly of the saints, and to be had in reverence of all those that are about him. (Psalm 89:7)

Vengeance belongeth unto me, I will recompense, saith the Lord. (Hebrews 10:30)

God judgeth the righteous, and God is angry with the wicked every day. (Psalms 7:11)

For the Lord your God...loveth the stranger, in giving him food and raiment. (Deuteronomy 10:18)

Patron saints are assigned to protect particular groups and places on the basis of the saints' imagined character traits and talents.

In summary, Christian theology assumes the presence of a variety of invisible spirits that can affect events of the world. The spirits are located on three tiers, representing three major levels of power that range from God's omnipotence at the top, through the assigned acts of angels in the middle, to the saints' limited roles at the bottom. Humans can seek help from the spirits through prayer and the ceremonies described later in Chapter 6.

INDIAN SPIRITS

Whereas Christian spirits form a rather obvious power hierarchy that extends from God down through angels and saints, the arrangement of Indian spirits is more complex and controversial.

For example, consider Indian counterparts of Christianity's supreme power, God. Over the decades, scholars of Amerindian history have disagreed about whether the original Native Americans' spirit pantheon (a) included an all-powerful supreme spirit that reigned over a host of lesser deities, (b) consisted of multiple spirits that acted independently rather than under the rule of a paramount deity, or (c) was initially polytheistic but, after the arrival of the European colonists, copied the Christian spirit structure by adopting a top god to head the spirits' chain of command. My review of diverse Amerindian historical accounts suggests that all three of those patterns have existed. Whereas some tribes originally had a supreme god, others never did, and still others copied the Christian model. Hence, from at least the early nineteenth century forward, each of the three patterns could be found someplace on the continent (Clements 1986, 28; Heizer 1978, 655; Lowie 1954, 165; Powers 1973, 109). By way of illustration, Heizer (1978, 656) has proposed that among Central California tribes, the Kuksu had a supreme-creator god, but among tribes farther south (Costanoans, Esselen, Miwok, Yokuts) this supreme deity was missing, with his place "taken by a pantheon of animals—Eagle at the top, Coyote his chief assistant, and then Falcon, Hawk, Condor, Owl, Fox, Roadrunner, Antelope, Deer, Hummingbird, and Raven" in descending order.

Among Native North-American religions that include a supreme Great Spirit, that spirit's title—and to some extent its traits and powers—can vary from one tribe to another. For the Algonquin [Northeast, Great Lakes, Subarctic Canada] the spirit's name has been *Gitche-Manitou* or *Gitche-Manedo*. But the top god's name becomes *Tirawa* among the Pawnee [Great Plains], *Wakan Tanka* among the Sioux [Great Plains], *Glooskap* among the Wabanaki [Northeast], *Wakonda* among the Omaha [Great Plains], *Acbadadea* among the Crow/Apsaalooke [Great Plains], and *Quetzacoatl* among the Aztecs [Mexico]. The Great Spirit's title, when translated into English, is *Sun* for the Comanche [Great Plains], *Thunder* for the Cahto [California], *Great Turtle* for the Chippewa [Northeast], *Wolf* for the Shoshone [Great Plains], and *That-Old-Man-Above* for the Wiyot [California]. Pueblos and Navajos [Southwest] "recognize the sun as the most powerful creative source in the universe. Personified as the Sun Father, he is the great creator, the original impulse, the primal source of all life" (Waters 1950, 198).

The precise nature of the Great Spirit is an issue of continuing debate. For instance, *Manitou* and *Wakan Tanka* have each been conceived as (a) a kind of ethereal energy or miraculous power pervading everything in the universe (called *manito* by Algonquin tribes, *wakanda* by the Sioux, *orenda* by the Iroquois) and also (b) a miraculous personage with humanlike character traits.

> Manitou combines the meanings of spirit, mystery, magic, and generally is applied to the manifestation of some form of power that is not readily understood or coming from elsewhere.
>
> (Musinsky 1997)

> Wakan Tanka, as the all-pervasive force, was eminent among gods. His being, as good and evil, was divisible. As good, his was a four-part being . . .again divisible into 16 gods. He thereby incorporated not only all the significant elements of the universe of which the Sioux were aware but also those elements which they knew they did not understand. Such a comprehensive cosmology. . .gave the Sioux people a framework within which they could carry out their activities with a sense of security in a very insecure world. As visible and invisible, as material and immaterial, as human and as animal, the gods embodied all manifestations of nature.
>
> (Hasssrick 1964, 246)

In some tribal traditions, the Great Spirit has been modeled after an admired animal. Consider the supreme god among the Cheyenne [Great Plains] who bears the title *Heammawihio*—"The Wise One Above." Embedded in the title is the word "spider" (*wihio*), a reference to the insect that "spins a web, and goes up and down, seemingly walking on nothing" (Grinnell in Hoebel 1960, 86). According to Cheyenne legend, this amazing ability reflects superior intelligence that equips the spider deity to know "more about how to do things than do all other creatures" (Hoebel 1960, 86).

Below the rank of Great Spirit, Indian lore describes a vast array of lesser gods, most of them fashioned after revered objects of nature. For instance, immediately below the Sioux *Wakan Tanka* are four superior deities—*Inyan* the Rock, *Maka* the Earth, *Skan* the Sky, and *Wi* the Sun. Beneath those four is a quartet of associate gods—*Hanwi* the Moon, *Tate* the Wind, *Whope* the Great Mediator, and *Wakinyan* the Winged. Then another four subordinate spirits appear on the next lower level—Buffalo, Bear, Four Winds, and Whirlwind (Hassrick 1964, 247).

Of particular note among tribes' deities is the trickster, an Amerindian type of spirit that has no equivalent in Christian culture. Although the trickster is usually envisioned as a coyote—admired for his cunning—a few bands liken him to some other creature, such as the spider *Iktomi* among the Lakota Sioux [Great Plains], the wolverine *Lox* among the Algonquin [Northeast], and a raven in the Northwest (Rice 1998, 5; Nichols 2002). The Kiowa [Southern Great Plains] trickster is not an animal but, rather, a personified being called *Saynday*, "funny looking, very tall and thin, with bulging arm and leg muscles, and a little moustache that hung down over his mouth" (Marriott & Rachlin 1975, 57). But in most Indian religions, Old Man Coyote is society's mischief-maker—playing practical jokes, causing ventures to go awry, and incessantly teasing. On one occasion he is good and helpful, on another bad and destructive. Often his mischief is not aimed at an intended goal but, rather, is "for the sheer joy of prankishness" (Bright 1993, 31). He has been blamed for the night sky's irregular arrangement of stars, for cooking his daughter, for being grossly erotic, and for death being eternal rather than only temporary (Nichols 2002). Although Coyote is neither satanic nor the embodiment of evil, people are wise to be wary, for one never knows when this charlatan will spring an unwelcome stunt. One deceptive trait of tricksters is their ability to adopt different guises, such as morphing from the body of a coyote into that of a young buffalo or changing from a wolverine into a pretty maiden (Marriott & Rachlin 1975, 73; Leland 1884, 161).

In contrast to benevolent deities and tricksters are Amerindian religions' truly evil spirits, the equals of Christianity's Satan and his angels. For the Sioux, the headmaster of deviltry is *Iya*, aided by such companions as Two-Faced Woman, *Waziya* the Old Man, his wife *Wakanaka*, and their daughter *Anog-Ite* (Hassrick 1964, 248). For the Great Lakes Algonquin, the evil one is *Matche Monedo*, sometimes depicted as a great serpent. The epitome of evil among the Saginaw [Great Lakes] is *Mudjee Monedo*, capable of altering his appearance to suit the occasion, such as during a footrace changing from a fox into a wolf and then into a deer (Clements 1986, 29; Williams 1956, 13, 199).

So it is that a seemingly infinite number of spirits bearing specific assignments populate Indian religions, with the range of spirit types and their duties suggested by the following examples.

Algonquin [Northeast, Great Lakes] mythology identifies demigods in charge of the winds from the four cardinal directions of the compass. *Kabeyun* controls west winds while his sons manage winds from the other three directions—*Kabebonicca* the north, *Shawondasee* the south, and *Wabun* the east. Algonquin spirits also include: *Iagoo*, teller of tales; *Weeng*, bringer of sleep; *Pauguk*, spirit of death; and *Kwasind*, strong man, who clears rivers of fallen trees (Williams 1956, xiii).

Iroquois [Great Lakes] legends tell of a pair of feuding brother spirits, *Tawiskaron* (the Ice King or God of Winter) and *Teharonhiawakhon* (friend of humans and the creator of animals along with lakes and rivers to water the arid earth). The brothers' grandmother, *Awenhai*, had originally fallen out of the sky to land on the back of the Great Turtle where she conceived and bore a daughter.

In due time the daughter matured and was impregnated by the Wind. [At the time of the brothers' birth], Teharonhiawakon was delivered normally, but Tawiskaron performed his own Caesarian section through [his mother's] navel, an easy operation because his flint head was shaped like an arrow point.

(Williams 1956, xiv)

Lipan Apache [Southwest] mythology includes a hero named Killer of All Enemies, who not only rid the world of monsters and the tribe's foes but created useful animals (deer, horses) and schooled the Lipans in warfare and raiding (Newcomb 1961, 128). The Pueblos [Southwest] revere: Earth Mother; the fire god, *Huehueteotl*; the chief of the hunt, Mountain Lion; and the celestial power, Eagle (Kehoe 1981, 130).

Chippewa [Great Lakes] legends tell of *Manibozho* (the Great Hare) who rebuilt the world after evil beings destroyed it with a flood (Waldman 1999, 14).

Wichita [Great Plains] tradition locates the supreme deity, *Kinnikasus* (Man Never Known on Earth), at the pinnacle of a spirit hierarchy, followed in descending order by a Sun God, Morning Star (ruler of other stars), South Star (guardian of warriors), and North Star (people's guide to their location and the source of shamans' power). The Comanches, like other Great Plains peoples, have cast thunder as a huge bird of great power, larger and stronger than the eagle and much to be feared because of Thunderbird's capacity to do harm with devastating storms. Comanche theology also assigns human abilities to common animals. Buffaloes can talk and occasionally transform themselves into people. The wolf is admired for craftiness in combat. Because eagles were believed to be powerful in warfare, Comanche warriors wore eagle feathers into battle. Elk are esteemed for their great strength, which is shared with whoever adopts the elk as a guardian spirit (Newcomb 1961, 190–191, 270–271).

The Lakota Sioux [Great Plains] rely on animal spirits for courage and healing, depending especially on buffalo, bear, eagle, and elk deities. The Lakota also believe that some spirits are the souls of dead friends or enemies who, in their postmortem existence, act according to the personalities they displayed when alive. A modern-day Lakota woman, Edna Two Dogs, insisted that the spirit of deceased Chief Crazy Horse had attended tribal ceremonies to urge the Sioux to retain ownership of the Black Hills (in South Dakota and Wyoming) in defiance of the U.S. Government's attempt to annex the region (Rice 1998, 79).

In addition to deities, Indian worldviews have included frightening ghosts. Among Great Plains tribes, ghosts are often regarded as spirits of the dead who were scalped and then returned as specters to where they had lived (Mails 2002, 12). In Cheyenne [Great Plains] tradition, ghosts (*mistai*) are invisible poltergeists that reveal their presence by making strange noises in dark places, tugging at people's clothing, and tapping on lodge coverings (Hoebel 1960, 86).

The Dineh Navajo [Southwest] believe that mysterious *chinde* are malevolent shades of the dead that cause accidents and illness (Waldman 1999, 160).

Eastman (1986, 216) has noted that there are no angels in Sioux [Great Plains] religious lore, a characteristic apparently true of all Native North-American religions. But "in the mind of the Indians, animals and birds often take upon themselves a *holy* character, and in every tribe tales and traditions have grown up which have for their central motif the unique powers exercised by certain creatures" (Mails 2002, 13).

For the Navajo [Southwest] most spirits—known as "the Holy People"—are

> mercurial and capricious. The sun, whose rays bring life from the soil, may at any time disappear from the sky, causing the fields of corn and squash to wither and die....In addition, there are many lesser but still threatening divinities, such as Big Fly, Corn Beetle, Gila Monster, Big Snake Man, Crooked Snake People, Wind People, Thunder People, Cloud People, and Coyote, the trickster. Each being or group of beings has its own power, which it can use for good or evil. Every Navajo knows that the goodwill of all the Holy People must be retained or, if lost, regained.
>
> (Reader's Digest 1973, 238)

In summary, by assuming that all objects of the natural world contain souls or a divine essence, Indian religions have accumulated millions of spirits. The Nomlaki [California] have viewed mountains, lakes, springs, caves, and forests as animate and ever ready to influence human affairs. As a Nomlaki explained, "Everything in this world talks, just as we are [talking] now—the trees, rocks, everything; but we cannot understand them, just as White people do not understand Indians" (Heizer 1978, 651).

This seemingly endless assortment of divinities was identified early by the seventeenth-century French explorer Nicholas Perrot (1644–1717) when he described the deities of Great Lakes tribes as ones

> in the air, on the land, and within the earth. Those of the air are the thunder, the lightning, and in general whatever [people] see in the air that they cannot understand—as the moon, eclipses, and extraordinary whirlwinds. Those [divinities] which are upon the land comprise all creatures that are malign and noxious—especially serpents, panthers, and birds like griffins; they also include in this class such creatures as have... unusual beauty or deformity. Lastly, are those [animals] within the earth, [especially] the bears who pass the winter without eating. The savages pay the same regard to all the animals that dwell in caves, or in holes in the ground, and invoke these [animals' images] whenever [people who] have, while asleep, dreamed of any of these creatures.
>
> (Perrot in Blair 1911, 49)

TRADITIONS COMPARED

As a means of summarizing this chapter's content, the two religious persuasions can now be compared in terms of their likenesses and differences.

Similarities

One way that Indian religions and Christian culture are alike is in their both recognizing multiple deities. In Christian culture and in most—if not all—Indian cultures, the spirits are arranged in a hierarchy, with those on the upper steps of the structure wielding greater power and commanding larger realms of life than those on the lower steps. Thus, the Christian God is more potent and affects more aspects of life than do either the angels or Christian saints. In like manner, the Algonquin *Gitche Manitou,* the Sioux *Wankan Tanka,* and the Cheyenne *Heammawihio* are more influential than any other deities in those tribes' spirit registries.

In both Indian and Christian traditions, believers can adopt guardian spirits to ward off evil and furnish aid in time of need. For Christians, that protector can be Jesus, the Holy Ghost, an angel, or a saint. For Indians, the guardian has most often been an animal—a bear for its strength, a spider for its cleverness, or an eagle for its imposing power and air of command. Hassrick (1964, 167) has suggested that the Sioux "deliberately placed themselves upon a lower plane [than the animals] with respect to rapport with the universe and its Controllers. With complete devotion, the Sioux appealed to the animals as emissaries in tune with the gods for guidance and help in all matters."

Differences

Perhaps the two most dramatic differences between Amerindian and Christian spirit worlds are in (a) the far greater number of deities in the Indian pantheon than in the Christian and (b) the Indians' assuming that animals and inanimate objects of nature can be spirits while Christians limit the concept *spirit* to select humans (saints) and personified deities (God, angels).

The combined total of spirits in American Indian religions extends beyond the billions, if we grant that all things in nature have spirit qualities. In contrast, the number of spirits in Christian tradition is perhaps in the thousands, composed of the Trinity (God, Jesus, Holy Spirit), an indeterminate quantity of angels, and perhaps 10,000 saints.

Not only have Indian religions taught that animals can assume spirit form but, in at least some tribes' belief systems, animals rank above humans because they allegedly arrived in the universe before people and wield power over events. "The Sioux may have been envious of animals, whom they unconsciously felt have a more efficient ecological adjustment" (Hassrick 1964, 267). This notion of animal superiority is a claim rejected by Christian clerics.

Part of the argument about animals functioning as spirits hangs on the question of whether animals do, indeed, possess a powerful invisible essence, such as a soul. This is a question pondered by Christian theologians in the past. As a result, an apparently common Protestant belief in colonial America was that the human soul is not a unitary object, but like the Christian God, it is a trinity consisting of a *vegetative* soul, a *sensible* soul, and a *rational* soul. The vegetative soul has the powers of nourishing and propagating—characteristics that people share with the earth's plant life. The sensible soul has not only powers of nourishing and propagating but also additional equipment possessed by animals—external senses (eyes, ears, nose) and the internal senses of memory and emotions as well as the musculature (*sinews*) that makes mobility possible. But it is the rational soul, the highest in the trinity, which distinguishes humans from the earth's other living things. The rational soul contains all the powers of the other two souls, plus the faculties of reason and will (Miller 1963, 240). However, even being blessed with a rational soul does not qualify an individual to be a spirit that can affect what happens in the world. Something additional— a special holiness—is also needed. And, according to Christian doctrine, animals not only lack rationality but the required sanctity as well.

A final way that Indian and Christian traditions differ is in the sources they trust for identifying spirits and spirits' traits. Christian culture depends on the Bible for knowledge of the trinity and angels, whereas church organizations create saints. In contrast, Indian cultures accept as spirits all those beings depicted as deities in the thousands of stories recounted by tribal tellers of tales.

· 4 ·

Places

For present purposes, *places* are considered to be of two sorts—mundane, perceptible sites and invisible, otherworldly locations. Mundane sites can be directly seen and verified, but otherworldly sites cannot be viewed and thus must be accepted on the word of a trusted authority, such as holy scripture or a seer capable of extrasensory awareness. The places significant in Christian tradition differ in most cases from those important in North-American Indian tradition.

SIGNIFICANT CHRISTIAN SITES

The viewable mundane locations in Christianity include sites mentioned in the Bible, places associated with individuals who were canonized as saints over the past two millennia, places of worship (churches, cathedrals, chapels), and burial grounds.

Some viewable sites are large expanses in which important events occurred over an extended period of time. Such territories include Egypt, where early Israelites were held in bondage, and Sinai, the mountainous desert region through which the Israelites wandered for 40 years after escaping from Egypt.

Other noteworthy locations are towns and cities where battles were fought or critical incidents occurred. One example is the city of Jericho, whose walls Joshua's followers allegedly blew down, thereby demonstrating how God-given powers could promote the welfare of the Lord's chosen people. Another significant place was Jerusalem, the center of Jewish culture under King David. In the Bible's New Testament, Bethlehem was notable as the birthplace of Jesus.

Perhaps the most controversial biblical description of a place is the portrayal of the universe in the first chapter of Genesis—with the world represented as a flat Earth under a dome-shaped sky referred to as a "firmament" in which the sun, moon, and stars were embedded. It is difficult today for many Christians to accept this conception of the universe, because it is a far cry from modern science's version of a cosmos in which a ball-shaped earth revolves in endless space.

Places of note in the evolution of Christian tradition since Jesus's day are locations associated with miracles attributed to saints. Lourdes, France, is visited by thousands of pilgrims each year for healing that is credited to St. Bernadette Soubiroux, who had visions of the Virgin Mary at Lourdes in 1858. Catholic pilgrims in search of cures also visit Mugnano, Italy, the town of St. Philomena's martyrdom at age 14 in 1802. St. Peter's Basilica in Rome is built where Jesus's disciple, Peter, was martyred. In the Italian town of Assisi, a basilica holds artifacts from the life of St. Francis (1182–1226), including "the crucifix from which Jesus spoke to St. Francis, asking him to rebuild His church" (Shrines of Italy 2006).

Places of worship are usually churches, cathedrals, and chapels. When European colonists settled in America, they erected churches in each village and town to serve as the community's most important meeting place (Figure 4.1). As towns expanded into cities, and as immigrants from diverse Christian denominations arrived, a greater variety of churches appeared. And as city congregations became increasingly affluent, churches grew more elaborate—colonial copies of ornate European cathedrals (Figure 4.2).

Christians traditionally have buried their dead in graves or tombs regarded as sacred places to be revered. And Christians memorialize the life of the deceased by marking the burial site with a grave stone or tomb that displays the name and the birth and death dates of the departed. Sometimes a carved epitaph follows the name:

"At last at peace with Jesus."

"Gone, but not forgotten."

"This lovely flower of fairest bloom,
Thus early met a sudden doom
From her fond parents torn away
Now lives and blooms in endless day."

"Faithful husband, thou art at rest until we meet again."

"I am persuaded that neither death nor life
Shall be able to separate us from the love of God,
Which is in Christ Jesus, our Lord." (Greene 1962)

Figure 4.1   A Typical Protestant Village Church of Colonial Times.

Over recent decades, cremation has rapidly become a popular Christian alternative to interment. For example, cremations in Canada increased from 4 percent of all deaths in 1958, to 8 percent in 1978, to 24 percent in 1998, and 31 percent in 2004. Cremations in the United States rose from 3 percent in 1958, to 17 percent in 1978, to 42 percent in 1998, and 56 percent in 2004 (Cremation Association, 2006).

In contrast to viewable, mundane places are those invisible locations whose description is accepted from a trusted source—a document or a respected person—or from personal extrasensory revelation not accessible to other people. Four such locations in Christian tradition are heaven, hell, purgatory, and limbo. Each is a site to which a person's soul might go after death.

Heaven

The Bible speaks often of heaven and identifies its location—high in the sky —but rarely describes heaven's contents and living conditions. Although Jesus said that in heaven ("in my father's house") there "are many mansions" (John 14:2), the precise nature of those mansions and their surrounds was not made clear.

In the book of Revelation, John envisioned heaven as featuring God on a throne.

And he who sat there appeared like jasper and carnelian, and round the throne was a rainbow that looked like an emerald. Round the throne

Figure 4.2   A Modern Christian Cathedral—Montreal, Canada.

were twenty-four thrones, and seated on the thrones were twenty-four elders, clothed in white raiment; and they have on their heads crowns of gold. And before the throne burn seven torches of fire, which are the seven spirits of God; and before the throne there is as it were a sea of glass, like crystal.

And round the throne, on each side of the throne, are four living creatures, full of eyes in front and behind: the first living creature like a lion, the second living creature like an ox, the third living creature with the face of a man, and the fourth living creature like a flying eagle. And the four living creatures, each of them with six wings, are full of eyes round about and within, and day and night they never cease to sing "Holy, holy, holy, is the Lord God Almighty, who was and is and is to come!"

(Revelation 4:1–8; 7:9–17)

Ever since early Christian days, theologians—and particularly saintly ones during the Middle Ages (St. Gregory the Great, St. Ambrose, St. Augustine, St. Jerome. St. John Chrysostom, St. Basil, St. Gregory Nazianzen)—have offered their own versions of heaven, versions apparently discovered through divine inspiration. One example of the present-day inheritance of such views is this segment from the *Catholic Encyclopedia* (2006).

> In heaven there is not the least pain or sadness; for every aspiration of nature must be finally realized....[The souls of the deceased] delight greatly in the company of Christ, the angels, and the saints, and in the reunion with so many who were dear to them on earth.
>
> (Heaven 2006)

Conceptions of heaven have also appeared in folk culture, as in Negro spirituals that envision newcomers to heaven

> A-settin' down with Jesus
> Eatin' honey and drinkin' wine
> Marchin' round de throne
> Wid Peter, James, and John....
> I'm gonna tell God all my troubles,
> When I get home...
> I'm gonna tell him the road was rocky
> When I get home. (Brown 1953)

Among well-known depictions of heaven, perhaps the most complex is the version in the third part of the epic Italian poem, *The Divine Comedy,* written by Dante Alighieri in the early fourteenth century. The parts of the poem are titled *Inferno, Purgatory,*and *Paradise.* In Dante' vision, heaven or paradise consists of nine spheres, ranging from the least desirable to the most desirable in recognition of the fact that people arriving in heaven can vary in their degree of holiness, that is, in their ability to love God. The first level is for good people, but ones who renounced their vows, such as a nun who left her convent. The second level is for individuals who did good on earth out of a desire for fame. The third level is for those who did good out of love. The fourth is for the wise, the fifth for ones who fought for Christianity, the sixth for the just, the seventh for the contemplative, and the eighth for the blessed, such as saints. The ninth sphere is occupied by angels. "Thus, there is a heavenly hierarchy, but everyone is satisfied with his post, because he understands the fact that he is not capable of any greater experience" (Divine Comedy 2006).

Christian denominations do not all agree about how people get to heaven. The Puritans in colonial times believed that sincerely receiving Jesus as their savior would convince God to accept them into heaven. Doing good works on earth was important, but it would not ensure believers a place in heaven, because admission to heaven depended solely on God's decision—on God's grace.

Conservative Christians believe that the natural tendency of every human is to reject the Gospel and thus be destined to spend eternity in Hell. However God grants his grace to a small percentage of the human race so that they are receptive to the Christian message. God chooses who will receive this gift, using criteria that humans are not aware of.

(Robinson 2006)

More liberal Protestant denominations teach that people can earn their way into heaven by believing in Jesus, faithfully abiding by God's commandments, repenting of their sins, and doing good works.

Hell

Whereas heaven is a joy-filled, pain-free destiny for souls after death, hell (*hades* or the Hebrew *Shoel*) is quite the opposite. By long tradition, hell is said to exist in the depths of the earth where deceased sinners suffer eternal torment. One present-day conservative American theologian has suggested that

Historically, hell has been portrayed in evangelical sermons as fire and brimstone. The most we should say is that hell is a place of unexplainable mystery. The reality is probably far worse than our most vivid imaginations can conjure up. The reality of both heaven and hell are both greater than we can express.

(George in Robinson 2006)

The most detailed, best-known estimate of conditions in hell is found in the *Inferno* section of Dante's *Divine Comedy.* Dante's hell is composed of nine circles, each inflicting punishment in keeping with the arriving soul's chief sin when on earth. The first circle (Limbo) is for virtuous people who had no chance to accept Jesus, either because they were not baptized (as in the case of new babies) or were pagans, such as the Greek authors Homer, Aristotle, and Plato who lived before Jesus's time, and Roman authors Virgil, Horace, and Ovid who were Jesus's contemporaries but were not among his followers. Occupants of Limbo are not actively punished. Instead, they suffer psychologically by regretting that they were not Christians when alive (Divine Comedy 2006).

In the second circle, souls that were lustful on earth are whipped about by violent storms. In the third, gluttons lie in the mud under constant rain and hail. In the fourth, people who spent life greedy for worldly wealth are forced to move enormous weights. In the fifth, souls of chronically angry people fight each other in swamp water while slothful souls gurgle beneath the water. In the sixth, heretics are trapped in fiery tombs. In the seventh, the violent, the suicidal, and the blasphemous are immersed in a river of boiling blood, transformed into thorny bushes, or cast into a desert of flaming sand. The eighth circle is for souls that were intentionally evil when on earth—flatterers, sorcerers, false prophets, corrupt politicians, hypocrites, thieves, trouble-makers, counterfeiters, perjurers, impersonators, and simonists who sold sacred objects for profit. They suffer punishments ranging from snakebites and boiling pitch to horrible diseases and immersion in human excrement.

The ninth circle is entirely ice. Satan is frozen into the center of a pit. His companions, also encased in ice, are the souls of people who were traitors on earth—traitors to their kin (such as Cain who killed his brother, Abel, in the biblical book of Genesis) or traitors to their city or country, to their guests, or to their benefactors. Dante portrays Satan as a beastly, six-winged, three-headed giant chewing on the bloody bodies of traitors (Divine Comedy 2006).

Robinson (2006), after reviewing present-day Christian fundamentalist conceptions of the afterlife and after inspecting data on church attendance and people's belief systems, speculated that

> Those [individuals] who have repented of their sins and have trusted Jesus as Lord and Savior are "saved." They will go to heaven. This represents a minority of those North Americans who identify themselves as Christians. Those who have heard the Gospel and have not been saved will be tortured without relief in hell after they die. Most North American Christians will share this fate.

Purgatory

In Roman Catholic doctrine—and for some Anglicans—the souls of Christians may, upon death, still be stained with sin, unworthy of immediately entering heaven. Those souls are thus obliged to spend time at a way station called *purgatory*, where they will be cleansed of sins before deserving eternal heavenly bliss.

As with heaven and hell, Dante's version of purgatory continues to influence Christians' ideas about life after death. According to *The Divine Comedy*, purgatory is a terraced mountain, with each of the seven terraces representing one of the deadly sins—pride, envy, wrath, sloth, avarice, gluttony, and lust. The terrace that a soul occupies is suited to the most prominent of the sins the person committed while alive. On that terrace the soul must suffer a suitable punishment until repentance permits the soul to ascend to the mountain summit that represents the Garden of Eden from which the first man and woman, Adam and Eve, had been ejected for disobeying God. The purged soul is then permitted to pass from the garden into heaven (Divine Comedy 2006).

Limbo

As noted earlier, limbo is the afterlife dwelling for souls of good people who did not have a chance to become Christians because they either died before being baptized or else lived before Jesus's time. Because limbo is populated by virtuous souls, it is a happy place, with the joy of the residents marred only by feelings of distress over their not qualifying as Christians.

SIGNIFICANT INDIAN SITES

Viewable worldly places of religious importance in Indian lore include power centers, ceremonial sites, and burial grounds.

Indian religions have presumed that divine power exudes from works of nature that are impressive in size and character—particularly mountains and waterways. For example, the Iroquois of the Great Lakes region revere Niagara Falls, which derived its name from the Iroquois word Nijhgarrah, meaning "thundering waters."

For centuries, the Iroquois believed that the sound of the waterfall was the voice of the mighty spirit of the waters. Until the mid-eighteenth century, they sought the favor of the Water Spirit by sacrificing a maiden to the Falls each year—sending her in a white canoe decorated with fruits and flowers over the brink of the falls. To be sacrificed was the greatest honor, and insured special gifts and happy hunting grounds in the afterlife (Yupanqui 1998).

According to Iroquois legend, death changed humans into pure spirits of strength and goodness, with their spirits living forever far beneath the falls where the water's roar sounds like music. When the French explorer Sieur de La Salle (René-Robert Cavelier) in 1679 observed the annual sacrificial rite, he was appalled and tried to convert the Iroquois to Christianity, urging the Indians to accept Christ as their savior. The Indians responded by asking why their form of sacrifice was considered bad while Christ's crucifixion was considered good (Yupanqui 1998).

As with Niagara Falls, other centers of power are linked to religious lore. Consider, for example, the Klamath Indians' legendary account of the origin of Crater Lake in Oregon. During ancient times, there were two neighboring volcanic peaks, Mount Mazama and Mount Shasta, each controlled by a potent spirit—Llao (the spirit of the Underworld) who dwelt beneath Mount Mazama and Skell (the spirit of the Above-World) who roamed the sky high over Mount Shasta. One day Llao rose from the Underworld to stand on the summit of Mount Mazama, and from there he beheld Loha, the beautiful daughter of the Klamath chief. When Llao sought her as his lover, she rejected him for being ugly and for dwelling in the Underworld. Infuriated by thus being cast off, Llao vowed revenge on the Klamath tribe—he would exterminate them with fire. In reply, Loha's chieftain father begged for help from the spirit Skell, who dropped from the sky to the peak of Mount Shasta and engaged Llao in combat. The two giants' furious battle caused the earth to thunder and tremble as, in their volcanic rage, they hurled blazing boulders at each other from their mountain tops. Skell's final blow felled Llao, who retreated through a hole into the Underworld below Mount Mazama. Skell, to ensure that Llao could never return, smashed the mountain peak, collapsing it on top of the vanquished underworld spirit and then turned the crater into a stunning setting by filling it with cool blue water. Thus Mount Mazama became Crater Lake (U.S. Geological Survey 2006).

In the past, Crater Lake not only inspired awe among the Klamath, but fear as well. Nineteenth-century visitors to the Plateau Region reported that

The Indians...lived on the Klamath Lakes not many miles away, yet before the white man came none but the medicine men dared to look upon Crater Lake, [because members of the Klamath band] long believed that only punishment could come to men who looked upon a lake that was sacred to the spirits. "Do not look upon this place," the legend warned, "for it will mean death or lasting sorrow."

(Indian perceptions 2006)

In 1873, an observant visitor to Klamath territory wrote,

Here their medicine-men still come, as they always came in the olden time, to study spiritual wisdom and learn the secrets of life from the Great Spirit. In the solitude of these wilds they fasted and did penance; to the shores of the weird lake they ventured with great danger, to listen to the winds that came from no one knew where—borne there to roam the pent-up waters and bear the mysterious whispers of unseen beings, whose presence they doubted not, and whose words they longed to understand. They watched the shifting shadows of night and day; the hues of sun-light, moon-light, and star-light; saw white sails glisten on the moon-lit waters; caught the sheen of noiseless paddles, as they lifted voiceless spray, and having become inspired with the supernal, they bore back to their tribes charmed lives and souls fenced in with mystery.

(Indian perceptions 2006)

Another sacred site is Bear's Lodge (*Mato Tipi*), a giant outcropping on the plains of the Black Hills of Northeastern Wyoming (Figure 4.3). For untold centuries, Cheyenne, Lakota, and Tsististas tribes have worshipped this stone

Figure 4.3   Bear's Lodge/Devil's Tower.

edifice as a place of great spiritual power. In 1906 it became the first of the nation's national monuments, so designated by President Theodore Roosevelt. Early white settlers in the region, apparently out of Christian piety, sought to defame *Mato Tipi,* condemning it as a pagan religious site by renaming the rock Devil's Tower, the label by which it's still widely known today. One Indian legend, to account for the Bear's-Lodge label, tells of seven children playing in the woods when a great bear came upon them. The frightened children prayed to Mother Earth for help. She responded by promptly lifting them up out of the animal's reach. The striations on the side of the tower are claw marks the bear made while trying to reach the children as they were borne skyward (Devil's Tower National Monument 2006).

Far east of Bear's Lodge in the Black Hills of South Dakota lies Bear Butte (*Mato Paha*), long venerated by the Cheyenne and Lakota (Figure 4.4). To those who named the site, the hill looked like a sleeping bear. According to Indian lore, nearly 4,000 years ago a Cheyenne holy man named Sweet Medicine received spiritual guidance and gifts for the tribe near this place. Since that time, members of the Cheyenne and Lakota bands have continued to visit the monument to fast and pray (White Face 2006).

For the Navajos [Southwest], San Francisco Peak in Arizona is the sacred western boundary of their world. The site is actually a combination of three mounts that bear non-Indian names—Humphrey Peak (11,940 feet), Agassiz Peak (12,300 feet), and Fremont Peak (11,940 feet). The Navajo name for the place is *Diichilí Dzil,* meaning Abalone Shell Mountain, in keeping with Navajo mythology that portrays the area in ancient times as adorned with abalone shells. It was also the home of the spirits *Haashch'éélt'i'í* (Talking God), *Naada'algaii 'Ashkii* (White Corn Boy), and *Naadá 'Altsoii 'At'ééd* (Yellow Corn Girl). The peaks continue to be an abundant source of herbs and natural medicines, but only Navajos intent on collecting herbs are bold enough to climb the sacred hills. San Francisco Peak is also revered by the Hopis, who regard the mountain as the abode of the hallowed kachina spirits (San Francisco Peak 2006).

Additional sacred places abound in other regions of North America, with members of Indian tribes continuing to visit them for guidance, spiritual power, and visions. Prominent among such locations are California's Trinity

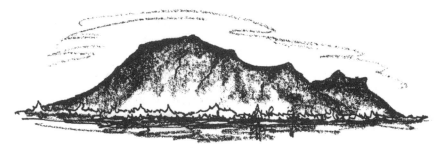

Figure 4.4   Bear Butte.

Alps and Lake Tahoe, Wyoming's Yellowstone National Park, the Great Smoky Mountains of North Carolina and Tennessee, sectors of the Allegheny Mountains (Pennsylvania, Maryland, West Virginia, Virginia), Idaho's Upper Priest Lake, and Washington's Mount Rainier (Lake-Thom 1997, 179).

In the past, Indian religions rarely had true counterparts of Christianity's permanent meeting houses—churches, chapels, and cathedrals. Instead, people would conduct religious rituals outdoors or use buildings that also served other purposes, such as the longhouse dwellings of the Iroquois [Northeast, Great Lakes]. Or they would erect temporary quarters designed for particular celebrations.

Among the exceptions to this general practice were temples maintained by such tribal confederacies as the Caddo [Southeast]. The temples were like ordinary dwellings but larger. A typical one contained an altar made of reed mats, other mats, benches, a bed, and a low table displaying tobacco, a feathered pipe, and pottery vessels in which fat and tobacco could be burned. Worshippers could place food offerings to the supreme deity in a pair of boxes beside the altar (Newcomb 1961, 310). Among the Comanches and other plains tribes, individuals seeking divine guidance would sometimes visit a high and lonely place where they would build a sepulcher of stones and pay homage to the spirit they venerated, hoping to dream of the counsel for which they yearned (Berlandier 1969, 93).

An example of a temporary construction is the medicine lodge built for the Sun Dance, which is a summer festival celebrated by diverse tribes of the Great Plains, with the dance's settings differing somewhat from one band to another. Among the Crow, it has been customary to erect a tall, straight trunk of a cottonwood tree (with a forked top) as the center pole of a temporary lodge (Figure 4.5). That centerpiece is ringed by 12 smaller forked trees, joined across the tops with rafters of lodgepole pine covered with foliage (Greaves 2002, 34). For the Kiowa variation of the Sun Dance,

> The completed medicine lodge was some 60 feet in diameter, with an entrance to the east. Around the center post were 17 equally-spaced cottonwood posts, 12 feet high or more. Small cottonwoods were tied to them horizontally, and against them others were set up vertically to form a leafy wall. Here spectators would sit unobtrusively in the shade. More cottonwood limbs were laid from the center pole to the outer poles, and other branches were placed across these to form a roof.
>
> (Newcomb 1961, 215–216)

As with Christians, burial has long been Amerindians' principal means of disposing of the dead, especially in the East, Midwest, and Far West. Throughout North America, archeologists continue to find Indian burial mounds, some dating back nearly 2,000 years. However, the most prominent of the mounds were apparently constructed during the centuries referred to as the Middle

Figure 4.5   Raising the Center Pole for the Sun Dance.

Woodland time period, about 200 BCE to 300 CE. During that era, burial mounds were built across the eastern third of the continent from Kansas to New York and from the Great Lakes to the Gulf of Mexico (Hanson 2006). One major site still preserved today is at Albany, Illinois, where more than 100 mounds are distributed across 205 acres.

The number of skeletal remains varied from a few to nearly a hundred with a mixture of men, women, and children, indicating the mounds contained the remains of the general populace. The majority of the mounds were conical in shape, although there are some linear and oval mounds. They varied in size from one foot to 32 feet in height and from 200 feet to 15 feet in diameter. After selecting a burial site, the natives cleared the topsoil away. A central pit or crypt was dug into the subsoil. It was lined with stones, plaster, or logs to form a tomb. After the remains were interred, they were covered with logs or stones, then earth. Often more burials were added as the mound was built higher (Hanson 2006).

The construction of a mound excavated in Racine County, Wisconsin, was sketched by a Smithsonian Institution archeologist in 1860 (Figure 4.6). The bodies of two adults, along with several clay pots, had been laid in a gravel pit about three feet below ground level, then a rounded earthen mound was heaped over the grave.

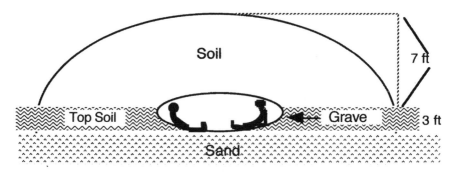

Fgiure 4.6   Burial Mound—Racine County, Wisconsin.

Source: Adapted from Lapham, 1855.

In mound burials, objects were usually interred with the bodies. For example, excavations at the Albany, Illinois, grounds yielded such a variety of items as ceramic jars, pots, arrow points, stone tools, copper awls, polished stone pendants, bracelets and necklaces of shell beads or river pearls, and knife blades from meteoric iron.

That the Albany tribe traded throughout North America was suggested by mound objects made of "obsidian from the Rocky Mountains, copper from Michigan, mica from the Appalachian Mountains, conch shells from the Gulf coast, seashells from the south Atlantic coast; galena from northwestern Illinois, chert from southern Indiana and southern Illinois, pipestone from the Rock River valley, and pottery from lower Illinois River valley" (Hanson 2006).

In more recent times, Indian graves have often featured markers. For example, the Chumash on California's seacoast topped graves with stone slabs, wooden planks, grave poles, or the rib bones of whales. Designs in red, black, and white paint were added to planks. Painted poles three or four times the height of a slab would be decorated with symbols or with favorite possessions of the deceased, and burials were preceded at night by a wake with singing and dancing around a bonfire.

> The body was then carried to the cemetery [on a rise adjacent to the village] amidst much lamentation by the relatives and other mourners. The deceased was buried in the flexed position, knees roped together against the chest and placed in the grave with the face down. Then his personal objects, effigies, steatite bowls, beads, flint knives, charmstones, wands, pipes, and bone whistles were placed in the grave.... Sometimes these personal objects were deliberately broken and scattered in the grave.
>
> (Miller 1988, 128)

A second mode of disposing of the dead, particularly among Great Plains tribes, was to first attach the body to a scaffold. Then when the scaffold decayed and fell, close relatives of the deceased buried the bones. However, clans often did not bury the skulls. Instead, they laid them "in circles of a hundred or more on the prairie, placed some eight or nine inches apart with the faces all turned toward the center where they were diligently protected and preserved...as objects of religious and affectionate veneration" (Mails 2002, 184).

Like Christianity, Indian religions include a spiritual afterlife that begins with a person's physical death. The concept of an abiding spirit, soul, or ghost has varied from one tribe to another. Many Native North Americans believe people have two souls, one that animates the body and another that travels through space, as during dreams, and that survives after death. Naskapis [Northeast, Labrador] and Cherokees [Southeast] include both intellectual and emotional characteristics in the soul.

> Mandans [Great Plains] thought that humans possessed four spirits. A white spirit was associated with the white sage plant. The second spirit was light brown and was associated with the meadowlark. The third spirit was identified more closely with the particular dwelling place of the dead person. The fourth spirit was black and was associated with a ghost that might frighten people. The white and brown spirits united after death, traveling to the village of the dead, while the third spirit remained near the lodge where the person had died.
>
> (Harrold 1996, 156)

The fourth spirit sometimes left the village but periodically returned to frighten the residents (Lowie 1954, 165).

Indian religions have offered diverse explanations of where a person's spirit goes after death. For the Blackfeet [Great Plains] the destination was the Sand Hills somewhere out on the plains. For some Hidatsas [Great Plains] it was under North Dakota's Devil's Lake and for others it was a land in the sky. The Sandpoils [Northwest] thought the dead lived on a river island, and the Laguna Pueblos [Southwest] suggested that the deceased turned into clouds or kachina spirits that brought rain (Harrold 1996). For most tribes, living conditions in the hereafter were believed to be similar to those on earth, but always with plenty of game to hunt, a bountiful supply of food, good weather, no sorrow or suffering, no war, no darkness, and everyone was youthful. In preparation for such an afterlife, a warrior's personal possessions were buried with him—clothing, weapons, a favorite horse (Powers 1973, 113–114). A few bands, such as the Blackfeet and Gros Ventre [Great Plains] held a dour view of the afterlife, conceiving it to be a "land of unrealities, where ghostly shadows of the departed endured an existence which was only a mockery of earthly life" (Mails 2002, 176–177).

Very seldom have Native American religions included the equivalent of the Christians' hell. For nearly all Indians, postmortem destinations have been pleasant realms in which the departeds' "spirits would forever rest, but not without periodically returning, manifested in symbolism the living understood; and they would return as bearers of beautiful thoughts and promising messages from the supernaturals who shaped the destines of all creatures" (Terrell 1979). However, some belief systems have included the conviction that individuals who committed especially wicked deeds on earth would have difficulty entering the land of the dead—a notion somewhat akin to Christianity's purgatory. Comanches [Great Plains] associated the soul with the breath, so that death by strangulation prevented the soul from leaving the body, eternally imprisoning the soul within the lifeless frame. Others among the deceased who would not go to a blessed afterworld were ones who had been scalped after death, died in the dark, or were mutilated (Newcomb 1961, 189).

> For the Cheyenne [Great Plains] there is no Hell or punishment of any sort in afterlife; no Judgment or Damnation. Although Cheyennes sin when they commit murder and they often do wrong, murder is expiated in the here and now, and wrongdoing builds up no burden of guilt to be borne beyond the grave. When at last the Cheyenne soul shakes free of its corporal abode, it wafts free and light up the Hanging Road to dwell thereafter in benign proximity to the Great Wise One and the long-lost loved ones. Only the souls of those who have committed suicide are barred from this peace.
>
> (Hoebel 1960, 87)

An interim of travail and pain after death is described in Fox (*Meskwaki,*) [Great Lakes] tradition for people who had behaved badly during their lifetime. Good people who died could travel a pleasant road to the enjoyable habitation that the Great Spirit provided for them in the afterworld. But bad people were unable to find that road and, instead, ended up traveling a difficult, crooked, rocky path that led to turbulent rivers they had to cross. By forcing the wicked into such a troublesome trip, the Great Spirit punished them until they repented, and only then did he guide them to the proper road.

> They soon reached their friends and the country of their future residence, where all kinds of game was plenty, and where they had but little to do but to dance by night and sleep by day.... Most of the Indians say that their deceased friends appear occasionally to them in the shape of birds and different kinds of beasts.
>
> (Marston in Blair 1911, 174–175)

Among the rare Indian equivalents of the Christian hell is the Lipan Apache [Southwest] site to which dead humans' souls may return. The site is an underworld or afterworld of vague location in whose northern compartment the spirits of wicked people and sorcerers are plagued with fog and fire while their food consists solely of snakes and lizards. Lipans fear that spirits of the dead might return to the earth as ghosts and haunt those who had wronged them when they were alive. Because a ghost will most likely appear when the name of the deceased is spoken, a dead person's name should never be uttered (Newcomb 1961, 129).

TRADITIONS COMPARED

The following comparison of Indian religions and Christianity identifies ways that significant places in the two traditions have been alike and different.

Similarities

Indian religions and Christian culture are comparable in several ways. Both revere centers of spiritual significance and power. Both have special sites for worship, honor the dead with burial services, and envision places where souls or spirits of the deceased reside in their afterlife. However, the form of each of these practices differs between Indian and Christian traditions.

Differences

Christianity's revered, viewable locations are mainly places mentioned in the Bible (such as Jerusalem and the Sea of Galilee) and sites in which miraculous events have been reported during last two millennia (healing at Lourdes, the annual Miracle of the Holy Fire at The Church of the Holy Sepulchre in Jerusalem). In contrast, Indian religions' mundane sites are wonders of nature, such as inspiring mountains, unusual rock formations, and impressive waterways (lakes, rivers, springs, falls).

Whereas most Christian ceremonies are conducted in permanent buildings constructed as places of worship and fellowship (churches, chapels, cathedrals), most Indian rituals are performed outdoors, in temporary quarters erected for the particular occasion, or in structures also used for purposes other than religious rites.

In their burial practices, American Indians, far more often than Christians, have placed in graves those possessions the deceased had found useful or had valued during life—clothing, amulets, pottery, weapons, pets.

The destination of the soul of the deceased in Christian culture has typically been one of four places—heaven, hell, purgatory, or limbo—with general agreement about the location of at least two of those sites. Heaven has been envisioned as a kind of land—a "firmament"—above the sky. Hell has often been cast as a vast fiery dungeon in the depths of the earth. In contrast, different Indian tribes have located the site of decedents' blissful afterlife in diverse places—in the sky, on the back of a giant turtle, in mountains some distance from the band's village, in the sea, and more.

Of particular note is the absence in Indian lore of the hell that is so important in Christian doctrine. Christians have traditionally used the threat of spending eternity in hell to motivate followers to abide by the religion's beliefs and rules of behavior. Indian religions have no such place as hell for the souls of the departed. Nearly all of the dead can expect a wondrously enjoyable eternity.

· 5 ·

Creating the Universe

Both Indian and Christian religions offer explanations of how the universe was formed, with the Indian versions far more diverse than the Christian. Descriptions of the world's origin in both traditions include a creator, a creation process, and a creation product.

The following account opens with Christian views of the universe's origin, continues with American Indian beliefs, and finishes with a comparison of creation theories.

CHRISTIAN PERSPECTIVES

Present-day Christians' conceptions of how the universe and its occupants originated appear in two main varieties: the literal account in the Bible and a modern-science account that considers the biblical description to be ancient observers' naïve estimate of how the world and its occupants came into being.

Creation According to Genesis

The traditional explanation among Jews, Christians, and Muslims of how the universe began is the description that appears in the first two chapters of the book of Genesis in the Jewish Torah and Christian Bible. The following summary of that creation story is from the Protestant Bible authorized by King James I of England in 1611.

In the beginning God created the heaven and the earth. And the earth was without form and void; and the darkness was upon the face of the deep. And the Spirit of God moved upon the face of the waters. And God said, "Let there be light," and there was light....And God called the light Day, and the darkness he called Night. And the evening and the morning were the first day.

(Genesis 1:1–4)

On the second day God formed a region—a dome-like firmament—that he called heaven. On the third day, he created dry land below heaven which he called earth; and he produced waters that he called seas, along with grass and fruit trees. On the fourth day he created the sun to light the day and the moon and stars to light the night, and he attached stars to the heavenly firmament. On the fifth day he created all sorts of fish for the seas and fowl for the skies. On the sixth day he declared, "Let the earth bring forth every living creature after his kind—cattle, and creeping thing, and beast of the earth after his kind: and it was so."

And God said, "Let us make man in our image, after our likeness: and let them have dominion over the fish of the sea, and over the fowl of the air, and over the cattle, and over all the earth, and over every creeping thing that creepeth upon the earth. So God created man in His *own* image... male and female created He them. And God blessed them and...said unto them, "Be fruitful, and multiply, and replenish the earth, and subdue it: and have dominion over...every living thing that moveth upon the earth."

(Genesis 1:1–28)

In a more detailed passage, the second chapter of Genesis explains that

The Lord God formed man of the dust of the ground, and breathed into his nostrils the breath of life; and man [named Adam] became a living soul....And the Lord God caused a deep sleep to fall upon Adam... and took one of his ribs...[from which he] made a woman [Eve].

(Genesis, 2:7, 21–22)

In summary, the creator was God, the creation process was a six-day series of acts, and the creation product was the earth and its life forms—plants, animals, and humans in essentially the same condition as they exist today. And, as noted in Chapter 3, the final product in Christian lore includes invisible elements of the cosmos—God, a Holy Spirit, angels, souls of the dead—in addition to the earth's viewable contents.

Today there are several versions of the biblical creation story's details. One is *young-earth creationism,* which proposes that (a) God produced the universe and everything within it during six days and (b) Earth is only a few thousand years old—perhaps 4,000, maybe 6,000, or possibly 10,000. Another version accepts the notion that Earth is millions of years old but holds that God originally created humans complete in their present form, distinctly different from all other manner of life. A third version rejects the notion of macro-evolution (all species tracing their origins back to a common simple-celled organism) but accepts micro-evolution (changes within a given species as the result of selective breeding or adjustments to changed environments, as with humans in intense-sunlight tropical regions developing more protective dark skin pigment than humans in temperate zones).

Among Christians in colonial North America, virtually everyone subscribed to the young-earth biblical account. To do otherwise would be heresy. Such was the case until the late nineteenth century when the Bible story was contested by a view of creation derived from secular empirical science.

Creation According to Modern Science

Although across the centuries the biblical account was accepted in Jewish, Christian, and Muslim societies as the true story of human beginnings, a few people doubted that the Genesis version was literally true, because the story contained logical inconsistencies. For instance, how could God differentiate day from night on the first day of creation when he did not create the sun and moon until the fourth day of creation? However, most Jews, Christians, and Muslims accepted the Genesis account as God-given truth.

Then, in the mid-nineteenth century, Europeans and Americans alike were stunned by a proposal that men and women had not been created suddenly in their mature form by a supreme heavenly power. Instead, in the opinion of a group of scientists, humans had evolved gradually over eons of time from simpler forms of animal life through a process of mutation and natural selection by which varieties of animals that were well suited to survival as their environments changed would prosper, and those not well suited would die off. Therefore, humans were not unique beings, entirely separate from other animals. They were part of a complex pattern of linked life forms. The detailed version of that proposal appeared in the book *The Origin of Species* (1859) by Charles Darwin, an English naturalist; and the scheme became known as a theory of evolution.

Darwin's theory was not greeted with great joy in his day, nor is it universally accepted by Christians today. In the late nineteenth century, the theory was condemned from most pulpits; and the general public did not welcome the unattractive likelihood that their close biological relatives might have been apes and monkeys and that more distant ancestors could have been chickens, toads, and garden slugs. However, a massive accumulation of empirical evidence over the decades gradually convinced scientists of the theory's worth, so that today most of biological science is founded on an updated version of the theory of evolution called neo-Darwinism.

Whereas Darwin's proposal explained how humans represented one link in a chain of connected forms of life, it did not explain how the universe itself began. Such an explanation came later. During the twentieth century, the most popular secular-science account of cosmic origin was labeled the *big-bang theory.* According to the theory, about 13.7 billion years ago the cosmos was born from the explosion of an extremely hot, dense core of matter and energy. Since that time, the galaxies, stars, and planets produced in the explosion have been traveling through space in all directions, producing an ever-expanding cosmos. However, scientists continue to puzzle over what might have been the original source of the scorching, dense matter that produced the big bang. Present-day Christians who accept the Darwinian and big-bang explanations in preference to the Genesis account usually contend that God was the source of that energy and of the processes by which the universe continues to enlarge and life forms evolve.

Therefore, in this revised Christian account of the origin of the cosmos and its life forms, God is still the creator, but the creation process consists of the universe's contents gradually evolving from simpler to more complex forms with the passing of time. Hence, the product of creation—the cosmos and its elements—is not fixed or static but is ever-changing.

In the twenty-first century, Christian denominations known as *conservative, fundamentalist,* or *evangelical* have clung to the Genesis story, whereas church groups labeled *moderate or liberal* have accepted Darwinian and big-bang explanations, with God identified as the original force behind those phenomena. Fundamentalist groups have included Southern Baptists, Jehovah's Witnesses, Mormons, Pentecostals, and Conservative Lutherans. Moderates have included Presbyterians, Episcopalians, Liberal Lutherans, Methodists, Christian Scientists, and Unitarians. Whereas the most recent popes of the Roman Catholic Church have subscribed to a biblical view of creation, most Catholic high schools and colleges in North America teach Darwinism and the big-bang theory in their science classes; the Vatican's chief astronomer has endorsed those secular-science theories (Thomas 2007).

INDIAN PERSPECTIVES

In contrast to Christian doctrine, American Indian tribes can differ dramatically from each other in their conception of the creator, the creation process, and the precise nature of the final product. The following account first describes (a) Indian versions of the creator, the creation process, and the ultimate form of the universe, then turns to (b) likely Christian influence.

The Creator

With rare exception, Indian cosmologies identify a supreme being—*Manitou, Wakan Tanka, Glooskap,* The Great Hare, or the like—as the creator of the universe. Among the exceptions is the early Yurok [Northern California] view that did not posit a beginning of the universe but simply accepted the existence of the world and its contents. Yurok lore reports a prehuman race of spirits, but those beings did not create humans. Rather, they merely organized the world and its operation prior to the arrival of humans who would become the land's proprietors (Heizer 1978, 654). Likewise, the Hupas [Northern California] believed that the world had always existed and that humans had merely sprung into being (Readers Digest 1978, 271–272).

Just as analysts of the Christian story of creation often ask about where the creator—God—came from, so also analysts ask about the source of the initial creator in Indian religions. The usual answer is that the creator "just appeared" or else "was always there." But some Indian worldviews are more specific about the creator's origin. For example, in Caddo or Kadohadacho [Southeast] theology, before the world existed there was a woman with two daughters, one of whom was pregnant. When the daughters were alone, they were attacked by a monster that tore the pregnant girl apart and ate her. Her sister escaped and reported the attack to her mother, who searched the location of the tragedy and found a drop of the dead girl's blood in an acorn shell. When the mother returned home, she sealed the blood in a jar. The next day, she heard a scratching noise from the jar and discovered inside a perfectly formed boy the size of her finger. She replaced the jar top, and the following day when she opened the container again she found a perfectly shaped man, who flew to the sky where he would become the universe's supreme creator and ruler (Newcomb 1961, 309).

The Original Form of the Universe

Accounts of the initial state of the world have varied from one tribal tradition to another.

The French commandant in the Great Lakes region in the late 1600s, Nicholas Perrot, reported the nearby tribes' belief that before the earth was created, the universe consisted entirely of water on which an enormous wooden raft floated. The raft contained all of the earth's animal species. The group's leader, the Great Hare, realized that if he could obtain at least one grain of soil, he could turn it into land sufficient to accommodate and feed all of the animals. So he delegated the beaver to dive to the ocean bottom and retrieve some soil. But the beaver's long search ended in failure, as did the attempt of the next candidate, the otter. Finally the muskrat volunteered for the task. After being submerged for 24 hours, he rose to the surface exhausted and with a single grain of sand clutched in his paw. The Great Hare cast the grain onto the raft, where the grain began to multiply, soon forming a mountain and then a widespread, spacious earth that the Great Hare inspected but judged to be incomplete.

Since then [the Great Hare] continues to increase what he has made, by moving without cessation around the earth. This idea causes [the Indians] to say, when they hear loud noises in the hollows of the mountains, that the Great Hare is still enlarging the earth; they pay honor to him, and regard him as the deity who created it. [The Indians believe the world is] always borne upon that raft. As for the sea, [they say it has] existed for all time.

(Perrot in Blair 1911, 34–36)

A Shasta-Karuk [California] version of the world's origin tells that the Great Spirit initially cast the earth in the form of a woman, with the soil as her flesh, the rocks her bones, the wind her breath, and the rivers her veins. She lay down in a nurturing position so people and animals could dwell on her body. When people misbehaved, she warned them by shaking, thereby causing floods and earthquakes. The Great Spirit next rolled bits of damp earth into mud balls that became the first living beings. Some were half human and half animal, others were half human and half bird, and still others half human and half fish. These early creatures communicated through silent telepathic messages. Intellectually they were a mixture of cleverness and stupidity, smart enough to hunt but unable to distinguish between people and animals, "so sometimes they ate humans" (Lake-Thom 1994, 60). In addition to the half-humans/half-animals, the Great Spirit produced real people who became the ancestors of present-day Indians. And certain animals that were blessed with wisdom and special power shared their own wisdom and power with the Indians.

In those days [the animals and humans] even sang and danced with each other to celebrate good fortune, or to give thanks to the Great Creator, and to pray and give thanks to the Earth.…Some of the original creatures have disappeared, but their spirit side is still around in [sacred] places on the Earth. That is why [people must] be careful about what they do to the Earth…[for] otherwise the spirits of Nature and the Earth itself will turn against us.

(Lake-Thom 1994, 60)

A Sequential Process

During the creation process, the sequence in which the world's contents appeared could vary from one Indian religion to another.

In the lore of Central California tribes, animals are described as the *first people,* occupying the land before the arrival of humans (Heizer 1978, 655). In a linked-species version of this sequence, the Huron and Iroquois [Great Lakes] believed that when the first animals on earth died, men were born from their corpses—some men from fish and others from cranes, bears, beavers, deer, moose, and more. Villages were named after the imagined animal ancestors of the villages' residents. Then the Great Hare decided that men needed female companions as helpmates, so he created women whose assigned roles would include cooking, sewing, dressing animal skins, making moccasins, and performing "all the tasks that are proper for women" (Perrot in Blair 1911, 37–40).

The creation process for the Navajos and Pueblos [Southwest] began with
the birth of Changing Woman from the mating of Earth Mother and Sky
Father. Changing Woman's name derived from the patterning of her life,
which revealed a different aspect of her nature with each new season—"young
in the springtime [when] fructified by the sun and copious spring rains, bearing
abundantly in summer, and aging in the fall to die and be born anew" (Waters
1950, 195). When Changing Woman first appeared, the universe was still an
amorphous combination of the preceding worlds of fire, air, and water. As
she matured, the earth-world "solidified into form and substance; earth and
sky, the mountains and the stars, plants and animals assumed their proper
roles. Impregnated by sun fire and water, she immaculately conceived the dual
Hero Twins and then gave birth to a new race—the Navajos [and Pueblos]"
(Waters 1950, 194).

Algonquin [Northeast] theology pictures the supreme spirit, *Glooskap,* as
first creating elves who dwelt in the rocks. Then, with his bow he shot arrows
into ash trees, causing Indians to emerge from the bark. After thus creating
humans, *Glooskap* produced all of the animals—moose, wolf, squirrel, white
bear, dog, loon, and the rest (Leland 1884, 18–19).

An Osage [Great Plains] legend tells of a snail that became stuck in the mud
on the bank of the Missouri River, where he suffered from the baking sun until
suddenly his shell burst open. His head rose above the ground, his lower body
sprouted feet and legs, and arms grew from his upper body. After a single day
in the sun, he turned into a tall, noble man—the world's first human. Over the
coming days, as he wandered about, he spotted birds and beasts but knew not
how to hunt them for food. Weak and starving, he lay down to die when a voice
called him by name—*Wasbasas.* And he saw it was the Great Spirit, sitting on a
white horse, hair aglow like the sun and eyes sparkling like the stars. In his
hand, the Great Spirit held a bow and arrow and showed *Wasbasas* how to
shoot game for food, then how to remove a deer's skin to make himself a garment. Next, the Spirit draped a string of wampam shells around *Wasbasas's*
neck, announced that the wampam was the sign of *Wasbasas's* authority over
all the animals, and vanished. As *Wasbasas* began his travels in search of his
native land, he came across the king of the beaver nation and was invited to
the king's village. The beaver chief taught *Wasbasas* how to fell trees, build
dams, and construct lodges cemented with leaves and clay. And it was there
that *Wasbasas* met the king's beautiful daughter whom he would wed in a
ceremony attended by all the beavers and other friendly beasts. "The Snail-
Man and the Beaver-Maid were thus united, and this union is the origin of
the Osages. So it is said by the old people" (Schoolcraft in Williams 1956,
263–264).

The struggle between good and evil plays a central role in many Indian creation stories. An example is Iroquois [Great Lakes] tradition in which human
life began after Sky Woman was pushed out of heaven. She fell onto the islands
that had been created when a muskrat brought a bit of mud from the sea floor
and dropped it on a turtle's shell, where the mud expanded to form the vast

earth. Before Sky Woman fell from heaven, she had already been impregnated by Earth Holder. Now on earth, she gave birth to a daughter who herself became magically impregnated and bore twin sons, Great Spirit and Evil Spirit. The daughter died in childbirth, and Great Spirit honored her by fashioning the sun, moon, and stars from her body. Great Spirit's next task was to create the earth's components—mountains, valleys, streams, people, animals, and plants. Meanwhile, Evil Spirit was introducing into the world such features as anger, fear, strife, warfare, and creatures that would threaten peace on earth. The inevitable conflict between the two bothers' acts led to a furious two-day battle that Great Spirit won. Evil Spirit was then forced to dwell in the netherworld for the rest of eternity, but his creations remained in the world to bring misery into people's lives (Readers Digest 1978, 131–132).

In some versions of Indian theology, the master creator leaves to others — either by intent or default—the job of producing features of the universe not yet completed. An example is the set of tasks assigned to the Iroquois and Algonquin [Great Lakes, Northeast] deity *Teharonhiawagon,* a son of *Awehai,* the Earth Mother, and a personification of the life force. It was Teharonhiawagon who made the earth's plants and animals before he created humans. And from "his father of mysterious origin he had learned the art of fire-making and agriculture and how to build a house; and these arts he communicated to mankind" (Hewitt in Blair 1911, 271–272).

Wichita [Great Plains] tradition teaches that *Kinnikasus* (meaning "Not-Known-to-Man" because he is beyond human comprehension) created the universe and all of its contents, then assigned various duties to deities lower in the spirits hierarchy. Morning Star, created as the first man, was charged with ushering in daylight and supervising the other stars. South Star guarded warriors, North Star enabled people to identify where they were located on the earth, and Great Bear bore duties similar to those of Sun and Morning Star (Newcomb 1961, 371).

Pawnee [Great Plains] legend has identified *Tirawa* as the supreme deity who existed forever and who, at the world's beginning, appointed Evening Star (Mother of All Things) to issue his commands to the other gods. He ordered Morning Star to wed Evening Star, who produced the first girl, and he then directed Sun to mate with Moon and produce the first boy. When the boy and girl married, they became the ancestors of much of the human race. But, according to Pawnee lore, other deities also created humans (Lowie 1954, 165).

Certain Indian religions attribute the creation of death to particular spirits. The Blackfeet [Northern Great Plains] tell of Old Man (*Napi*) arguing with Old Woman in primordial times about whether people should die or should live forever. To settle the question, Old Woman cast a rock into a pool and prophesied that if the rock floated, the dead would come back to life within four days. But if the rock sank, people would remain dead forever. Because the rock sank, everlasting death became a fact of human destiny. In a different version of death's origin, Apache [Southwest] lore blames the creation of death on a pair of mean-spirited rascals, Coyote and Raven (Howard 1996, 155).

As another instance of delegated creation tasks, a Lummi [Northwest] story tells of Raven being assigned by the Great Spirit to distribute certain of the earth's contents—streams, trees, birds—so they would not all be crowded into the same region (Lake-Thom 1997, 54).

In contrast to creation beliefs that cast animals as earlier arrivals on earth than humans is the Chemehuevi [Southwest] tradition, which envisions the earth's contents—mountains, rivers, plants, animals, and humans—as appearing simultaneously at the very beginning, then "interacting in a great drama that put the world into motion" (Greaves 2002, 8).

The Universe in Final Form

Indian traditions have depicted the nature of the world in a variety of ways. In general, they have conceived the earth to be in the same form as did early Christians—a flat, rather bumpy surface that is circular, drops off vertically at the edges, and is surmounted by a blue, domed canopy overhead that is embellished with a sun, moon, and stars (Clements 1986, 213–214; Heizer 1978, 651). But different tribes have had their particular renditions of this general pattern.

Among the early Yuroks [Northern California], the world consisted of a small bounded region with the Klamath River flowing through it to the edge of the Pacific Ocean (Heizer 1978, 651).

Chumash [California] legend has depicted three worlds, one above the other, each in the shape of an island suspended in a dark void. The lowest island (*C'oyimashup*) is the dwelling place of gloomy, misshapen beings — *Nunashish*—that may sneak up into the middle island to cause evil mischief. Humans live on the middle island that is surrounded by a great sea and is held up from below by two giant serpents who occasionally move, thereby causing earthquakes. Long before humans appeared, the First People ("supernatural beings with the human attributes of will, reason, and emotion") lived on the middle island until a great flood engulfed the universe, killing *Nunashish* in the lower world and driving many of the First People onto the top island. But some of the First People remained in the middle world in the form of animal and plant spirits or such natural forces as thunder, wind, and water. The topmost world (*'Alap'ay*) is supported by the Great Eagle whose powerful wings change phases of the moon and move the heavenly bodies along their assigned paths. The Sky People of the upper world include the most powerful beings in the universe—such deities as the Sun (male), Moon (female), Morning Star (Venus), Sky Coyote, Great Eagle, and Lizard. Following the great flood, the upper world deities held a council during which they agreed to create humans. With that act, *life* and *death* originated, leading to "the Chumash belief that all earthy things are in flux in a natural cycle of reincarnation" (Miller 1988, 120).

The Sioux [Great Plains] have also believed in reincarnation, with people who were virtuous during their lives being returned in death to the presence of the Great Spirit. However, wicked people were sent back to the world as one of the lower animals. Then, if obedient as animals, they could be returned to their original condition as humans (Clements 1986, 215).

The Navajos [Southwest] defined the boundaries of their world by four sets of mountains that mark the extremes of the cardinal directions—east, south, west, and north. Mount Blanca (*Tsisnaasjini'*—Dawn or White Shell Mountain) is the eastern boundary in Colorado's San Luis Valley near the city of Alamosa. Mount Taylor (*Tsoodzi*—Blue Bead or Turquoise Mountain) north of Laguna, New Mexico, forms the southern boundary. San Francisco Peak (*Doko'oosliid*—Abalone Shell Mountain) near Flagstaff, Arizona, marks the western border. Mount Hesperus (*Dibé Nitsaa*—Big Mountain Sheep or Obsidian Mountain) in Colorado's La Plata range is the Navajo universe's northern outpost.

In Navajo lore, each day carries individuals' lives through a cycle of quadrants that begins when the sun dawns in the east, requiring people to plan for the day. As the sun advances past the south and into the west, the plan is carried out. When the sun sets in the west, the north comes into play as the time for appraising how the day worked out. "This is where we get our satisfaction and evaluate the outcome of what we first started in the east. Here is where we determine to change things to make life better or to see if we are on the right path as we continue the cycle" (Introduction to the Navajo 1997).

Navajo cosmology portrays the universe as at least five worlds, each one atop another. Both people and animals started in the lowest world, then gradually crawled up to the second world. In one Navajo version, the world began as a black island floating in the mist. Above it were four clouds, black, white, blue, and yellow. The first cloud, the black one, represented the female within whose being were contained all the forms of life. The white cloud contained the male substance. When the black and white clouds met, the forms of life—plant and animal—emerged; the worlds had become real. The first and lowest world (*Ni'hodilqil*) was like black wool. To escape the blackness, the people and animals crawled up into the second or blue world, which was occupied by blue birds, blue hawks, blue jays, blue herons, and other blue-feathered beings. When the angry blue residents attack the newcomers, First Man directed his followers to crawl up to the sunless yellow third world, which consisted of six mountains and two great rivers, the north-to-south Female River and east-to-west Male River.

> On the mountains lived the light and dark squirrels, chipmunks, mice, rats, the turkey people, the deer and cat people, the spider people, and the lizards and snakes. The beaver people lived along the rivers, and the frogs and turtles and all the underwater people in the water. So far all the people were similar. They had no definite form, but they had been given different names because of different characteristics.
>
> (O'Byran 1997)

Then up to the fourth world, which First Man decided was too small. And a huge flood had so thoroughly soaked the earth that growing corn became impossible. Thus, First Man delegated the locust to climb up a tall reed to that world's vaulted ceiling and dig his way into the fifth world above. Now First Man and his companions could follow the locust into the sunny fifth world, which was bounded by the four sets of mountains where the Navajos live today. Some shamans say there are two additional worlds above the fifth—one called the World of the Spirits of Living Things and the other called the Place of Melting into One.

(O'Bryan 1956)

Now, after all the people had emerged [to the fifth world] from the lower worlds, First Man and First Woman dressed the Mountain Lion with yellow, black, white, and grayish corn and placed him on one side. They dressed the Wolf with white tail feathers and placed him on the other side. They divided [their followers] into two groups. [The ones] who had the Mountain Lion for their chief turned out to be the people of the Earth. They were to plant seeds and harvest corn. The followers of the Wolf chief became the animals and birds; they turned into all the creatures that fly and crawl and run and swim.

(O'Bryan 1997)

The European Immigrants' Influence

As noted earlier, before Native Americans adopted the European immigrants' written form of language, they transmitted their religious beliefs orally from one generation to the next. Therefore, Indian shamans, in the tales they told, could be influenced by such recent experiences as missionaries teaching them Christian doctrine. Charles Leland (1884) speculated that such was the case with an Algonquin [Northeast] creation tale that pictured a spirit mother (perhaps Mary?) descending from above (heaven?) and producing twins, one of whom was good (God or Jesus?) and the other evil (Satan?). The twins fought for control of the universe, with the good spirit emerging victorious and the bad spirit sinking into the underworld (hell?). The following is a brief version of that story and its apparent merging of original Algonquin beliefs with elements of Christian lore. Note how several aspects of the tale are much like those of the Iroquois variation described earlier, thereby suggesting theological borrowings between the two neighboring nations.

A woman spirit who fell from "the higher world" landed on the earth, which was at that time a gigantic turtle encased in darkness. The woman soon bore twins who displayed opposite personality traits. One, named *Enigorio* or Good Mind, was blessed with a multitude of virtues; he desired that the earth be turned bright and pleasant. The other, *Enigonhahegea* or Bad Mind, wanted darkness to prevail. Good Mind, in an effort to turn desire into reality, started the work of creation by making his mother's head the sun and her body the moon. Then, after producing rivers and animals, he fashioned soil into two images, male and female, and gave them human souls by breathing into their nostrils. Meanwhile, Bad Mind created tall mountains, waterfalls, and deep valleys, where he placed reptiles that could threaten people's welfare. Bad Mind also formed clay into two images that he intended to be humans, but they turned out to be apes. As a means of settling the conflict over which twin's plan for the universe would prevail, the pair engaged in a furious two-day battle that Good Mind won. "The last words uttered by the Bad Mind were that he would have equal power over the souls of mankind after their deaths, and so sank down to eternal doom and became the Evil Spirits" (Leland 1884, 25).

The likely influence of Christian lore is also reflected in the Saulk [Subarctic Eastern Canada] tale in which the Great Spirit formed two men out of the soil. Then, to alleviate the men's loneliness, the Spirit took a rib from each man to produce a pair of women (Marston in Blair 1911, 174).

A different effect of Europeans on Indians' worldview is found among the Kiowas [Southwest], whose traditional conception of human beginnings has acquired an addendum focusing on the European immigrants. One popular form of the Kiowa creation story begins with the Great Spirit first producing the world's physical features (sun, night, mountains, plains, streams) and then making animals. Finally, he creates Kiowas by pounding on a hollow log from which frightened men, women, and children emerge. But the Spirit tells them not to fear, for they are his children. And because some were born imperfect, the Spirit corrects their deformities, teaches them how to use tools and weapons, and sends them on their way.

Now for the later addition to the Kiowa tale. After the Spirit meets the Great White Man who had created the Europeans, he returns to the Kiowas and instructs them in ways to resist the white enemies who had come to steal their land. Finally, the Spirit changes the Great White Man into the moon and turns himself into a group of stars (Newcomb 1961, 219–220).

TRADITIONS COMPARED

In the following paragraphs, Christianity and Indian religions are reviewed —first their similarities, then their differences.

Similarities

Christian cosmology and nearly all Indian belief systems attribute the creation of the universe and its contents to invisible spirits. For Christians, the creator is a single deity, God. Most Indian religions, like Christianity, credit a single spirit—Manitou, Wakan Tanka, the Great Hare, and such—as the creator of all things. However, in some Indian religions, minor spirits are considered responsible for producing certain of the world's contents. And a few Indian worldviews do not attempt to account for how the universe came into being. They simply accept the universe as a given.

A second similarity is in the story form used for describing the world's beginnings. Both Christian and Indian depictions are cast as tales involving personified spirits, animals, and humans.

Third, Christian and Indian portrayals are alike in neglecting attention to changes in the world's social structures and technology, particularly during recent centuries. Christian doctrine and most Indian tales describe a process by which the earth's geography, the contents of the sky, and the earth's plant, animal, and human life developed in a very distant past. However, neither Christian nor Amerindian theologies explain shifts in modes of governance (monarchy, oligarchy, anarchy, democracy, autocracy) or technological innovations (radio telescopes, electron microscopes, airplanes, television, computers, space travel). Some present-day critics suggest that Christian and Indian conceptions of societal governance and phenomena of nature are now badly out of date.

Consider, first, styles of governance. We can recognize that Christianity was born, and for centuries nurtured, in monarchies or oligarchies, so that conceiving God as *The Lord* and Jesus as *King of Kings* was compatible with the mode of authority under which Christians lived. But in modern-day democratic or socialistic nations in which the ultimate responsibility for decisions is vested in the voting citizens, a Christian conception of a kingly deity determining the fate of societies is obliged to exist rather awkwardly—perhaps blindly—alongside secular democracies. This same problem of who's really in charge of social decisions and actions—including wars and economic depressions—also confronts Indian religions that locate the control of worldly affairs in one or more deities.

Next, consider science and technology. Orthodox Christian and Amerindian beliefs about the shape, scope, and contents of the universe are obliged to live uncomfortably beside astrophysicists' depictions of a vast, expanding cosmos and biologists' neo-Darwinian evidence that the world's living things evolved gradually from simple matter over eons of time rather than being created all of a sudden by a divine spirit.

As a result of the seeming incompatibility of traditional religious explanations and modern-day social or scientific views of the creation and subsequent operation of the universe, arguments continue among North Americans who concern themselves with such matters.

Differences

Perhaps the greatest difference between Christian and Indian views of creation is in Amerindian versions' greater diversity. As described early in this chapter, Christian creation beliefs are of two main types—the literal biblical description in Genesis and a modified version that credits God as the creator but regards the Genesis description as no more than the crude speculation of ancient theologians. In contrast, Amerindian religions offer a multitude of creation accounts that can vary dramatically from one tribe to another. Such diversity resulted to a great extent from Indian creation descriptions being communicated orally rather than in written form, with descriptions depending on the accuracy of tale-tellers' memories and their inclination to embellish stories with their own imaginings.

A second difference is in the role assigned to animals in Christian and Indian worldviews. Christian belief distinguishes sharply between humans and animals, with humans displaying intelligence and skills that extend far beyond the inferior traits of animals. With few exceptions (the snake in the Garden of Eden, Daniel in the lions' den), people are not depicted as engaging in meaningful relationships with birds and beasts. In contrast, Indian religions not only populate their lore with great hosts of animals, but also invest animals with traits and powers often superior to those possessed by people, so Amerindian legendry is replete with descriptions of animals serving as people's guardian spirits and sources of wisdom.

·
· 6 ·
·

Causes and Ceremonies

The word *cause,* as intended throughout this book, refers to explanations of why an event occurred the way it did. The analysis of causes in the present chapter distinguishes between two interpretations of cause, the *direct* and the *mediated* (Figure 6.1).

The term *direct* is applied to explanations that propose that an event—such as a thunderstorm or the loss of a car key—was the result of an earlier observed condition or event. Thus, an observed configuration of clouds, humidity, and temperature change is said to have caused the thunderstorm. The motorist's carelessness is said to have caused him to misplace his ignition key somewhere around the house. Secular scientific explanations of cause are of this direct variety. In effect, the scientist's task consists of (a) observing conditions that preceded an event, (b) identifying which of those conditions have consistently been correlated with the event, and (c) adducing a persuasive line of logic showing that the selected conditions inevitably lead to such an outcome and therefore can be considered the cause of the event. So, from this perspective, there is a direct connection between a previous condition and a subsequent event.

In contrast to direct explanations of events, *mediated* explanations assume that a supernatural being or power has served as an intermediary between an initial condition or event and a subsequent one. Hence, the thunderstorm occurred because, (a) as an initial event, a group of people performed a dance of appeal to a supernatural power to end a drought and (b) the mediating supernatural spirit responded favorably to the appeal by (c) producing a rainstorm. In another application of a mediation viewpoint, unwanted events can be blamed on people's having angered a mystical spirit or power. For instance,

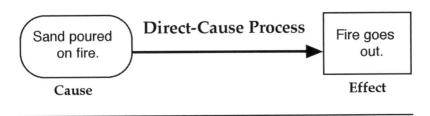

Direct-Cause Process

Sand poured on fire. ⟶ Fire goes out.

Cause   Effect

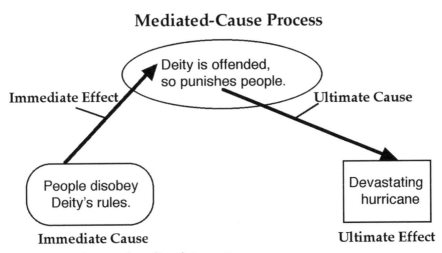

Mediated-Cause Process

Immediate Effect

Deity is offended, so punishes people.   Ultimate Cause

People disobey Deity's rules.   Devastating hurricane

Immediate Cause   Ultimate Effect

Figure 6.1   Direct and Mediated Cause Processes.

(a) a motorist used a supernatural spirit's name as a curse word, thereby (b) offending the spirit, who responded by (c) distracting the attention of the motorist so the motorist lost his car key. Or, perhaps the key was lost only inadvertently ("accidentally") and not because an invisible spirit was displeased. However, the motorist can still trust mediated cause in order to recover the key. He can (a) appeal for the spirit's help in finding the key on the assumption that (b) the all-wise spirit knows where the lost key fell and (c) will reveal that location to the motorist or perhaps to a confidant of the motorist.

People who subscribe to a religion are apt to employ both direct and mediated causal reasoning. When the connection between an initial event and a subsequent event seems obvious, nearly everyone will attribute the outcome to the direct influence of the initial event. Thus, throwing sand on the fire is judged to be the cause of the fire going out. Slapping the mosquito is said to be the reason the mosquito died. Failing to water the corn patch is blamed for the corn stalks withering. But religious people are prone to apply a mediated interpretation when an event's origins and causal process are not readily apparent. Thus, assuming the influence of a spirit-mediator seems necessary for solving such questions as: Why did the child contract the fatal illness? Why did the volcano erupt and bury the village under lava? Why did the enemy win the war? Why did the economy fail? Why did the ship sink in the storm? Why did the swarm of locusts arrive to devour the crop? Why did I win the lottery?

North-American Indian religions and Christian doctrine both depend heavily on mediated explanations of events whose causes seem puzzling. Thus, differences among religions are not about whether supernatural beings cause events but, instead, the differences are about the way the mediation process operates and, especially, about how people can make the process operate in their favor. In other words, how can people most effectively appeal to the spirits in order to achieve people's aims? The answer, for both Indians and Christians, is by prayer and ceremonies.

For present purposes, *prayer* and *praying* consist of remarks, silent thoughts, or observable actions that people address to one or more invisible deities. Prayers can be intended to serve diverse purposes, such as,

- Giving thanks for one's good fortune and for blessings received.

  "We gratefully thank Thee, Lord, for this bountiful meal Thou hast provided."
  "We raise our voices in thanks to the Great Spirit for protecting our people during the snowstorm."

- Exalting and paying tribute to a deity.

  "Allah be praised."

- Appealing for a deity's help.

  "We beseech Thee to give us the strength to endure the hardships ahead."
  "Do spare our hunters from harm, revered Takuskanskan."

- Drawing a deity's attention to a problem that should be remedied.

  "Blessed Wakan Tanka, the Sioux nation is in dire need of food for the winter."

- Issuing advice, suggestions, or orders for a deity to perform particular tasks.

  "Stop the hurricanes that are destroying the lives of so many good folks."
  "Lead us not into temptation, and deliver us from evil."
  "Bless our missionaries who labor in foreign lands."
  "Guard our warriors as they defend the tribe."

- Asking forgiveness and mercy for having done wrong.

  "Forgive us our sins, as we forgive those who sin against us."

- Expressing faith in, and respect for, a deity's wisdom and power.

  "We know that Almighty God will not forsake us in our hour of need."

- Doing penance for having behaved badly.

  "To compensate for what I did wrong, I will give baskets of food to the needy this holiday season."

- Appealing to be transported to a place of eternal bliss.

  "Manitou, may our aged father be welcomed in the Great Beyond."
  "Lord, we deliver the soul of this dear departed child to thy keeping in heaven."

- Bargaining with a deity.

  "If you fix it so our side wins, I'll faithfully attend all the weekly religious services the rest of this year."

To add strength and conviction to a prayer, supplicants may close their plea with "good words"—a *benediction*. A typical Christian benediction reads, "In the name of the Father, the Son, and the Holy Ghost," in reference to the trinity of God, Jesus, and the Holy Spirit.

Prayers can be cast in various forms. The most common forms are oral remarks and silent thoughts. However, prayers can also assume the guise of actions—fingering Catholic prayer beads, twirling a Buddhist prayer wheel, sacrificing a sheep or goat in Judaic tradition, preparing a Navajo sand painting, carving a Hopi kachina doll, performing an Ojibway jingle-dress dance, singing an Anglican anthem, and more.

Ceremonies are activities, infused with ritual significance, that are performed on special occasions for their symbolic value as prescribed by a group's religious tradition. Whereas most religious ceremonies are intended to serve one or more of the foregoing aims of prayer, some are designed for other purposes—to initiate newcomers into the religion, to honor a worthy member of the faith, or to commemorate a significant event.

CHRISTIAN RELIGIOUS PRACTICES

Christian tradition includes multiple forms of prayer and ceremony.

The Nature of Christian Prayers

Three types of oral prayer are the *established, self-prepared,* and *spontaneous.* An established prayer is a conventional written or memorized oration that an individual or group recites verbatim. The most popular established prayer in Christian tradition is known as The Lord's Prayer, designed to venerate God and appeal for divine guidance and support.

Our Father which art in heaven, hallowed be thy name. Thy kingdom come. Thy will be done in earth, as it is in heaven. Give us this day our daily bread. And forgive us our debts, as we forgive our debtors. And lead us not into temptation, but deliver us from evil: For thine is the kingdom, and the power, and the glory, forever. Amen.

(Matthew 6:9–13)

Other established prayers—such as ones used in marriage and funeral services—are found in publications like the Anglican *Book of Common Prayer*, whose best-known edition, issued in 1662, was popular throughout the American colonies, and was adopted by missionaries in their effort to convert Indians to Christianity. In revised editions, the book is still used today by several denominations (Howell 1662/2006).

An established prayer can also be one passed orally from generation to generation, as with this bedtime verse for young children.

Now I lay me down to sleep, I pray the Lord my soul to keep.
If I should die before I wake, take me to heaven for Jesus's sake.

Self-prepared prayers are formally composed by an individual—usually a minister, priest, or rabbi—then read to a congregation at a later date, such as during a Sunday sermon.

Spontaneous prayers are oral or silent communications directed to God by an individual who creates the prayer on the spur of the moment, often at a time of crisis (a threat of danger, a loved one's death or injury) or at a time of good fortune (winning a game, finding money).

Christian prayers are frequently in the form of poems and songs, either selections from the Bible or hymns created by Christian composers over the past two millennia. Perhaps the most revered of the 150 verses attributed to King David in the Bible's book of Psalms is the twenty-third, which praises God for his guidance and assures believers that they will enjoy not only a blessed earthly life but also a heavenly afterlife.

The Lord is my shepherd, I shall not want. He maketh me to lie down in green pastures; he leadeth me beside the still waters. He restoreth my soul: he leadeth me in the paths of righteousness for his name's sake. Yea, though I walk through the valley of the shadow of death, I will fear no evil; for thou art with me: thy rod and thy staff they comfort me. Thou preparest a table before me in the presence of mine enemies: thou anointest my head with oil: my cup runneth over. Surely goodness and mercy shall follow me all the days of my life: and I will dwell in the house of the Lord forever.

(Psalms 23:1–6)

Typical themes of Christian religious songs can be illustrated with the opening stanzas of three well-known hymns—*Amazing Grace, In the Garden,* and *The Navy Hymn.*

Amazing Grace, with lyrics by John Newton (1725–1807), extols God's power and offers thanks for his mercy and generosity.

> Amazing grace! How sweet the sound that saved a wretch like me!
> I once was lost, but now am found; was blind, but now I see.
> 'Twas grace that taught my heart to fear, and grace my fears relieved;
> How precious did that grace appear the hour I first believed!
> Through many dangers, toils and snares, I have already come;
> 'Tis grace hath brought me safe thus far, and grace will lead me home.
> The Lord has promised good to me, His Word my hope secures;
> He will my Shield and Portion be, as long as life endures.

In the Garden, composed by Charles Austin Miles in 1913, expresses the comfort and emotional support derived from a vision of Jesus that appears to a believer during a quiet period of meditation.

> I come to the garden alone while the dew is still on the roses
> And the voice I hear, falling on my ear the Son of God discloses.
> And He walks with me and He talks with me and He tells me I am His own,
> And the joy we share as we tarry there none other has ever known.

Some songs are intended for particular occasions or types of people. Such is *The Navy Hymn,* written in 1861 by two English clergymen, William Whiting (the words) and John B. Dykes (the music). The hymn—now the official anthem of the U.S., British, and French navies—is a plea for God's protection.

> Eternal Father, Strong to save, whose arm hath bound the restless wave,
> Who bid'st the mighty Ocean deep its own appointed limits keep;
> O hear us when we cry to Thee, for those in peril on the sea.
> O Christ! Whose voice the waters heard and hushed their raging at Thy word,
> Who walked'st on the foaming deep, and calm amidst its rage didst sleep;
> Oh hear us when we cry to Thee for those in peril on the sea!

The Nature of Christian Ceremonies

Christian ceremonies that serve functions of prayers are of two general types—those that take place on customary holidays and those performed at irregular times in relation to a significant event in the life of some individual or group.

The two customary holidays most widely celebrated by Christians are Christmas (in honor of Jesus's birth) and Easter (in honor of Jesus's return to life after he was put to death). Next in popularity is the day of Jesus's crucifixion, the Good Friday that precedes Easter. Other holy days or holy periods are observed by selected Christian sects:

Feast of the Epiphany (January 6) by the Roman Catholic Church

Ash Wednesday (first week of March) by Protestant and Catholic Churches

First Day of the Feast of Unleavened Bread or Passover (mid April) by the United Church of God

Ascension Day (May 25) by Catholic and Protestant Churches

Day of Pentecost (June 2) by the United Church of God

The Exaltation of the Holy Cross (September 14) by the Russian Orthodox Church

Feast of Trumpets (October 4–5) by the World Wide Church of God

Day of Atonement (October 13) by the Global Church of God

Reformation Day (October 31) by the Lutheran Church

All Saints Day (November 1) by the Roman Catholic Church

As these examples illustrate, rarely does an important Christian celebration depend for its form and timing on seasons of the year or on the celebrants' locations or lifestyles. Instead, form and timing are dictated by events in Jesus's life—his birth, his ministry, his death, his reappearance on earth, and his ascension to heaven. Exceptions to this pattern are ceremonies honoring saints, with the time of such events usually determined by the date of a saint's birth, death, or most prominent miracle.

The timing, but not the form, of Christian ceremonies that signify religious milestones in an ordinary person's life (baptism, confirmation, marriage, funeral) depends on that person's birthday and availability. The form of such events is basically the same everywhere.

Ceremonies can include a variety of activities—group prayers, individual prayers, meditation, choral music, instrumental music, pageants, processions, dramas, the lighting of candles, feasting, and the Eucharist (the commemoration of the last supper that Jesus had with his disciples that involves using bread and wine to symbolically ingest Jesus's flesh and blood to signify faithful believers' communing with the divine).

Therefore, two tasks assumed by adherents of the Christian faith since early colonial days have been those of teaching Native Americans that

- Almighty God is the ultimate cause of events in the world, so that God must be respected and his commandments obeyed.

- Prayer, in the form of words and ceremonies, is the essential means of communicating with God in order to express veneration, to seek aid in time of trouble, and to suggest matters that warrant the Lord's attention.

INDIAN RELIGIOUS PRACTICES

The following discussion addresses (a) spirits' mediating ability and their transfer of power, (b) the nature of Indian prayer, (c) the nature of Indian ceremonies, (d) imitative magic, and (e) sickness and its treatment.

Spirits' Mediating Ability and Their Transfer of Power

Two beliefs underlying Indians' high regard for spirits concern (a) spirits' role as cause-and-effect mediators and (b) spirits' willingness to transfer power to humans.

The opening paragraphs of this chapter distinguished two kinds of cause attribution—mediated and direct. A mediated interpretation of cause assumes that (a) when people act in a way that either pleases or displeases an invisible spirit, (b) the spirit's resulting pleasure or anger at such an act motivates the spirit to respond by (c) either rewarding (if pleased) or punishing (if displeased) the people. Based on this belief in spirits as mediators, people hope by means of prayer and ceremonies—and often with the aid of a shaman—to engender spirits' goodwill and assistance in time of need.

A direct interpretation of cause assumes that people, on their own initiative, can produce an observed effect or outcome. A hunter shoots an arrow into a rabbit, and the rabbit dies. In order to accomplish that feat, the hunter needs *power,* which in this instance consists of arm strength, sharp eyesight, and precise eye-hand coordination. Indian religions generally assume that humans, when left to their own talents, are rather weak and helpless—"endowed by nature only with limited *sicum,* or spiritual power" (Hassrick 1964, 266). In contrast, spirits—and especially those in the guise of animals—command immense power that they can often transfer to people. Thus, people are wise to treat spirits in a manner that encourages them to yield power to individuals who solicit it through vision quests, prayers, rituals, songs, fetishes, feathered regalia, herbs, potions, tobacco (smoked in a pipe), or peyote (chewed or as a tea).

Each animal, by its nature, commands a particular variety of power—the hawk, the deer, the swallow, the elk, the buffalo. Therefore, individuals direct their appeals to the sorts of animals that are famous for special kinds of power.

The eagle is considered the biggest, strongest, and most courageous of all the birds. It can fly higher than any other bird....This is why you will see some Native people dancing like [an eagle], even using eagle wing-bone whistles in ritual ceremony....When I need the raven's help, I go outside and make a special prayer, hold the bird's feathers in my hand, and call out like a raven.

(Lake-Thom 1997, 33)

Prayers and ceremonies can be intended not only for good spirits (begging for their aid or expressing appreciation for past blessings) but also for bad spirits (mollifying them so as to fend off ill fortune that they might generate). Hence, spirits that populate Indian religions can function as either potent friends or dreaded enemies, so prudence dictates that all spirits be honored and gratified. Consider, for example, the Holy People in Navajo lore—those "strange and powerful spirit-beings who travel on the wind and on sunbeams, on rainbows, thunderbolts, and lightning flashes" (Reader's Digest 1978). If pleased, Holy People can provide such services as those of the Sun (who nurtures the corn crop), Spider Woman (who teaches Navajos how to weave), Spider Man (who warns of danger), and Hero Twins (who kill threatening monsters). But if offended, Holy People can withhold their services. Thus, cautious Navajos humor the Holy People with conciliatory ceremonies.

The Nature of Indian Prayer

Prayers in Indian cultures have assumed three main forms—words (spoken, sung, or silent), symbolic acts, and symbolic objects.

Before praying, tribe members frequently engage in purification rites—fasting or cleansing their inner selves with emetics and purgatives so the deities will agree to accept their solicitations.

Objects that function as prayers are often gifts and sacrifices, such as special foods intended by the Algonquin [Northeast] and Kwakiutl [Northwest Coast] for the souls of the deceased. The so-called prayer sticks of the Kickapoo [Northeast] also serve as symbolic prayers, just as prayer beads and candles do for Christians.

The Nature of Indian Ceremonies

The media that Indian tribes use to communicate with the spirits include songs, dances, rituals, tobacco smoked in pipes, costumes, amulets, bird feathers, herbs, and potions. Ceremonies serve a variety of functions—honor the spirits, prepare hunters and warriors for their tasks, memorialize important occasions, keep a tribe's history alive, and test participants' skills and stamina.

In a culture without a written literature, the ceremonies became living dramas which kept the good things of old alive by renewing their memory in an annual cycle of ceremonial rites. [Ceremonies] told the Indian who he was, and what to do to preserve the culture for future generations.

(Mails 2002, 173)

The kinds of ceremonies associated with Indian religions, and the times those ceremonies are held, are strongly influenced by tribes' sources of food and shelter, the climate, and the characteristics of other people in the region that the particular Indian nation inhabits. Furthermore, ceremonies can vary markedly in their complexity and in the amount of time they require. An observance can be as brief and simple as an Iowa [Great Plains] shaman blowing a puff of pipe smoke toward a sky spirit. Or it can be as extended and complicated as the Mandan [Great Plains] version of the Sun Dance that continues over a dozen days after weeks of preparation.

SOURCES OF FOOD

Among tribes that depend on agriculture for their livelihood, ceremonies are conducted at key junctures in the crop-growing cycle. Prior to planting time, rituals are designed to forecast the nature of the upcoming growing season. For example, among the Caddoes [Southeast] elderly shamans in late winter would drink a tea of laurel leaves, then cast eagle feathers and tobacco on a fire to aid them in predicting the preparations needed for the kind of crop yield they could expect. Additional ceremonies would be performed at planting time to plead for the spirits' good graces so they would nurture the seeds. Then, in late summer, joy and gratitude at a successful harvest were signified by the Caddoes' first-fruit rites at the beginning of the harvest season, an occasion marked by great feasts and dancing (Newcomb 1961, 313).

Typical of rituals practiced in numerous Indian agricultural communities are the Corn Dance and the Rain Dance.

Green Corn Festival and Corn Dance

At the close of summer, Creeks and other tribes of the southeast signaled the end of the growing season and the start of a new year by celebrating the four-to-eight-day Green Corn Festival. The ceremony's intent was to rid the tribe of impurities from the past year, thereby rendering the village and its residents faultless at the onset of the next year. To ready the village for the festival, men repaired the communal buildings while women cleaned their homes and quenched their hearth fires. Villagers cleansed themselves internally by fasting and by swallowing the Black Drink, a tea made from a poisonous shrub, tobacco, and other herbs that induced vomiting.

The ceremony itself began with hot coals from the Sacred Fire being carried to rekindle hearth fires, and food was cooked for a great meal featuring corn and venison. Some villagers performed the Green Corn Dance and engaged in lacrosse and archery contests. The festival ended with everyone bathing in the river for final purification; and "all past wrongdoings were forgiven, except murder" (Waldman 1999, 76).

A Pueblo [Southwest] form of the Corn Dance features two lines—one of men, the other of women—that move in slowly shifting circles to the chanting of a chorus of old men and the beat of a drummer. The dancers pantomime the stages of corn growth—the right hand with an attached rattle raises skyward, then lowers to represent descending clouds. A shaking arm gesture signifies lightning, then jerky hand motions toward the ground bring falling rain, and gentle upswept hands finally symbolize corn shoots and the stalks of growing corn (Waters 1950, 202).

Rain Dance

Rain Dances have been performed mainly among agricultural tribes that live in hot, dry climates, such as that of the Southwest where the Apache, Hopi, Navajo, Pueblo, and Zuñi have developed their particular versions of the ceremony. A Rain Dance's tripartite purpose is to induce rainfall for the crops, to cleanse the community of evil spirits, and to persuade the deities to bless the people with all sorts of prosperity. The dance is typically scheduled during the month of August when crops are in greatest need of water, with the form of the dance varying from one band to another.

In a Zuñi version, masked men and women in separate lines execute intricate steps accompanied by chanting. In many Indian dances the performers move in circles, but the Zuñi dancers—wearing turquoise jewelry to symbolize rain and feathers to represent the wind—move in lines that trace zigzag patterns.

> The mask of the men is turquoise in color—a straight strip about six inches deep, and reaching from ear to ear across the face. At the bottom is a band of painted rectangles, alternately red, blue, and yellow. From this band hangs a horsehair fringe, long enough to hide the throat. There are three white feathers at the top of the mask, one hanging over the face at the middle of the top, and one over each ear. They wear a tuft of macaw feathers on top of the head. The mask of the women is similar, but white instead of turquoise, and with no colored band above the fringe. There is a short fringe of goat hair around the whole head at the top of the mask. A soft white eagle feather falls over the face, attached above the top fringe.
>
> (Rain dance of the Zuñi 2007)

A traditional Hopi rendition of the Rain Dance was known also as the Snake Dance, because the participants (members of the Snake and Antelope fraternities) began by spending four days capturing snakes that were then kept in earthen jars, "washed, fondled and readied for the ceremonial dance to invoke the gods to provide rain." A participant explained that, to prepare for the dance, members of the two societies "smeared pink clay over our moccasins and other parts of our costume and corn smut mixed with 'man medicine' (a concoction of root juices and whatnot) over our forearms, calves and the right side of our head. We whitened our chin and blackened the rest of our face. Around our waist we placed the customary brightly woven fringed belt and in the rear, we hung a fox skin, which moves in rhythm of the dance" (Curtis

1912). During the ceremony, the men pranced wildly around the plaza, with snakes draped around their necks or grasped in their lips. Following the dance, chiefs of the Snake and Antelope societies retired to their kivas to offer four days of prayer directed at the spirits who controlled rain.

The nature of music that can accompany a Rain Dance is suggested by this translation of a Sia-Pueblo rain song.

> Let the white floating clouds—the clouds like the plains—the lightning, thunder, rainbow, and cloud peoples, water the Earth. Let the people of the white floating clouds—the people of the clouds like the plains— the lightning, thunder, rainbow, and cloud peoples—come and work for us, and water the Earth.
>
> (Rain song 2007)

In contrast to the tribes that depended primarily on agriculture for sustenance are ones that hunted game as their main source of food, clothing, and shelter. Such was the case of many bands in the Great Plains. Among their important ceremonies were the Buffalo Dance and the Deer Dance.

Buffalo Dance

For tribes of the Great Plains, the buffalo (bison) provided all that was needed for survival.

- Buffalo rawhide was fashioned into medicine bags, buckets, clothing, moccasin soles, headdresses, food, shields, drums, drumsticks, rattles, splints, ropes, thongs, saddles, cinches, stirrups, knife cases, quirts, armbands, lance cases, horse masks, horse forehead ornaments, bullet pouches, belts, and bull boats (wooden frame covered with buffalo hide).
- Buckskin became moccasin tops, cradles, winter robes, bedding, breechclouts, shirts, leggings, belts, dresses, pipe bags, pouches, paint bags, quivers, teepee covers, gun cases, lance covers, coup flag covers, and dolls.
- All meat parts were eaten or converted into jerky or pemmican (dried pulverized meat mixed with dried berries).
- Horns were turned into cups, fire carriers, powderhorns, spoons, ladles, headdress ornaments, signal horns, and toys.
- Bones were carved into knives, arrowheads (ribs), shovels, splints, winter sleds, saddle trees, war clubs, scrapers (ribs), quirts, awls, paint brushes (hipbones), game dice.
- Muscles provided sinews for thread, bowstrings, and glue.
- Buffalo chips were used for fuel, sending smoke signals, and ceremonial smoking.

- Tails served as medicine switches, fly brushes, lodge decorations, and whips.

(Buffalo-Bison 2007)

With such an array of uses, buffalos were viewed by Indians as symbols of the abundant life. Prior to a buffalo hunt, the community would gather for a dance to encourage the deities to furnish a bounteous supply of animals and safe traveling for the hunters (see Figire 6.2).

The featured participants in a typical performance were a dozen or more dancers—the simulated buffalos—clad in buffalo heads and tails, with the heads formed from bear hair and from cow horns or from tree leaves if no actual buffalo heads were available. The procession included a hunt chief, a few hunters, and a chorus of singers. During the dance, the buffalos milled

Figure 6.2   Buffalo Dancer.

about, moved in a circle, or arrayed themselves into several lines, all accompanied by the chanting of a chorus.

Deer Dance

Among Indians of the Southwest—Navajos, Pueblos, Yaquis—the Deer Dance has been accompanied by a chant intended to mesmerize the animals and lure them toward the singer. According to legend, the God of Sunrise (*Hastyeyalti*) created the hunting chant and gave it to the Navajos. The song's refrain tells how a deer follows a trail from the top of Black Mountain, through flower-covered meadow dewdrops, until the animal nearly reaches the hunter. Then, startled at the sight of the hunter, the deer stamps and turns to run, but the hunter shoots a single arrow into the animal's heart. The hunter, with his skill and good fortune, will then slay many another.

The dance performers—deer and hunters—enact the theme of the chant. Bare to the waist, the dancers wear carved oval wooden masks with long tufts of hair. They carry a gourd rattle in each hand and wear strings of cocoon rattles wrapped around their legs, dancing off and on throughout the night to the music of the harp, violin, flute, water drum, and rasps (Deer Dance 2007; "Yaqui and Mayo" 2007).

WARFARE

War among Indian tribes and against European settlers was frequent from earliest times through the nineteenth century. Intertribal warfare was most common among bands that encroached on each other's territory or ones that stole a neighboring tribe's horses or women. War dances were performed both before a battle and after a victory.

War Dance

The mandatory Pawnee [Great Plains] dance before men went to war was designed to call the supreme spirit, *Tirawa,* to the warriors' aid. The rhythm for the dance was set by drums beating in a simple rhythm—a single accented stroke followed by a single unaccented stroke. The drumbeats were supplemented with the shaking of rattles made of dry gourds filled with gravel. Dancers, carrying war clubs and other weapons, chanted as they stomped about, with the chants recalling former victories or lauding the achievements of some chief or brave (Waters 1950, 269–270).

Following a battle in which the Pawnee were triumphant, the tribe held a victory celebration in which all of the dancers were women, joined by drummers and a chorus that might include men. The dancers and members of the chorus spontaneously created songs from incidents in the recent fight. As the performers moved from right to left in a circle, they waved scalps in the air—scalps taken in the recent battle (Waters 1950, 271).

Arrows Renewal

The Cheyenne [Great Plains] Renewal of the Sacred Medicine Arrows is a rite promoting both hunting and battle success for the tribe's braves. In ancient times, the personified great spirit, *Maiyn,* gave four magic arrows to a mythical youth named Sweet Medicine. Two of the arrows had power over buffalo; the other two had power over humans. When the first pair was pointed at a buffalo herd during a hunt, the buffalo easily succumbed to the Indians' shots. When the second pair was pointed at the enemy force during a battle, the foe was blinded and confused, so the Cheyenne emerged victorious.

The Medicine Arrows symbolize the collective existence of the tribe. In a sense, they may be called the embodiment of the tribal soul. As the Arrows prosper, the tribe prospers; as they are allowed to suffer neglect, the tribe declines in prosperity.

(Hoebel 1960, 7)

Therefore, the aim of the biennial renewal ritual is to ensure that the spirits represented by the arrows continue to be revered. The ceremony continues over four days, with the sacred arrows eventually unwrapped from their medicine bundle, their feathers smoothed, and offerings presented while each male of the tribe passes by to receive the arrows' blessing. On the final night, shamans sing four sacred songs that *Maiyn* had taught Sweet Medicine; and just before daybreak, the participants enter a sweat lodge "to ritually decontaminate themselves. The tribe is now renewed, purified, and strengthened because it has been resanctified" (Hobel 1960, 10).

Sun Dance

Although the Sun Dance was not designed as preparation for battle, it bore links to war themes by testing braves' courage and their ability to bear the pain associated with the warrior tradition.

As described in Chapter 4, a special arena or lodge was built for the annual Sun Dance, which was late-springtime's or summer's crowning ceremony in most Great Plains traditions. Tribe members from throughout the region arrived to surround the lodge with their teepees. All variations of the Sun Dance focused on the arena's center pole, a forked cottonwood tree to which thongs were tied. The other ends of two thongs were then attached to skewers inserted in slits in each participating warrior's breast flesh. When the warrior began to step away from the pole, the thongs tightened and the flesh began to tear, causing extreme pain. The object of this exercise was to have the youth strain backward enough to tear his flesh loose from the ties, thereby testing his capacity to suffer without wincing. According to a Sioux legend, the act of suffering at the pole transferred to the warrior much of the agony of the tribe. It was a manner of worship that offered the participant's body and soul to the

Great Spirit represented by the sun. The tearing of flesh was believed to free the sufferer and the tribe from ignorance and to renew the world for another year (Mails 2002, 159–161).

Among the Cheyenne, the Sun Dance was a complex ceremony lasting eight days that included not only the flesh-tearing exercise but four days of dancing around the center pole that was accompanied by singing and the rhythm of rawhide rattles. Dancers would rise "up and down on their toes while standing in one place. As they rise, they blow piping, short blasts on eagle-wing bone whistles held between their teeth" (Hoebel 1960, 15).

The torture involved in the Sun Dance caused the U.S. Government to ban the ceremony in the late nineteenth century. However, the event was later revived without its flesh-tearing component.

OTHER PROMINENT ANIMAL CEREMONIES

Dances and songs have also focused on animals other than the buffalo and deer. Wolves were featured in an Animal Dance that the deity Sweet Medicine taught the Cheyenne as an aid to hunters in their pursuit of game. The festival was a five-day riotous affair in which Bowstring Society members dressed as animals to perform silly antics and regale their audience (Waldman 1999, 53).

For Indian nations that envision the world beginning on the back of a giant turtle, the Turtle Dance signifies the advent of life on earth. In a Pueblo [Southwest] variety of the dance, two dozen men emerge from a kiva, clad in breechcloths and moccasins, each with a band of paint extending from one ear to the other to represent the mouth of a giant turtle. The dancers' bodies are painted the dark brown of turtle shells. During the dance, each man stands on the same spot, barely lifting his feet, and sways in time with the song that recalls humans emerging from the water of the third subterranean world into the present world.

The Eagle Dance honors the most powerful bird in Indian lore, the one who flies higher than any other bird and serves as the emissary connecting heaven and earth. In a typical modern-day performance, two dancers appear with yellow-painted forelegs and breast. Their upper legs are white and their bodies are painted dark blue. Their short white skirts are embroidered in colors. Fringed red garters circle the legs above the knees, and bells jangle on a belt around the waist. The headdress is of white feathers fronted by a yellow beak. Wings are attached to the dancers' arms, while a bustle simulates a tail. The performance features the dancers swooping about, accompanied by a drum and a chorus of a half-dozen singers (Eagle dance 2007). The dancer in Figure 6.3 wears leggings and a simulated eagle-head bonnet.

Additional animals are depicted in such ceremonies as the Apache [Southwest] Rabbit Dance, Pueblo [Southwest] Antelope Dance (Figure 6.4), Quechan [Southwest] Night-Hawk Dance, several California tribes' Bear Dance, and the Haida [Northwest] Salmon Dance, Shark Dance, and Raven Dance.

Figure 6.3   Eagle Dance.

Imitative Magic

Attempts to control life's events include Indians' symbolically simulating a chosen event—a procedure that Lowie (1954, 155) has labeled *imitative magic.* During a Comanche [Great Plains] antelope hunt, a warrior crossed two sticks decorated with antelope hooves in an effort to prevent the herd's escape. Crow [Great Plains] drummers, at a key juncture in their tobacco dance, pointed their drumsticks skyward to foster tobacco-plant growth. Among the Mandan [Great Plains], having women perform the White Buffalo Cow dance was considered an effective way to lure buffalo herds close to the village. A Wichita [Great Plains] technique for provoking the death of an enemy involved placing a lock of the victim's hair in the mouth of a toad, then killing the toad (Newcomb 1961, 275).

SICKNESS AND ITS TREATMENT

Illness in Indian cultures has often been thought to result from evil spirits or dangerous objects entering the body as the result of a person's failing to respect taboos, ignoring required rituals, or suffering the evil influences of a vindictive shaman. Dangerous objects include insects, arrows, stones, or poisonous plants that witches will into the victim's body. The medical lore of the Sioux [Northern Great Plains] warned that worms which spirits injected into a person's body would squeeze the flesh, causing spasms, rheumatism, colic, diarrhea, or headaches. Boils and carbuncles were thought to result from eating goose eggs. Scabs and black splotches on the face came from a woman's tanning a bear hide during her menstrual period (Hassrick 1964, 289).

The typical cure for such maladies consists of a healer—usually a shaman—sucking the evil contents from the affected regions of the body, sweating the irritants out, or extracting the foreign substances by slight-of-hand tricks. A

FIgure 6.4   Antelope-Dance Mask.

member of the Kiowa [Southern Great Plains] tribe described such a healing session in the following manner.

> [The shaman doctor] danced four times around the [sick man], and then he went four times around the bush arbor. One of the herd boys, who was watching the doctor instead of the sick man, thought he saw the doctor put something in his mouth the fourth time he danced around the arbor. Nobody else was looking [at the shaman]. The doctor came back, and stood over his patient. "Now I can get it," he shouted. He bent over the wound and began to suck. He sucked four times, and the last time he stood up, held out his hand, and spat a little gray rock-spider into his hand. He threw it into the fire, and it shriveled up and was gone.

Whatever the herd boy thought to himself, the sick man got better from that moment on.

(Marriott & Rachlin 1975, 149)

Finally, it is important to recognize that the Indian ceremonies described in this chapter represent only a small sample of the multitude of rituals practiced by tribes in both the past and present. Many additional varieties appear in the sources among the references following Chapter 15.

TRADITIONS COMPARED

The following comparison of Indian religions and Christianity begins with the two traditions' likenesses, then turns to their differences.

Similarities

Both Indians and Christians pray to deities, with prayers assuming three main forms—spoken or silent words, songs, and symbolic objects intended to solicit aid or to honor the spirits.

The key participants in Indian and Christian rituals usually don special garb on ceremonial occasions. For Christians, robes and caps are worn by ritual leaders (priests, ministers) and their supporting casts (acolytes, choir members). Among Indians, the directors of ceremonies (shamans, chiefs, heads of special societies) dress in elaborate costumes featuring animal hides, bird feathers, beads, garments embroidered in bright colors, and facial and body paint. Indian dancers wear costumes symbolizing the animals and spirits that their performances are intended to portray.

Differences

Christians and Indians differ in their bases for scheduling religious ceremonies. The timing and nature of a Christian ritual is usually determined by happenings in a revered individual's life. The most important of those individuals has been Jesus. Key events in his life and afterlife have set the dates for such celebrations as Christmas, Easter, Good Friday, and Pentecost (fiftieth day after Easter). Less important, but still significant, are saints' birthdays or the dates on which saints had performed exceptional miracles. In marked contrast to Christian tradition, the timing of Indian celebrations has depended on the seasons (climate, weather) and significant junctures in tribal history (legendary events, wars, moving to a different region). For Indian agricultural societies, the time for planting, for nurturing, and for harvesting crops (mainly corn) have been ceremonial occasions. For societies that depended on hunting, celebrations were scheduled before and after a hunt. Warfare also called for rituals before and after a battle. And while Christians have not engaged in the elaborate warrior rites celebrated by Indian tribes, Christian priests and ministers, along with parishioners, (a) have typically declared that their soldiers and sailors were doing God's will by going to war and (b) have prayed for God to bless and protect their nation's war effort.

One of the most salient contrasts between Indian and Christian ceremonies is seen in the major role that dance plays in Indian rituals. Dance is not only absent from Christian rites, but some Christian sects condemn dancing as tool of the devil.

Finally, Indian and Christian ceremonies differ in the musical instruments used. Christian services are most often accompanied by a piano, organ, guitar, or an orchestra composed of stringed instruments (violins, cellos), woodwinds (flutes, clarinets, oboes, saxophones), brasses (trumpets, French horns, trombones), and drums in a modest supporting role. On the other hand, Indian celebrations feature such percussion instruments as drums, gourd rattles, and whistles.

· 7 ·

Maxims and Tales

Maxims are concise wise sayings, such as proverbs or adages. Tales are stories, often in the form of parables or allegories. Religious maxims and tales are intended to teach moral lessons or to tell something about the philosophy, practices, or history of a religion.

CHRISTIAN MAXIMS

Two abundant sources of Christian aphorisms are the Bible and the sermons of ministers, priests, and evangelists.

Adages from the Bible

The chief compendium of Christian wise sayings is the Bible. The most frequently quoted adage from the New Testament is the verse known as the Golden Rule, a moral principle that Jesus recommended: "As ye would that men should do to you, do ye also to them likewise" (Luke, 6:31, 1611). Additional virtues that he advocated were:

Mercifulness. Love your enemies, do good to them which hate you. Bless them that curse you, and pray for them which despitefully use you. (Luke 6:27)

Tolerance. Judge not, and ye shall not be judged: condemn not, and ye shall not be condemned; forgive, and ye shall be forgiven. (Luke 6:37)

Generosity. Give, and it shall be given unto you....For with the same measure that you mete withal it shall be measured to you again. (Luke 6:36)

The advice Jesus offered included nine Christian beatitudes:

Blessed are the poor in spirit: for theirs is the kingdom of heaven.

Blessed are they that mourn: for they shall be comforted.

Blessed are the meek: for they shall inherit the earth.

Blessed are they which do hunger and thirst after righteousness: for they shall be filled.

Blessed are the merciful: for they shall obtain mercy.

Blessed are the pure in heart: for they shall see God.

Blessed are the peacemakers: for they shall be called the children of God.

Blessed are they which are persecuted for righteousness' sake: for theirs is the kingdom of heaven.

Blessed are ye, when men shall revile you, and persecute you, and say all manner of evil against you falsely, for my sake. Rejoice, and be exceeding glad: for great is your reward in heaven. (Matthew 5:3–12)

The most frequently cited Jewish and Christian guide to proper human behavior is the set of Ten Commandments (the Decalogue) in Chapter 20 of the book of Exodus in the Jewish Torah and Christian Old Testament. Those ten rules—said to have been dictated by God to Moses—include three ways people should act and seven ways they should not act. Thus, people should (1) worship only the one true God, (2) respect one's parents, and (3) respect the Sabbath day by not working. People should not (4) use God's name in an insulting fashion, (5) worship idols, (6) kill, (7) steal, (8) commit adultery, (9) tell lies about others, or (10) yearn for anyone else's property or spouse.

In the Bible's Old Testament, the richest source of adages is the book of Proverbs, which offers 30 chapters of such advice as:

Mercy and truth. Let not mercy and truth forsake thee: bind them about thy neck; write them on the table of thy heart. So shalt thou find favour and good understanding in the sight of God and man. (Proverbs 3:3–4)

Wickedness. Enter not in the path of he wicked, and go not in the way of evil men. . . . The way of the wicked is as darkness: they know not at what they stumble. But the path of the just is as the shining light, that shineth more and more unto the perfect day. (Proverbs 4:14, 18–19)

Tattling. A talebearer revealeth secrets; but he that is of a faithful spirit concealeth the matter. (Proverbs 11:13)

Obedience to God. The fear of the Lord is a fountain of life to depart from the snares of death. (Provers 14:27)

The role of punishment in child rearing. He that spareth his rod hateth his son: but he that loveth him chasteneth him betimes. (Proverbs, 13:24)

Jesus often cast his advice in similes, illustrating principles of behavior by comparing people's actions to easily recognized events in daily life.

Whosoever cometh to me, and heareth my sayings, and doeth them, I will show you to whom he is like: He is like a man which built a house, and digged deep, and laid the foundation on a rock; and when the flood arouse, the stream beat vehemently upon that house, and could not shake it; for it was founded upon a rock. But he that heareth, and doeth not, is like a man that without a foundation built a house upon the earth; against which the stream did beat vehemently, and immediately it fell; and the ruin of that house was great.

(Luke 6:47–49)

Adages from Sermons

Preachers frequently include maxims in their sermons. A very popular style of preaching consists of a minister first quoting a verse from the Bible to serve as a theme that will be elucidated in detail in the body of the sermon. Non-biblical aphorisms can also serve as the focus of a sermon when the origin of the maxim is a popular saying, the title of a book or song or movie, or the preacher's own invention. The intent of including an adage in a sermon is often to cast a religious belief in a concise form that members of a congregation can easily remember. The following are maxims extracted from a selection of modern-day sermons.

Reclaimed poachers make the best gamekeepers; and saved sinners make the ablest preachers.

At the point of greatest despair in life, when we feel that we cannot go on, that is the moment of opportunity in which we can open up for moments of profound transformation.

The heroes are the ones that quietly do not give up. They just gently persist through life when all seems to be lost.

Scatter your wealth around the world. We flourish by causing others to flourish.

As Christians, we are deeply committed to doing God's will. God will show us when his plans conflict with ours. We need to listen for God's guidance.

There can be no truthfulness among friends without judgment—without that risky, sometimes painful willingness to confront a friend. Judgment—the assignment of right and wrong, the acknowledgement of genuine injustice, the naming of real hurt, the telling of truth—can be an act of deepest love.

CHRISTIAN TALES

For convenience of discussion, Christian stories can be divided into two types, examples from the Bible and tales told by people engaged in religious instruction. Christian tales typically are intended to relate history, explain the cause of some phenomenon or event, or teach a moral lesson.

Stories from the Bible

The following seven examples illustrate stories from the Bible that are commonly taught to the young in Christian families or are told to people—such as American Indians—who are considered to be potential recruits to the faith. The stories include (a) noteworthy historical events that signify God's wisdom and power and (b) lessons about proper and improper moral behavior.

PASSOVER

According to the Bible's Old Testament (the Hebrew Torah), people from Israel in ancient times migrated south from their homeland on the eastern border of the Mediterranean Sea to settle in Egypt. As the decades passed, the immigrants "increased abundantly, and multiplied, and waxed exceeding mighty; and the land was filled with them" (Exodus 1:7). This worried the king of Egypt, who complained that the Israelites were "more and mightier than we." So the Pharaoh ordered the Hebrews into hard labor and decreed that newborn Hebrew males be put to death. He also refused to let the people of Israel leave Egypt. When the oppression of the Israelites grew unbearable, God told a young leader named Moses that God would punish the Egyptians for tyrannizing the Hebrews. The punishment would consist of a plague designed to kill "all the firstborn" Egyptians. But to avoid making the mistake of killing Israelites as well, the residents of each Hebrew house were to mark the door-lintel and doorposts with the blood of a lamb.

For the Lord will pass through [at night] to smite the Egyptians: and when he seeth the blood upon the lintel, and on the two side posts, the Lord will pass over the door, and will not suffer the destroyer to come in unto your houses to smite you.

(Exodus 12:23)

Thus, the Passover event served as the first step in freeing the people of Israel from bondage in Egypt, enabling them to escape through the Red Sea and trek north to "the promised land." Ever since ancient times, Jews have annually celebrated the Passover in gratitude for God's arranging their ancestors' flight from Egypt. Some Christian denominations also deem the tale of the Passover a significant historical incident.

DAVID AND GOLIATH

The importance of bravery, skill, and faith in God is illustrated in the Old Testament story of a confrontation between Israel's army and an army of Philistines. The two armies had been facing each other in a standoff for 40 days when a giant Philistine named Goliath came onto the battlefield to challenge the Israelites. The Bible lists his height at six cubits and a span, making him over 11-feet tall. (A cubit is the length of a man's arm from elbow to fingertips —about 21 inches. A span is the distance from the tip of the thumb to the tip of the little finger when the hand is spread out—about 9 inches.)

> [Goliath] had a helmet of brass upon his head, and he was armed with a coat of mail....And he had greaves of brass upon his legs, and a target of brass between his shoulders. And the staff of his spear was like a weaver's beam; and his spear's head weighed six hundred shekels of iron. And he stood and cried unto the armies of Israel and said unto them... Choose you a man of you and let him come down to me. If he be able to kill me, then will we be your servants; but if I prevail against him, and kill him, then shall ye be our servants, and serve us.
>
> (1 Samuel, 17:4–9)

No soldiers in Israel's army accepted the challenge, which they saw as a form of suicide. At that moment, a young shepherd named David was bringing food to his three brothers who were in Israel's army. And David, upon hearing Goliath's challenge, volunteered to confront the giant. David's brothers scoffed, pointing out that he was a mere youth with no military experience. But David said he had killed a bear and a lion that had attacked his sheep, so "The Lord that delivered me out of the paw of the lion and out of the paw of the bear will deliver me out of the hand of this Philistine." Finally King Saul, the head of Israel's army, agreed, "Go and the Lord be with thee." David refused the heavy coat of armor, helmet, and sword he was offered and, instead, picked up five smooth stones from a nearby brook.

When Goliath saw the lad who intended to do battle, he invited David to "Come to me, and I will give thy flesh unto the fowls of the air, and to the beasts of the field." David replied,

> Thou comest to me with a sword, and with a spear, and with a shield; but I come to thee in the name of the Lord of hosts, the God of the armies of Israel, whom thou hast defied. This day will the Lord deliver thee into

mine hand; and I will smite thee, and take thine head from thee; and I will give the carcasses of the host of the Philistines this day unto the fowls of the air, and to the wild beasts of the earth; that all the earth may know there is a God in Israel. And all this assembly shall know that the Lord saveth not with sword and spear: for the battle is the Lord's, and he will give you into our hands.

(1 Samuel, 17:45–47)

As the giant approached to slay the youth, David slipped a stone into his slingshot and slung it at Goliath, striking the giant in the forehead, just below the helmet. As Goliath fell to the ground, mortally wounded, David ran forward, grabbed the giant's great sword, and severed the Philistine's head from his body.

The men of Israel and Judah arose, shouted, and pursued the Philistines. And the wounded of the Philistines fell down by the way to Shaaraim, even unto Gath and unto Ekron. And the children of Israel returned from chasing after the Philistines and spoiled their tents.

(1 Samuel 17:52–53)

Therefore, faith in the Lord saved the day, and David would grow to be a man and become Israel's greatest king.

SOLOMON'S JUDGMENT

Upon King David's death, his son Solomon became king of Israel. Solomon's wisdom was demonstrated in the case of two prostitutes, each of whom claimed to be the mother of a particular infant son. Solomon thus faced the task of deciding which of the claimants was the true mother of the child. When the two women appeared before Solomon, one said,

Oh, my lord, I and this woman dwell in one house; and I was delivered of a child with her in the house. And it came to pass the third day after I was delivered, this woman was delivered also....This woman's child died in the night, and she arose at midnight and took my son from beside me while I slept and hid it in her bosom and laid her dead child on my bosom. And when I rose in the morning to give my child suck, it was dead. But when I had considered it in the morning, behold, it was not my son which I did bear.

(1 Kings 3:17–21)

But the second woman protested and swore that the live infant was indeed her own. To solve the conflict, Solomon asked a servant to bring him a sword, and he ordered, "'Divide the living child in two, and give half to the one [woman] and half to the other.'" In response, the first woman, horrified at the prospect of the child being killed, told Solomon to give the child to the second claimant "'and in no wise slay it.' But the other [woman] said, 'Let it be neither mine nor thine, but divide it,'" whereupon Solomon gave the infant to the first woman for "'she is the mother thereof.' And all Israel...feared the king, for they saw that the wisdom of God was in him to do judgment" (1 Kings 3:25–28).

Thus, the tale of the two harlots served to illustrate how God's wisdom can be channeled through a revered religious figure to affect events in the world.

JOB'S TRIAL

The Old Testament book of Job opens with Satan debating with God over whether Job, a wealthy member of God's earthly devotees, truly loved and honored God. When God assured Satan that Job was indeed "perfect and upright, fears God, and eschews evil," Satan replied that if God took away Job's riches (extensive lands, thousands of sheep, camels, oxen, and donkeys), Job would no longer venerate the Lord. God accepted Satan's dare by removing Job's worldly goods. When Job, now impoverished, still honored God, Satan challenged the Lord to further test Job's loyalty by afflicting Job with physical ailments. God responded by burdening Job with painful boils from head to toe. When three of Job's friends came to help their despondent companion, they spent days arguing with Job as he bemoaned his fate. The tale then continues, chapter after chapter, with Job claiming injustice ("Why me, Lord?") and his friends giving advice. Finally, God spoke to Job, describing the wonders that God had performed in the world. As a result, Job reaffirmed his faith in the Lord's infinite wisdom and power, and he admitted to God that

> I know thou canst do every thing, and that no thought can be withholden from thee....I uttered [things] that I understood not; things too wonderful for me, which I knew not...but now mine eye seeth thee [as thy true self]. Wherefore I abhor myself and repent in dust and ashes.
>
> (Job 42:2, 5–6)

Following this declaration of faith, humility, and loyalty, God restored Job's health and gave him twice the riches he had held before Satan's challenge. "After this, Job lived 140 years" (Job 42:16).

Thus, the lesson Christians have been taught through the story of Job is that unwavering faith in God during troubled times will eventually be rewarded in great measure.

JESUS'S PARABLES

During Jesus's three-year ministry before his death, a favorite device he used to teach moral lessons was the parable or allegory. For instance, when a group of Pharisees (religious scholars who adhered to strict laws inherited from Moses) criticized Jesus for welcoming sinful people and dining with them,

Jesus told his critics three brief stories—the lost sheep, the lost coin, and the lost son.

When a single sheep was lost out of a flock of 100, the shepherd went to great lengths to find the lost one.

> And when he hath found it, he layeth it on his shoulders, rejoicing. And when he cometh home, he calleth together his friends and neighbors, saying unto them, "Rejoice with me, for I have found my sheep which was lost."
>
> (Luke 15:5–6)

Then Jesus interpreted for the Pharisees the significance of this tale for explaining his own habit of consorting with sinners whom the Pharisees held in contempt.

> I say unto you, that likewise joy shall be in heaven over one sinner that repenteth more than over ninety and nine just persons which need no repentance.
>
> (Luke 15:7)

Apparently Jesus did not trust one parable as sufficient for making his point about tolerance and compassion, so he followed the story of the lost sheep with two additional anecdotes. The first concerned a woman who lost one of her ten silver coins, then went to great trouble hunting until she found it. Like the shepherd, she collected her friends to rejoice in retrieving the coin. And again Jesus, in his effort to instruct the Pharisees, drew a parallel between the recovered coin and the significance of remorseful souls.

> Likewise, I say unto you, there is joy in the presence of the angels of God over one sinner that repenteth.
>
> (Luke 15:10)

The third tale was about a son—a spendthrift, prodigal son—who begged his father to give him the inheritance he would receive upon his father's death. The indulgent father did so, only to have the son leave home to waste the funds in riotous living in a far country. Years later, the son, now reduced to poverty, returned home to tell his father,

> I have sinned against heaven and in thy sight, and am no more worthy to be called thy son.
>
> (Luke 15:21)

In response, the father neither rejected or admonished the son but, instead, ordered servants to

Bring forth the best robe, and put it on him; and put a ring on his hand and shoes on his feet. And bring hither the fatted calf and kill it, and let us eat and be merry. For this my son was dead, and is alive again; and he was lost and is found. And they began to be merry.

(Luke 15:22–24)

THE GOOD SAMARITAN

When Jesus was about to send his disciples off to teach the gospel through-out the world, he created a parable illustrating the virtue of mercy and the importance of judging people by their deeds, not by their positions in society.

A certain man [a Jew] went down from Jerusalem to Jericho and fell among thieves which stripped him of his raiment and wounded him, and departed, leaving him half dead. And by chance there came down a certain [Jewish] priest that way; and when he saw [the wounded man], he passed by on the other side. And likewise, a Levite [a temple assistant] came and looked on [the robbery victim] and passed by on the other side. But a certain Samaritan [not a Jew], as he journeyed, came where [the victim lay], and...had compassion on him. And went to him, and bound up his wounds, pouring in oil and wine, and set him on his own beast, and brought him to an inn, and took care of him. And on the morrow when [the Samaritan] departed, he took out two pence and gave them to the host, and said unto him, "Take care of [this fellow]; and whatsoever thou spendest more, when I come again I will repay thee."

(Luke 10:30–35)

Then Jesus asked his disciples, "Which of these three [men] thinkest thou was neighbor unto him that fell among the thieves? [It was] he that showed mercy. Go and do likewise" (Luke 10:36–37)

TALES OF MIRACLES

Religious leaders profit from stories that invest themselves with magical powers—with abilities to perform feats beyond the talents of ordinary mortals. A frequently mentioned astonishing gift is the skill to communicate directly with invisible spirits, often through messages revealed in a dream or trance state. The Bible ascribes this gift of prophecy to such seers as Abraham, Joseph, Moses, Joshua, David, Solomon, and more who, according to the scrip-tures, spoke with God. Further evidence of mystical ability is provided by sto-ries of a religious celebrity's wondrous acts. Thus, over the centuries the New Testament accounts of Jesus performing miracles have served as persuasive evidence for Christians that Jesus was indeed divine and commanded super-natural powers. Among the amazing feats attributed to Jesus were those of walking on the sea (Matthew 15:25), reviving Lazarus, who had been dead four days (John 11:43–44), restoring a blind man's sight (John 9:1–7), curing a leprosy victim (Mark 1:40–42), healing the lame and deaf (Matthew 11:5), turning five loaves of bread and two fish into enough food to feed a crowd of 5,000 that had followed Jesus into the desert (Matthew 14:17–21), and, finally, his raising himself from the dead two days after he had been crucified (Matthew 28:1–20).

Stories Embedded in Sermons

Just as Christian sermons can contain non-biblical adages, sermons and Sunday-school lessons can include tales of everyday life. The stories may be descriptions either of actual past happenings or of imagined, make-believe, "what-if" situations.

As demonstrated in the following examples, stories can serve diverse purposes, including those of (a) explaining a religious process by means of nonreligious analogies, (b) tracing the steps by which a particular person became a Christian, (c) illustrating exemplary Christian behavior, (d) advising people how to cope with adversity, (e) imagining an important event, and (f) assuming a constructive attitude.

NONRELIGIOUS ANALOGIES

In a sermon entitled "Wicked and Righteous Comingled," one preacher sought to illustrate the need for people to be cleansed of the ungodly wickedness that was mixed with blessed virtues in their original character structure. The pastor first cited a passage from the book of Genesis, then told a brief story of a metallurgical process.

> Genesis 2:7—"And the Lord God formed man of the dust of the ground, and breathed into his nostrils the breath of life; and man became a living soul." This is equally true of all precious metal. In its original condition it is mixed with earth, which can only become separated out by the refining process. This is a symbol of the process God uses to remove the dross. Precious metals are found in the hills and in the ground and are from the dust, just as we were created. The refining process is used to separate those metals from the dust.
>
> ("Wicked and Righteous" 2007)

The analogy that another minister chose was intended to clarify the meaning of *born-again Christian*.

> Have you ever tried to explain to a person how to get to heaven? Going to church, being baptized, reading the Bible, praying, joining a church, giving money—all these are things a Christian *does*—but they are not means of getting to heaven. An Indian is not an Indian because he rides a horse or sleeps in a teepee or lives on an Indian reservation; he is an

Indian because he was born into an Indian family. A Christian is the same way; he is a Christian because he has been born into the family of Christ [by wholeheartedly accepting Jesus as the savior]. [In the Bible verse John 3:3], Jesus said, "Truly, truly,...unless one is born again he cannot see the kingdom of God."

(Can you tell me 2007)

TESTIMONIALS

Ministers often tell stories about how they themselves, or people they know, were "saved" by adopting Christianity. In one popular form, the tale describes how individuals, who were leading sinful destructive lives were caught in a crisis that both exposed the damage they were doing to themselves and others and demonstrated that the solution to their plight was to become a Christian, faithful to God's commandments.

Another variety of testimony is not that of a rescued sinner but, rather, that of a suddenly enlightened youth, illustrated in this account:

I was eleven years of age when I took an open stand for Christ on a profession of faith and joined Sardis Baptist Church....I know that my young heart was deeply impressed with the Gospel truth of God's Word. I never once questioned that I was saved.

At the age of sixteen I felt the burden of what I thought was the call to preach the Gospel of the Lord Jesus Christ, which was based largely on visions and outward manifestations. Yet, I was firmly grounded on the Bible, the Word of God, and believed its doctrines as taught by the old-time Missionary Baptist church....

Immediately following my call and my surrender to the Gospel ministry I became very active in church life; praying in public, teaching Sunday School classes, leading prayer meetings, taking part in young people's work, and pastoring small country churches as well as holding summer revivals. I was generally referred to as "the boy preacher," and large crowds attended upon my ministry from the very beginning. I never once doubted that I had received a divine call to the ministry.

(Shelton 2006)

EXEMPLARY CHRISTIAN BEHAVIOR

Particularly when a sermon is intended to honor a person who has died, the priest or minister lauds the deceased as one whose virtues the listeners could profitably emulate. In the following example, the virtue the minister emphasized was that of continuing to be a steadfast Christian throughout the entire life span. Thus, he opened the sermon with a verse from the book of Matthew 10:22—"He that endureth to the end shall be saved."

I have in my mind's eye one who has been for about sixty years associated with this Church, and who this week, full of years, and ripe for heaven, was carried by angels into the Savior's bosom. Called by divine grace, while yet young, he was united with the Christian Church early in life. By divine grace he was enabled to maintain a consistent and honorable character for many years; as an officer of this Church, he was acceptable among his brethren, and useful both by his godly example and sound judgment....He went to his bed without having any very serious illness upon him, having spent his last evening upon earth in cheerful conversation with his daughters. Ere the morning light, with his head leaning upon his hand, he had fallen asleep in Christ, having been admitted to the rest which remaineth for the people of God....Let us thank God and take courage—thank God that he has preserved in this case, a Christian so many, many years. "He that endureth to the end," and only he "shall be saved."

(Spurgeon 2006)

GUIDANCE IN COPING WITH ADVERSITY

Preachers often introduce their lectures with an anecdote that captures the congregation's curiosity and also leads into the sermon's theme. In this case, the theme is an approach people might profitably adopt when facing difficult times.

According to Greek myth, there was once a young woman named Pandora who was both beautiful and deceitful. She was taken into the household of Epimethus where stood a large box. Inside this box stood all of the evils of the world. Despite warnings, Epimethus left this woman into his household. The woman opened the box and let out all kinds of evils upon the world. Thus it was known as Pandora's Box....

In the story of Pandora's Box, the world is filled with all kinds of evil things when the lid is opened. What I didn't mention was that inside of the box, after all the other bad things had flown out, lay hope. In the midst of all kinds of evil, hope is the only thing that we can cling to.

We place our hope in the fact that one day Jesus will return and will make all things perfect. Until that time, we must simply wait patiently, enduring all things because we have to.

(Stine 2006)

IMAGINARY EXPERIENCES

Ministers can first ask listeners to envision themselves in situations that require decisions and then can propose the sort of decision that should yield the best result.

It's like the situation a man is in when he's trapped in quicksand. That's where we are spiritually in this world. Without a hope! There's nothing to grab—only the air as we thrash wildly about. And it's that useless grabbing—that desperate lunging at other religions—which makes us sink even faster into the quicksand of sin.

Then Jesus appears! He reaches out a stick. The stick of faith. [It's] His way to join us to Him....Boys and girls, every time you see that stick used, you don't just see a stick, you also think about everything that came with being saved. Imagine meeting your Mum and Dad for the first time after your rescue [from quicksand]. All that despair you went through when you honestly believed you wouldn't make it. And on your own you wouldn't have made it!

(Bajema 2005)

OTHERS' VIEWPOINTS

Another aim of including a story in a sermon is that of focusing attention on an attitude that Christians can properly adopt. In this case, that attitude is one of seeking to view life through other people's mental lenses.

Gerber Baby Foods! You know the brand? They have the picture of the very cute, chubby baby on the jar. Gerber is the staple diet of most babies growing up. When products enter into the African market, what they generally do, because of the language problem, is place a picture of the item being sold on the jar. So when Gerber went into Africa with a picture of a cute chubby baby on the front of their packaging, Africans panicked about what these crazy Americans were now doing—bottling young children. And so Gerber had to rethink their whole marketing approach in Africa.

The point that I want to make out of this is that we have to constantly check our assumptions about what is on the inside of another person. This becomes the basis for compassion and social justice.

(Lawton 2006)

Now, with the foregoing sketch of Christian maxims and tales as a background, we turn to Indian religions' wise sayings and stories.

INDIAN MAXIMS

Proverbial sayings in Indian lore have been (a) offered on solemn or festive occasions (birth, death, planting time, harvest time, preparation for battle), (b) issued as advice to the young, (c) declared as beliefs that guide behavior, or (d) attached to a tale as a summary of the story's theme or moral.

Solemn Occasions

An instance of an adage uttered during a somber event is the ancient proverb "Corn is the Hopi's heart" which signifies the linkage of each Hopi

[Southwest] generation to succeeding generations. On the Day of the Dead, when the harvest is over, a bit of corn meal is placed on each ancestor's grave, accompanied by the words, "I am the seed of the husk that lies here, and I am the seed of the husks which will follow after me, and this meal I now place here is the bond between us all" (Waters 1950, 197).

Advice

Wisdom is often passed on by elders to the young in the form of pithy sayings, such as "When you see a new trail, or a footprint you do not know, follow it to the point of knowing" (Uncheedah in Nerburn 1999, 78).

The form of adages is often important in Indian traditions, as in the Sioux [Northern Great Plains] practice of offering advice only in positive terms rather than as warnings about what not to do. An example of a positive form is the saying, "Be kind to women, for they are weak" (Hassrick 1964, 163–164). Likewise, advice to warriors is positive—"When you go to war, you should kill your enemy like a dog" (Black Elk in Rice 1998, 23).

Testified Beliefs

Adherents of Indian religions frequently explain their worldviews in the form of testimonials that can serve as maxims. For example, "We believe that the Spirit pervades all creation and that every creature possesses a soul in some degree, though not necessarily a soul conscious of itself. The tree, the waterfall, the grizzly bear, each is an embodied Force, and as such an object of reverence" (Ohiyesa in Nerburn 1999, 88).

Maxims in Tales

Adages appended to stories can have various purposes, such as (a) eliminating impudent behavior, (b) protecting nature's creatures, and (c) being true to one's own nature.

ELIMINATING IMPRUDENT BEHAVIOR

In a Shoshone [Southern Great Plains] legend, the trickster-hero Old Man Coyote wanted to be magically turned into a frisky buffalo calf by a buffalo bull's dancing around him. The bull agreed, but warned Coyote, "I'm not giving you my power. You will look like a young strong buffalo, but you will still be Old Man Coyote inside. Don't forget that." And the deed was done. Old Man Coyote, now a buffalo calf, "ran and wallowed in the shallow ponds, and he met a young buffalo woman and made love to her. My, he was happy."

Then one day he chanced upon a tired old coyote who begged Old Man to change him also into a buffalo. Old Man said he would do just that, using the same scheme the bull had used. But while dancing, Old Man hit the old coyote on the back, and the pair tumbled down the hill. That act turned Old Man Coyote back into his original self. Like his companion, he was just an aged Coyote. And the tale finishes with this advice—"Always remember, don't start anything unless you know you can finish it" (Big Turnip 1975, 72–75).

PROTECTING NATURE'S CREATURES

A Tsimshian [Northwest/Arctic] story tells of several youths from the Wolf Clan amusing themselves by catching salmon, cutting a slit in each fish's back, and inserting pieces of burning pitch pine before tossing the fish into the river, where the salmon frantically swam around "like living torches." When the village elders heard of the deed, they warned the youths that such wanton disregard for the welfare of living things would surely anger the deities. The village could expect dire consequences. Soon a great roaring noise came from the distance, "as if a giant medicine drum was being beaten." As the weeks passed, the noise grew louder and ended with an enormous explosion as the nearby mountain blew up. People fled in terror while rivers of lava engulfed the village and set the forest afire. The shamans said the spirit world was enraged at the torture of the salmon, so the errant youths needed to remember that "The powers of nature insist on a proper regard for all their creatures" ("Wolf Clan" 2007).

BEING TRUE TO ONE'S OWN NATURE

In the far distant past, a lazy hunter named Old Man wakened late one morning when the Sun Spirit—wearing flaming orange leggings—was already high in the sky. As Old Man watched, the Sun rushed through the fields and forests, with his burning leggings setting the grass, bushes, and trees on fire. The flames so frightened the deer and elk and rabbits that they ran into the open and were easy targets for hunters.

Old Man called out to the Sun, "Those are mighty leggings you wear. No wonder you are a great hunter. Give them to me and I shall be the great hunter and never be hungry."

And the Sun did as he was bid—gave the leggings to lazy Old Man, who slipped them on, hoping to catch lots of game with little effort. As he started searching through the thickets, the leggings turned hotter and hotter, so Old Man began to run. But the faster he ran, the hotter the leggings grew, and he cried out in pain, "Oh, Sun, take the leggings back. I don't want them."

But the Sun refused. So Old Man was forced to keep running until he came to a river. When he jumped into the water, the wet leggings stopped burning. Old Man pulled them off and tossed them onto the bank, where Sun would find them later that day.

And that's how Old Man learned this lesson: "Always be yourself. We should never ask to do things that Manitou did not intend us to do. If we keep this in mind, we shall never get into trouble" (Fire leggings 2007).

INDIAN TALES

The great majority of Indian religious beliefs have been conveyed to the populace in the form of stories, of which there are thousands. Even the religious ceremonies, with their dances and chants, are usually enactments of tales. Thus, stories function as the principal vehicles for informing Indians of their religious history, for explaining the causes of natural phenomena, and for teaching morality. However, some stories that feature spirits in the form of personified animals appear to have no religious purpose but are merely intended to entertain an audience.

(In order to fit a variety of tales into this chapter, I have condensed the stories into brief résumés of far longer narratives.)

Recounting History

As the following examples illustrate, both fancied and actual historical events have been recorded in accounts of the past.

THE NAVAJO CHRONICLE

Frank Waters (1950, 241–246) has observed that every Navajo [Southwest] chant and dance chronicles events in the lives of legendary tribal people and spirits. Each ritual or "way" bears its own title, characters, and plot.

- *Moving Up Way.* before humans emerged from the underworld
- *Blessing Way.* the birth of Changing Woman
- *Night Way.* the eventual emergence of people from the dark world into the present world of light
- *Monster Way.* Sun Father and Hero Brothers destroy monsters
- *Shooting Way.* more monsters are eliminated
- *Enemy Way.* ghosts of monsters and enemy aliens are exorcised in the Scalp Dance
- *Beauty Way.* Big Snake Man follows a maiden
- *Mountain-Top Way.* Bear Man follows the maiden's older sister
- *Flint Way.* a young man seduces a woman—the wife of White Thunder, who kills the youth with a bolt of lightning

So it is that all these countless myth-dramas lead into still more myths and ceremonials: the Navajo Wind Way and Chiricahua Wind Way, Hail Way, Water Way, Bead Way, Coyote Way, Ghost Way, and Down Way. All combine into one vast interlocked myth which is at once the complete story of The [Navajo] People and the whole story of man.

(Waters 1950, 246)

LEARNING TO MAKE FIRE

The Karuk [California] tell of ancient times when the only fire in the world was held by three Yellow Jacket sisters. Although the other animals were freezing, the sisters would not share fire with them. But Wise Old Coyote had a plan. He distracted the sisters with a whimsical tale, then snatched a burning stick from them and ran off. To elude the pursuing Yellow Jackets, Coyote tossed the stick to Eagle, who slipped it to Mountain Lion. And so the burning the stick passed from one animal to another until it came to Frog, who caught an ember in his mouth and dived to the river bottom. The distraught Yellow Jackets gave up the chase so that Frog could rise to the surface and spit out the hot coal, which Willow Tree swallowed. Now Coyote could show the animals how to extract fire by rapidly scratching willow sticks together over dry moss (Fire race 2007).

THE HISTORY OF SPOKANE

According to a Spokane [Plateau] legend, the region in which the city of Spokane, Washington, now rests was once a lake so large that it required days to cross it in a canoe. Great villages were built along the lake's shore and on its islands. Tribe members prospered from the abundance of fish in the lake and game in the forest. Thus, life was indeed pleasant until one morning the earth suddenly trembled, then wildly shook. The land buckled and broke open. Gigantic waves smashed boats and flooded villages. Clouds of sulfur dust suffocated animals, and the villagers who were not killed fled to the crest of Little Mountain, which had risen overnight from the rubble. Finally, the entire lake drained into the Below World, leaving the lake bed bare.

Over the coming months, the surviving tribe members scratched out a bare living until springtime, when the winter snows melted and a new river carved a channel through the earth to revive plant life. As the river cascaded over the rocks, it formed a waterfall with a rainbow shimmering in the spray above. The joy-filled Indians declared, "This will be our home." Today, that rainbow still glistens above the Spokane falls ("Historical Legend" 2007).

THE CHEROKEE ROSE

During the 1830s, when the U.S. government forced Indian nations to abandon their homelands in the Southeast and resettle in the Oklahoma territory, the Cherokees were among the bands that trekked west along the "Trail of Tears." The ones who did not die on the treacherous journey trudged ahead with broken hearts. To help the travelers survive, the elders called for the help of the Heaven Dweller, *Galvladiehi*, who answered their plea by promising a sign to strengthen the Cherokee trekkers' resolve.

In the morning, tell the women to look back along the trail. Where their tears have fallen, I will cause to grow a plant that will have seven leaves for the seven clans of the Cherokee. Amidst the plant will be a delicate white rose with five petals. In the center of the blossom will be a pile of gold to remind the Cherokee of the white man's greed for the gold found on the Cherokee homeland. This plant will be sturdy and strong with stickers on all the stems. It will defy anything which tries to destroy it.

(Warren 2007)

The next morning when the women looked back along the trail, they saw plants covering the path where they had walked. As they watched, rose blossoms slowly opened, causing the travelers' sadness to fade away. They once more felt strong and beautiful. So, just as the thorny stems were protecting the rose blossoms, the Cherokee mothers knew they would have the stamina and determination to protect their children as they built a new nation in the west.

Explaining Natural Phenomena

Indian descriptions of how the world's contents originated are typically in the form of fanciful tales.

THE BIRTH OF THE WINDS

In a Spokane [Plateau] legend, the earth's original atmosphere was motionless—no breezes, no gales, no gusts of wind. At that time, a husband and wife in a village on the Yukon River despaired because they had no child. Then one night *Igaluk*, the Moon Spirit, visited the wife in a dream, flew her through the sky on his sled, pointed to a tree, and said, "Make a doll from its trunk and you will find happiness." When she wakened and told her husband of the dream, they agreed to do as *Igaluk* had suggested.

While [the husband] carved the figure of a small boy from some of the wood, his wife made a little suit of sealskin and, when the doll was finished, she dressed it and set it in the place of honor on the bench opposite the door. From the remaining wood the man carved a set of toy dishes and some tiny weapons, a spear and a knife, tipped with bone. His wife filled the dishes with food and water and set them before the doll.

("Origin of the Winds" 2007)

Pleased with their work, they retired to bed. By morning the doll had become miraculously alive, able to run from the house and fly to the ceiling of the sky where he spied a hole covered with animal hide. With his knife, he cut the strands holding the hide, and a great blast of wind sprayed from the hole, carrying birds and animals into the world. When the boy-doll felt there was enough wind, he closed the hole in the sky and ordered the wind to "sometimes blow hard, sometimes soft, and sometimes not at all." Satisfied with his adventure, he returned to the Yukon River village where he told how he had let the winds into the world.

> Everyone was pleased, for with the wind came good hunting. The winds brought the birds of the air and the land animals, and they stirred up the sea currents so that seals and walrus could be found all along the coast. Because he had brought good fortune as the Moon Spirit had predicted, the doll was honored in special festivals afterwards. Shamans made dolls like him to help them in their magic and parents also made dolls for their children, knowing that they bring happiness to those who care for them.
>
> ("Origin of the Winds" 2007)

THE FIRST BEARS

Indian stories frequently tell of how humans magically evolved from animals, but this Cherokee [Southeast, Oklahoma] legend reverses the process.

In ancient times, a boy from the Anitsaguhi clan began spending long hours in the mountains, eventually staying there the entire day and refusing to eat at home. "I find plenty to eat there; it's better than the corn and beans we have in the settlements, and soon I am going into the woods to stay all the time." When his parents objected, he explained that he was changing into a different sort of being. To prove it, he showed them the dark hair that was growing on his body. He urged his parents and relatives to come with him to the woods where "there is plenty for all of us, and you will never have to work for it; but if you want to come, you must first fast seven days." So they agreed. Those seven days without food caused their human nature to change, and their bodies gradually became covered with fur. Before entering the forest, they explained to the clan members who were left behind, "Hereafter we shall be called *Yonva* (bears), and when you yourselves are hungry, come into the woods and call us and we shall come to give you our own flesh. You need not be afraid to kill us, for we shall live always." With that farewell, the cluster of bears retreated into the woods (Cherokee bear legend 2007).

THE VALLEYS AND HILLS

To account for the earth's bumpy surface, a Thunderbird legend describes the original world as a flat plain, a limitless prairie that animals and humans traveled across with ease. Among the Thunderbirds living at the time, a youth named *Wakâjagiciciga* (Bad Thunderbird) set out to hunt game, but was frustrated in his efforts as the elk and deer sped away before he could get close enough to shoot. Distressed, he approached a village to seek help, but the evil village chief told his people that *Wakâjagiciciga* was an enemy about to attack them. The chief's son, in response, shot the intruder full of arrows. When *Wakâjagiciciga's* Thunderbird uncles heard of his death, they were infuriated. They fasted, smeared their faces with charcoal, and marched about the countryside hammering the plain with great blows from their enormous war clubs. So it was that deep cervices and ravines were smashed into the earth, causing the valleys and hills that we see today. The frightened evil chief, along with his son, escaped into the Lower World, there to be transformed into earthworms, the meanest of Earthmaker's creations, destined to become mere food for fish (Dieterle 2006).

WHY WOODTICKS ARE FLAT

In a Dineh/Navajo [Southwest] story, Coyote entered a cave in which various starving animals were held captive. When he inquired about their plight, they informed him that the supposed opening to the cave was actually a giant monster's mouth, and they all were now in the monster's stomach. Coyote, unwilling to passively accept captivity, bragged to his frightened companions, "Giants don't scare me," (though he had never met one). "I always kill them. I'll fight this one too, and make an end of him."

To demonstrate his ingenuity and courage, Coyote used his hunting knife to carve meat from the giant's stomach, so his fellow hostages could eat and gain strength. Then in the distance he sighted what looked like a heaving volcano. It was the giant's beating heart. He told the animals that he would slash the heart open and "As soon as I have him in his death throes, there will be an earthquake. He'll open his jaw to take a last breath, and then his mouth will close forever. So be ready to run out fast!"

With that, Coyote drove his knife deep into the giant's heart. The monster's blood—in the form of lava—began to flow out, and the mouth opened wide.

"Quick, run now!" Coyote shouted, and the animals scampered out just as the mouth closed. The last one in line, a chubby woodtick, was caught in the monster's teeth. Coyote grabbed the tick and pulled him out.

"But look at me now," the woodtick cried. "I'm all flat!"

"You'll always be flat from now on," Coyote told him. "Just be glad you're alive."

"I guess I'll get used to it," said the tick, and so he did ("Coyote Kills a Giant" 2007).

HARE'S LEGACY

The question of why life for humans is imperfect is answered in tales about such magical spirits as Hare, who—though motivated by noble intentions—nevertheless spoiled idyllic human existence with his much-too-human inability to resist temptation.

For instance, after demonstrating that he could defeat evil spirits, Hare thought he could eliminate death for humans. To accomplish this, he would need to walk a perfect circle around the world without looking back at his grandmother. But he did glance back, so death ever since has plagued humankind.

On another occasion, Hare rescued a powerful spirit's red scalp. The spirit rewarded that good deed with the power to cause inanimate objects to behave voice commands. As a result, Hare could cook dinner by simply telling kettles and knives and spoons what to do. Furthermore, Hare could transfer that power to ordinary humans. But, alas, there was a beautiful girl behind a partition in Hare's lodge, and the spirit warned him not to touch her or else Hare would lose his newfound power, and the power transferred to people would also be lost. Again, temptation won out. Hare not only touched the maiden, but he slept with her. As a result, humans today must themselves toil to accomplish all of the tasks that make up daily living.

And it was Hare who sought to protect warriors' powers by requiring women, during their menstrual period, to retire to a seclusion hut separated a proper distance from men's quarters. Contact with menstrual blood, it was said, destroyed men's battle prowess. But, of course, Hare actually was the cause of this problem in the first place, because earlier he had created menstruation in women by throwing wildcat blood on the legs of Grandmother Earth (Dieterle 2007).

Teaching Morality

By depicting rewards earned by virtuous characters and by describing penalties suffered by wrongdoers, many stories teach which values are to be cherished and which despised.

EARN RESPECT BY BRAVE DEEDS

The Sioux [Great Plains] tale titled *Pah-Hah-Unndootah* or *The Red Head* tells of a father named Child of Strong Desires (*Odshedop Waucheentongah*). He returned home one late evening with a deer he had shot. Tired and thirsty, he asked his son to fetch water from the stream, but the son refused, saying he was afraid of the dark. In response, the annoyed father chided the lad, "If you are afraid to go to the river, you will never kill the Red Head"—a reference to the region's most potent and evil magician who terrorized tribes from an island in the middle of a lake. The son, humiliated by his father's taunt, left home the next morning with his bow and arrows, bent on confronting the Red Head. After days of fruitless travel, he came to the hut of a witch, who befriended him and planned a way to trick the fearsome sorcerer. She dressed the lad as an attractive girl, armed him with a blade of sharp grass as a weapon, and sent him to the Red Head's island in the guise of a potential wife. The trick succeeded. The Red Head invited the attractive "maiden" into his home, where the masquerading youth lulled the sorcerer to sleep and cut off his head with the blade of grass.

When the youth returned home after weeks away on his quest, his parents could not believe what he told them. But when he held before them his trophy—the severed head—"All doubts of the reality of his adventures now vanished. He was greeted with joy and placed among the first warriors of the nation. He finally became a chief, and his family were ever after respected and esteemed" (Schoolcraft in Williams 1956, 151–154).

DO NOT BRAG

In the Iroquois [Great Lakes] legend of *The Hungry Fox and Boastful Suitor,* a man carrying fish in a bag was riding his horse to his beloved's home and singing as he passed along:

> No one is braver than Heron Feather
> And I should know, for I am he.
> No one wears finer clothing.
> No one is a better fisherman.
> If you doubt this, look and see.

Ahead on the trail, a starving fox spotted the bag of fish that hung from the rider's saddle. Immediately the fox lay down on the roadside, pretending to be dead. When Heron Feather noticed the limp fox, he picked the animal up and decided to take it along, saying, "When Swaying Reed's mother sees this fox I caught, she will know I am a great hunter. Then she will surely allow her daughter to bring me marriage bread." He dropped the fox into the bag of fish and set off again, this time singing in praise of his beautiful clothes, the many fish he caught ("he actually had traded his mother's beaded moccasins for them"), and all the animals he hunted and trapped.

The fox, now inside the bag, began to chew a hole through which each fish could slip to the ground, followed by the fox.

When Heron Feather reached the village where Swaying Reed lived, he stopped in front of her mother's lodge, still singing of his exploits while a crowd gathered. As Swaying Reed and her mother came out of the lodge, Heron Feather reached for his bag and discovered the hole in the bottom. "Turning around, he rode silently away. He learned that day that boasting songs do not make a person great. It is one thing to find a fox and another to skin it" ("Hungry Fox" 2007).

ESCHEW GREED, EMBRACE FILIAL GENEROSITY

The Ottawa [Northeast] yarn *A Visit to the Sun and Moon* tells of four young men visiting a far-off country where each was granted a wish by a powerful spirit in the form of an old man. The first two youths wished to live forever and never be in need. The third and fourth asked to live only as long as most people do but to be highly successful hunters so they might provide for their parents and relatives. As the four were about to depart for their homeland, the old man granted their requests. He turned the first youth into a stone and the second into a tree, then sent the last two safely home to enjoy a bright future as hunters (Schoolcraft in Williams 1956, 143–144).

AVOID FALSE PRIDE

Some Indian stories combine traditional values (humility, bravery, obedience to elders), religious ceremonies (dances and chants to solicit the aid of spirits), and pathos (unfulfilled love, guilt). Such is true of the Chippewa [Northeast] tale of *The Red Lover.*

The beautiful daughter of a renowned warrior, *Wawanosh,* fell in love with a handsome young man of a nondescript family from an undistinguished village. When the youth sought to marry the daughter, *Wawanosh* scoffed, charging that the young man was a nonentity who had never proven his fortitude in battle "by suffering protracted pain, enduring continued hunger, or sustaining great fatigue." The youth, shamed by *Wawanosh's* challenge, gathered his village friends to perform a war dance and to chant a long poem that began with—

> Lance and quiver, club and bow,
> Alone attract my sight;
> I will go where warriors go,
> I'll fight where warriors fight.

But sadly, the youth was killed during the battle in which his brave acts proved his merit. The heartbroken maiden died of despair, and her father was consumed with guilt for having been moved by selfish pride to scorn the lad (Schoolcraft in Williams 1965, 41–45).

RITUAL ADVICE

Some stories illustrate religious rites that are to be practiced if tribe members are to avoid misfortune. For instance, the Kiowa [Great Plains] tale *Grandmother Spider and the Twin Boys* tells of two youths, the War Twins, who lived with Grandmother Spider. When several women begged Grandmother Spider to do something about giant bears that had killed their husbands, Grandmother Spider told the twins, "You are very young to start having your adventures, but you will have to go now....You are the Sons of the Sun, and nobody can kill the bears but you....And when you have killed a bear, bring me part of it, so I can be sure."

The twins searched east, south, west, and north. In each direction they found an enormous bear, which they speared to death after a vicious fight. Each time, they cut off the bear's ears, which they carried home to Grandmother Spider. She placed fawnskin bags inside rawhide cases to hold those trophies, and she ordered the twins to paint symbolic shields on the cases— "bear and lightning designs so the Kiowas will have great power in time to come."

Finally, Grandmother Spider and the twins took sweat baths to clean the bear power off their bodies, for as she explained, "Whenever [people] touch

holy things, or even look at them, they must sweat and rub themselves with
sage before they eat anything. And then they must eat very little, and drink only
a little water until the next day" (Marriott & Rachlin 1975, 41).

Entertaining

Indian stories—rather than chronicling history, proposing the cause of phenomena, or teaching a moral lesson—may simply be intended to amuse an
audience. The following examples have no more than a vague relation to religion, with that relation consisting only of the participants in the events being
personified spirits.

COYOTE AND ANOTHER ONE

A Chippewa [Northeast] anecdote tells of two coyotes—strangers to each
other—who were crossing a farmer's field together when the farmer shouted,
"There's a coyote." The first coyote called to the second one, "We'd better
run," whereupon the farmer yelled, "And there's another one."

When the two animals reached the safety of a grove, the first introduced
himself as "Wanderer. I'm a coyote like you."

The second answered, "I'm Sleek. But I'm not a coyote like you."

Wanderer objected, "Of course you are. What makes you think you aren't a
coyote."

"Because you heard what the farmer called us. He called you Coyote. He
called me Another One. So you are Coyote, and I'm Another One" (White
2006).

Whereas nearly all of the Coyote stories that abound in Indian oral literature elicit "much laughter and gaffawing and with exclamations of surprise
and awe," Barry Lopez (1977, xix) has claimed that most of the tales—unlike
the anecdote above—have not been "just a way to pass the time." Instead, they

> detailed tribal origins; they emphasized a worldview thought to be a cor-
> rect one; and they dramatized the value of proper behavior.... For
> youngsters, the stories were a reminder of the right way to do things—
> so often, of course, not Coyote's way.

BLUEHORN'S NEPHEWS

Entertainment narratives sometimes assume the form of a loose, rambling
plot that meanders from one incident to another without building to any logical
conclusion. It's as if the storyteller felt compelled to rattle on and on in an
effort to hold the listeners' attention for a long time. An example is the Hot-
câk/Winnebago [Great Lakes] saga *Bluehorn's Nephews,* which extends to
6,500 words in its English translation. Here are a few of the people and events
mentioned in the tale.

- A princess—the daughter of a chief—was to marry a brave but fearsome man who already had many wives, but she ran away to avoid the wedding.
- The princess met a beautiful woman, who turned out to be her older sister. Together they went to their brother, Bluehorn, a spirit who lived in a crystal lodge hidden in the bank of a stream.
- On Bluehorn's orders, the two princesses married the brave man, who happily served the wives as if he were their slave.
- The Thunders came and fought Bluehorn. He killed four until the remaining Thunders bound him with irons.
- Bluehorn's twin nephews—Flesh and Little Ghost—vowed to punish the Thunders.
- At an old woman's hut, the twins learned that the Thunders had carried Bluehorn off and eaten his legs up to his thighs.
- The nephews rescued Bluehorn, and his legs returned to him.
- Bluehorn crawled down to the bottom of the Earth, where he became chief of the buffalos and one of the great waterspirits.
- The nephews roamed the earth, killing everything that should not be killed. Once they killed and ate a bad bob-tailed waterspirit.
- A "thing" called *rucewe* chased the twins. To save themselves, they flew up to the Great One, who had created them. The Great One praised their works on earth and gave them a bird, a male turkey that would become the first one in the world.
- The nephews then settled where the Wisconsin River entered the Mississippi. They killed a waterspirit and shot a bear for a feast.
- Finally, as a sign of the great works they had performed during their adventures, the twins used waterspirit blood to paint a picture of the waterspirit.

They drew his face round, and they drew its tail very long, and they drew its body very long. Then they drew their own pictures. There they did their last work, and this was it. . . . The blood they pictured themselves with, some of it was scraped off and mixed with medicine because it was waterspirit blood that they had used. Now then, it is ended.

(Blowsnake 1912)

TRADITIONS COMPARED

The following comparison of Indian and Christian religious traditions begins with likenesses and ends with differences.

Similarities

The themes of Bible stories and Indian tales are often alike. There are plots in both traditions that focus on such matters as death, life after death, sexual attraction, loving kindness, bravery, generosity, friendship, self-sacrifice, vanity, pride, greed, hate, and revenge. Maxims in Indian and Christian traditions are also similar in teaching morality (truthfulness, bravery), constructive action (diligence, caution, high work standards), and prudence (filial piety, humility, respect for authority).

Robert Heizer has likened the tales of the Yuroks [Northern Califiornia] to the attitudes toward life and money of the European Protestant ethic and capitalism, with the Yurok myths being "slight in stirring plot and suspenseful narrative; . . . [but] full of examples of affection, homesickness, pity, and attraction to the place of one's birth; and with an overriding concern about the acquisition of wealth goods that would give a man status and influence in his society" (Heizer 1978, 654).

Differences

Identifying differences between Indian and Christian tales can include analyzing each tradition's (a) quantity of stories, (b) diverse versions of tales, (c) roles assigned to animals, and (d) the treatment of sex. The task of identifying true differences involves problems of translating oral Indian tales accurately into European languages and recognizing the influence of Christian teachings on Indian religious lore.

QUANTITY OF STORIES

Indian religions include far more tales than does Christian culture.

The number of stories that can reasonably be considered an established part of Christian doctrine is limited chiefly to ones in the Bible. That number probably doesn't exceed 100, or 200 at most. Of course, if anecdotes that Christian ministers and priests insert in their sermons were included in the Christian count, the total would be much larger. However, those stories are ephemeral, soon forgotten, and thus not part of the Christian canon.

The quantity of Indian tales that are permanent elements of religious belief extends into the thousands. Whereas some may be no more than passing fancies, a great many have become lasting components of Indian worldviews, repeated time and again in storytelling sessions, rituals, chants, and dances.

ALTERNATIVE VERSIONS

Among Indian nations, the same basic story can appear in different variations, suggesting that the narrative may have come from a single source, then transformed over the centuries as it filtered into different tribes' oral literature. Consider a Navajo [Southwest] story in which Coyote visits Wolf, who turns two flint arrow points into delicious minced meat by roasting them. But when Coyote attempts the same trick, he fails—the arrowheads remain flint points. This same theme is found in other Indian nation's lore, with a different dupe in each version. Among the Chinooks [Northwest], the hoodwinked fool is Bluejay instead of Coyote. The Comox, Nootka, and Kwakiutl [Northwest/Vancouver Island] versions picture Raven as the unlucky victim. For the Micmac [Northeast], Rabbit is the one who fails to pull off the stunt (Boas in Clements 1986, 220).

However, in Christian tradition, tales remain essentially the same over time and from one place to another. This is primarily due to the Bible stories having been in printed form for centuries, with the Bibles used in one society the same in content as those used in other societies. Inconsistent versions of Bible stories are rare. One such exception appears in the story of Noah (Genesis 7:2–9) where verses 9 and 10 explain that Noah took two of every living species aboard his ark while verses 2 through 5 say that Noah obeyed God's order to take along seven members of each clean species and two of each unclean species.

ANIMALS' ROLES

The characteristics and roles assigned to animals in Indian religious tales differ markedly from animals' traits and roles in Christian stories. Not only are animals extremely frequent in Native North-American narratives, but animals display human qualities (spoken language, complex thinking) and such magical skills as the ability to prophesy the future, flit about the world at will, and change themselves from one sort of beast or bird into another sort. In effect, Indians' animals are typically envisioned to be mundane forms of incredibly accomplished invisible spirits that deserve center stage in religious stories.

In contrast, animals in Christian accounts not only lack such human attributes as language, complex intelligence, and eternal souls, but they are assigned only passive roles in tales. Lambs in the Old Testament are objects of sacrifice or devices that serve human purposes, as in lambs' blood being used to mark Jewish homes in the Passover tale (Exodus 12:3–11). Job's 7,000 sheep, 3,000 camels, 5,000 oxen, and 500 "she assess" are not portrayed as personalities but are merely Job's possessions, symbols of his wealth (Job 1:3). And the donkey in the story of Jesus riding through the streets of Jerusalem is nothing more than a beast of burden (John 12:14–15).

THE TREATMENT OF SEX

Although both Christian and Indian tales include sexual incidents, the sexual encounters in Indian stories are far more frequent, more explicit in their descriptions, and more accepting of different types of sexual activities (masturbation, adultery, incest). The Bible's relatively few sexual episodes appear mainly in the Old Testament, as in Lot's daughters getting their father drunk and then going to bed with him (Genesis 19:33–38). And while the brief Old Testament book *Song of Solomon* is replete with sexual allusions, the accounts are mainly in symbolic images rather than blunt descriptions of sexual anatomy and activity. In contrast, consider the Navajo legend about the world's earliest women practicing masturbation.

> One used an elkhorn, one a feather quill, another a smooth stone stuck into the thick part of a leg sinew, and still another a whittled sour cactus. Hence, the first conceived a horned monster, the second a monster eagle, the third a monster bear, and the fourth a monster that killed with his eyes.
>
> (Waters 1950, 220–221)

TRANSLATING TALES

William Bright has drawn attention to problems encountered when translating Indian tales into European languages. Such problems are caused both by the lack of equivalent terms in the Indian and foreign tongues and by the fact that many Indian narratives presume a prior knowledge that is rarely held by people who did not grow up in the particular tribe's culture. The difficulty in conveying the sense of tales to non-Indians is further complicated by the use of symbolism in Indian lore. People without an intimate knowledge of the culture are apt to take symbolic characters or events literally or else to assume the wrong referent for a symbol. "From the Indian point of view, the stories are so well known that one does not need to hear every word in order to understand their meaning" (Bright 1993, xiii).

CHRISTIAN INFLUENCE?

A question is sometimes raised about whether —or to what extent— Christian culture, as introduced to Indians, affected Indian narratives over the centuries. Charles Leland, in his 1884 collection of Algonquin legends, proposed that

> When the Indians speak of Christian, or white, or civilized teachings, they say, "I heard," or, "I have been told." The Northeastern Algonquin always distinguish very accurately between their ancient lore and that derived from the whites. I have often heard French fairy tales and Aesop's fables Indianized to perfection, but the narrator always knew that they were not *N'Karnayoo*, "of the old time."
>
> (Leland 1884, 132)

· **8** ·

Symbols and Sacred Objects

Religious symbols are words, numbers, or graphic representations of a religion, its beliefs, or its adherents. Sacred objects are revered items either reminiscent of important people or events in a religion's history or ones used in the practice of the religion.

CHRISTIAN SYMBOLS AND VENERATED OBJECTS

Numbers, gestures, words, phrases, and graphic symbols have figured prominently in Christian life for more than two millennia.

Christians have often assigned religious meanings to numbers. For example, "3" has been interpreted to signify the trinity (God, Jesus, and the Holy Spirit), "5" to symbolize the five wounds Jesus suffered on the cross (hands, feet, and side), "6" to represent the number of days for God to create the universe, and "7" to stand for perfection, as God rested on the seventh day of creation, satisfied with his accomplishment. In addition, St. Paul cited seven gifts from the Holy Spirit and Jesus issued seven utterances from the cross. Finally, the number seven figures prominently in the Book of Revelation, which was originally in the form of a letter to seven churches in Asia Minor, with the letter including many references to quantities of seven.

A gesture signifying Christian belief is that of making the sign of the cross—moving one's hand vertically from forehead to waist, then moving it horizontally across one's chest from left to right.

Certain words and phrases have also been symbolic of Christian belief. Whereas some expressions have a positive connotation and are encouraged, others are deemed vile and their use prohibited. Esteemed language includes such expressions as:

The Lord be with thee.

Christ, the Redeemer.

Hail, Mary, full of grace.

Jesus saves.

Amen.

Among the Bible's Ten Commandments, the command warning people not to use the Lord's name in vain refers to such offenses as uttering the names of venerated biblical figures as curse words or in jest.

Christians' Graphic Symbols

The most popular Christian visual symbol across the centuries has been the cross, signifying the crucifixion of Jesus who died to atone for the sins of all who would follow his teachings. There are numerous versions of the cross (see Figures 8.1 and 8.2). The one most widely recognized in modern times is the Latin cross, which apparently first came into use during the second or third centuries.

The Celtic cross is said to have originated in Ireland in the early centuries of the Christian era, then carried in the sixth century by Colomba to the nearby island of Iona, thus accounting for the symbol's alternate name—Cross of Iona.

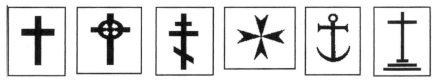

Figure 8.1   Christian Crosses (left to right): Latin, Celtic, Russian, Maltese, Anchor, Graded.

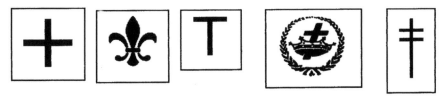

Figure 8.2   Christian Crosses (left to right): Greek, Fleur de Lis, Tau, Cross and Crown, Lorraine.

The three-bar Russian Orthodox cross has been adopted by many Eastern Orthodox churches and Eastern (Byzantine-rite) Catholic churches. One popular Eastern Orthodox interpretation of the bars on the cross proposes that the top bar symbolizes the sign that was placed above Jesus's head reading "King of the Jews." The bottom, slanted bar on the right side (from the vantage point of Jesus on the cross looking out) points up to the repentant thief crucified on Jesus's right, whom Jesus told, "Today you shall be with me in paradise." The left side, pointing down, is said to signify the death of the unrepentant thief crucified to the left of Jesus.

The Maltese cross—four spearheads pointing to the center—was the emblem of the Order of Hospitallers during medieval Crusades to the Christian holy land. Eventually the Hospitallers established their headquarters on the island of Malta, which accounts for the present-day name of their emblem.

The anchor cross originated in ancient Egypt and was used by Christians when they hid in Rome's catacombs. Over the centuries the anchor cross has served as the guardian symbol for seafarers.

The graded cross is erected atop three steps, with the highest step signifying *faith,* the middle step *hope,* and the bottom step *charity.*

The Greek cross, consisting of two simple bars of equal length, is the earliest of the Christian crosses.

The *fleur de lis* (literally in French, *flower of the lily*) is not a cross as such but has served the purpose of a cross by representing the Trinity (Father, Son, Holy Spirit) and by its association with Jesus's resurrection after he was crucified. According to legend, a lily sprang from the tears of Jesus's mother, Mary, as she wept at the foot of his cross.

The cross in the form of the Greek letter *tau* predates the Latin cross and is often associated with the Old Testament (the "T" is envisioned as the shape of the pole on which the brazen serpent appeared to Eve in the Garden of Eden) just as the Latin cross is associated with Jesus's death in the New Testament. The T-shaped symbol is also known as the Egyptian cross and St. Anthony's cross. St. Anthony was a fourth-century ascetic who established the first Christian monastery in the Egyptian desert.

The cross and crown is often interpreted as symbolizing the reward in heaven (the crown) after the trials of the earthly life (the cross). The words surrounding the symbol in the seal of the Christian Science Church reads, "Heal the Sick, Cleanse the Lepers, Raise the Dead, Cast Out Demons" (from the Gospel of Matthew 10: 8). The version pictured inFigure 8.2, with a palm wreath encompassing the symbol, was first published in the Jehovah's Witnesses' *Watch Tower* periodical in 1895 (Christian symbols 2006).

The cross of Lorraine is of ancient origin, dating back to the deified kings of Sumeria, the region surrounding the Tigris and Euphrates rivers in what is now Iraq. During the medieval Christian Crusades to the holy land, the double-bar cross was adopted as the emblem of the Knights Templars (*Poor Fellow-Soldiers of Christ and of the Temple of Solomon*).

Among Christian graphics, the image of a fish has become a distant second in popularity to the cross (see Figure 8.3). Fish symbols today are often displayed on Christians' autos and jewelry.

One popular form of the symbol features the Greek word for fish, *ichthus,* encased in a fish outline. In Greek letters, the word *fish* is spelled *Iota Chi Theta Upsilon Sigma.* Christians have often interpreted the Greek term as an acrostic "which has many translations in English. The most popular appears to be 'Jesus Christ, Son of God, Savior'—"I"esous (Jesus) "CH"ristos (Christ) "TH"eou (God) "U"iou (Son), and "S"oter (Savior)'" (Robinson 2005). Variations of the sign include the simple outline of a fish, the outline with the name *Jesus* inside, and the outline standing vertically and surrounding a cross.

Over the centuries, the cross and fish have been joined by other Christian symbols, including the skull and crossbones, lamb (St. Agnes), sheep (12 apostles), stag (St. Aidan), ship (Jude), Bible (St. Paul), sea shell (St. James), tree (St. Bride), harp (St. Cecilia), and more.

With the passing of time, some symbols have lost their original meaning and become anti-Christian. Such has been the fate of the pentagram and the swastika (Figures 8.4 and 8.5).

A pentagram or pentacle is a five-pointed star within a circle. In the somewhat distant past, Christians invested pentagrams with various sacred meanings. For example, the star's five points were associated with five wounds inflicted on Jesus by his crucifixion.

The pentagram was also called the *Star of Bethlehem* that allegedly guided three Zoroastrian kings to the baby Jesus on the night of his birth. In the legend of King Arthur, Sir Gawain emblazoned the pentagram on his shield, with the

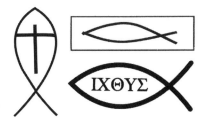

Figure 8.3   Fish images.

Figure 8.4   The Pentagram.

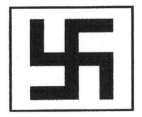

Figure 8.5   The Swastika.

five points signifying the knightly virtues of generosity, courtesy, chastity, chivalry, and piety. In the past the pentagram was worn by Christians as a protective amulet. It continues to serve as the emblem for the Order of the Eastern Star, the international women's humanitarian auxiliary of the all-male Masonic fraternal society. In North America, virtually all Masons and members of the Eastern Star are Christians (Robinson 2004).

However, in more recent times, as the pentagram has become identified with Wiccans and Satanists, Christians have generally rejected it as a revered sign.

> Wiccans have attempted to reconstruct a Pagan religion similar to that of the ancient Celts. They have adopted the upright pentacle/pentagram, since it was the symbol of Morgan, an ancient Celtic goddess. Many wear it as jewelry and use it on their altars. The symbol is frequently traced by hand using an athame (a ritual knife) during Wiccan rituals. It is used to cast and banish their healing circles. Some Wiccans interpret the five points as representing earth, air, fire, water, and spirit—the five factors needed to sustain life. Others relate the points to the four directions and spirit. Some Wiccans and other Neopagans bless themselves and others with the sign of the pentagram. Their hand passes from their forehead to one hip, up to the opposite shoulder, across to the other shoulder, down to the opposite hip and back to the forehead.
>
> (Robinson 2004)

The word *swastika* is a Sanskrit term meaning good luck. The figure is an ancient sign closely associated with Hinduism and Buddhism but found also among many other peoples, including American Indians—particularly the Navajo and Hopi.

Early Christians adopted the swastika as a revered symbol and carved it into the walls of Rome's catacombs. The image was considered blessed until adopted by the Nazi regime in Germany in the 1930s. Since then, the swastika has signified oppression and racism, traits so much in conflict with the traditional spirit of Christianity that the symbol has been renounced by most present-day members of the faith.

Revered Christian Objects

For convenience of analysis, sacred objects can be divided into two types—relics of historical significance and objects currently used in the conduct of religion.

VENERATED RELICS

Three of the most highly valued Christian relics over the centuries have been the *Crucifix*, the *Holy Chalice*, and *Jesus's Shroud*.

The *Crucifix* (Figure 8.6) is either a statuette or a painting of Jesus nailed to the cross when the magistrate Pontius Pilate condemned him to death. Today crucifixes are commonly seen in Christian locations, particularly in Roman Catholic churches, schools, and hospitals. In Italy, a law issued by Mussolini in 1924 required that each public-school classroom and every hospital room display a crucifix. Recent lawsuits challenging that practice have been denied by the highest Italian courts, thereby demonstrating the continued strength of a religious convention in an ostensibly secular state.

In Christian tradition the *Holy Chalice* is the vessel Jesus used at the Last Supper to serve wine to his disciples the evening before he was crucified.

Figure 8.6   The Christian Crucifix.

According to the Bible, "He took the cup when he had supped, saying, 'This cup is the new testament in my blood'" (1 Corinthians 11:25). Medieval legends declare that the Chalice was later used to catch Jesus's dripping blood when he was nailed to the cross. That chalice was the *Holy Grail* pursued by Sir Galahad in the King Arthur tales. Since Jesus's time, conflicting accounts have led to confusion about the nature of the chalice and its whereabouts. One version holds that St. Peter kept the vessel after Jesus's death and carried it to Rome where he became the first pope. The Grail was then guarded by succeeding popes until sent to Spain in the third century. Today, at least three cathedrals claim to house the authentic chalice. One vessel is the jewel-studded golden Chalice of Saint Gozlin (Figure 8.7), now in the treasury of the cathedral in the French city of Nancy. The relic in Genoa, Italy, is a green-glass dish rather than a cup. The one in Valencia, Spain, is a cup fashioned out of agate. Whether any of those vessels was used by Jesus at the Last Supper is doubtful, yet each is apparently honored by many Christians as the original one (Chalice 2006).

Equally uncertain is the authenticity of a shroud publicized as the cloth used to cover the crucified Jesus when he was placed in a tomb. Present-day debate continues over an ages-old, blood-stained linen cloth—14.5 feet long and 3.7 feet wide (436 by 110 centimeters)—displaying the shadowy image of a man (Figure 8.8). The cloth, currently at the cathedral in Turin, Italy, has been the recent subject of forensic study that has led some investigators to label it a clever medieval forgery made from a fabric created sometime between the years 1260 and 1390. However, other investigators have deemed the Turin shroud authentic (Trivedi 2004).

Three additional relics are (a) a blanket and a cloak in Aachen, Germany, that are claimed to be Jesus's baby blanket and his mother Mary's garment

Figure 8.7   Chalice of Saint Gozlin.

Figure 8.8   Face Segment of the Turin Shroud.

and (b) pieces of wood in various locations—most notably Santo Toribio de Liébana in Spain—that supposedly are from the cross on which Jesus died (Relics in Christianity 2006).

Centuries-old Christian memorabilia whose authors and locations are not in doubt include such art works as: (a) Michelangelo's statue of youthful King David and his painting of the creation of Adam on the ceiling of the Sistine Chapel in Rome, (b) Leonardo da Vinci's painting of the Last Supper, (c) Raphael's portrait of *Madonna and Child,* and (d) El Greco's painting *Assumption of the Virgin.*

SACRED OBJECTS IN CURRENT USE

Not only do Christians admire relics from the past but they also honor objects used in present-day religious ceremonies. The Bible is perhaps the most cherished item. Others include:

- Wine and bread (blessed by a priest or minister as the symbolic blood and flesh of Jesus) that communicants ingest during the communion ceremony.
- Statuettes and portraits of Jesus, his mother, and saints.
- Pendants, necklaces, rings.
- Church fonts for baptizing neophytes.
- Vestments of priests or ministers (tunic, hat, stole, and others).

In summary, Christianity is rich in symbols and revered objects that range from ancient signs and relics to present-day emblems and items used in the practice of the religion.

INDIAN SYMBOLS AND VENERATED OBJECTS

Because religious beliefs and practices often differ from one tribe to another, the variety of symbols and sacred objects is much greater than in Christian culture.

Indian Religions' Graphic Symbols

Types of visual symbols in Native American religions include (a) designs painted on the body and face, (b) decorations on pottery, utensils, weapons, clothing, blankets, and dwellings, (c) pictograms, and (d) emblems.

BODY AND FACE PAINTING

From long before Europeans settled in North America, Indians included body and face painting among their religious symbols (for example, see Figure 8.9), with the designs and colors varying from one tribe to another. Two of the main goals of such practices were to display evidence of the individuals' power and to identify their tribal affiliation. Particular colors were associated with the wearer's intended activity, imagined character traits, and tribe. Sometimes a design implied a message from a spirit or a vision the wearer had received. The paints for adorning the body and face were made from roots, berries, tree bark, and colored clay.

Sometimes half of the face would be painted in one color or style (dots, crisscross lines) and the other half in a different color or style, (stripes, zigzag lines), perhaps signifying dichotomies of human existence—life versus death, good fortune versus bad fortune.

Red was the color of war. In many bands, warriors about to go into battle painted red stripes on their faces and the backs of their hands. White usually signified peace, black typically denoted life (except among the Comanches

Figure 8.9   Cheyenne Brave of the Dog Soldier Society.

[Great Plains] who associated black with war), and yellow meant death. The Crow [Great Plains] painted their faces red, eyelids yellow, and chests and arms with horizontal stripes. The faces of the Blackfoot were decorated with stripes, circles, and dots in blue, yellow, red, black, and white, with an occasional warrior exhibiting a black face to remind others of a great deed he had performed. Green beneath the eyes was thought to improve night vision. (Indian face painting 2007; Selma 2007).

Painting was the way to display one's present mood or activity, such as going to war or performing a dance. Tattooing was the way to represent a permanent tribal affiliation, imagined character trait, or dedication to a guardian spirit.

DECORATIONS ON OBJECTS

Religious significance was often ascribed to designs on pottery, utensils, weapons, and dwellings. Repeated designs served as borders on jars, bowls, blankets, or clothing. The upper border in Figure 8.10 symbolizes clouds, implying movement and change in life, whereas the upright black images versus the inverted white images in the lower border stand for dichotomies—man/woman, night/day, or mountains/sky.

PICTOGRAMS

Before the arrival of European settlers in North America, the native peoples had no graphic writing system that would directly reflect language. However, many tribes did use drawings to represent events and beliefs. Warriors would sketch symbols of their deeds on buckskin shirts in order to gain the respect of tribe members. Pottery and the walls of teepees were decorated with

Figure 8.10 Symbolic Border Designs.

drawings that symbolized guardian spirits, historical incidents, and religious experiences.

Pictograms were also used as mnemonic devices that enabled chanters or storytellers to recall the sequence of events of lengthy songs and tales. Each succeeding symbol represented the theme of a verse whose words were associated in the chanter's mind with the memorized phrases that comprised the song or story. For instance, Figure 8.11 shows five of the 183 pictograms for a Delaware [Leni Lenape of the Northeast] chant describing the world's creation. Every verse had a drawing reminding the chanter of the verse's content, with each pictogram painted on a separate stick. In Figure 8.11, the five pictograms' meanings, from left to right, were (Squier 1848, in Clements 1986, 24–27):

- At first there were great waters above all the land.
- And above the waters were thick clouds, and there was God the Creator.
- He made also the first beings, angels, and souls.
- Then made he a man being, the father of men.
- He gave him the first mother, the mother of the early born.

EMBLEMS

The purpose of an emblem is either (a) to crystallize in visual form an abstraction—a deity, a tribe or nation, a virtue or a vice—or (b) to represent

Figure 8.11 Delaware Creation-Song Pictograms.

the imagined essence of a being or object. Emblems may be displayed on clothing, pottery, war shields, blankets, walls of dwellings, tobacco pouches, totem poles, and the like.

An example of an emblem representing an Indian nation is the Zia Pueblo [Southwest] sun image (Figure 8.12) with its rays pointing in the four primary directions of the compass. The number four is sacred in Zia culture, and the four rays in each of the directions have been invested with special meanings.

The lines pointing upward represent the seasons—spring, summer, fall, winter. Those pointing right signify the human life span—infancy, youth, adulthood, old age. Lines pointing down symbolize the four directions—north, east, south, west. Ones pointing left denote stages of the day—dawn, daylight, dusk, dark.

When New Mexico became a State, in 1912, the Zia symbol was adopted as the emblem for the state flag—a red sun on a yellow field. In recent years, Zia tribal leaders have sought to receive reparations from the New Mexico government for having adopted the sun emblem without the tribe's official permission.

Among the most popular emblems in Indian religions are images of animals that a person, band, or fraternal society has adopted as a guardian spirit revered for its assumed traits. The following are typical emblematic animals and some of their admired qualities (Lake-Thom 1997; Native-American designs 2007).

- Ant—good at planning, strong, psychical skills
- Antelope—messenger, visualizes the future
- Bear—special power, wisdom, abundance
- Buffalo—great strength
- Eagle—foresight, strength, spirituality
- Fox—pride, regality, loyalty
- Frog—fertility, brings rain
- Gopher—can cure illness
- Otter—wealth, good health

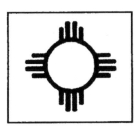

Figure 8.12   Zia Sun image.

Figure 8.13   Snake

- Snake—depicted as lightning, promotes fertility, moves undetected (Figure 8.13)
- Wolf—good hunter, clever, courageous

Revered Indian Objects

From among the host of venerated objects in Native-American religions, the six types inspected in the following section are pipes, medicine bundles, shields, masks, dolls, and musical instruments.

PIPES AND TOBACCO

Tobacco, indigenous to North America, was highly valued throughout the continent long before Europeans arrived. In many tribes, the practice of smoking tobacco was not merely a pastime, it was a sacred ritual.

Native American ceremonial pipes are often referred to as *peace pipes* because they traditionally functioned as key instruments of polite negotiations between individuals or groups. The groups could consist of tribes or could include representatives of such foreign entities as a European colonial power or the Canadian or U.S. government.

Throughout North America pipes continue to be among tribes' most hallowed possessions. A legend explains that the original Calf Pipe in ancient times was given to the Sioux [Great Plains] as a peace symbol by the goddess *Wope,* daughter of the Sun *Wi* and the Moon. *Wope* later became known among the Lakota Sioux as the White Buffalo Calf Woman. When people wished to have their own pipes blessed, they touched them to the Calf Pipe so its sacredness and force—*wakan*—would pass into their pipes.

Smoking a blessed pipe not only honors *Wope* (The Beautiful One) but also transforms her power into the tobacco smoke that serves as a mediator between earthly worshippers and the gods (Hassrick 1964, 259–261). Hence, pipes convey prayers, so they have been smoked at the outset of all religious ceremonies and prior to such risky ventures as hunting, traveling a great distance, moving camp, or going to war.

The materials from which pipes are carved have varied somewhat from region to region. The Iroquois [Great Lakes] and Cherokee [Southeast/Oklahoma] created ceramic pipes or made small, one-piece pipes from stone. Southwest tribes carved pipes from wood or antlers. However, the most famous have been the long-stemmed calumets (French for *hollow reed*) of the Great Plains bands (most notably the Sioux) as fashioned from soft pink pipestone quarried in Minnesota, South Dakota, and at the Pipestone River in Manitoba, Canada. The label *catlinite* has been used to identify pipestone ever since George Catlin, famous for his paintings of Indian life, visited the Minnesota quarries in 1835. In Figure 8.14 the top and bottom examples are catlinite pipes whose stems are detachable from the bowls. The wooden pipe in the middle has a catlinite bowl.

MEDICINE BUNDLES

A medicine bundle or medicine pouch is a collection of closely guarded sacred objects believed to contain the magical essence of the spirits that the objects represent (see Figure 8.15). A bundle can be either communal (owned by the tribe or family) or individual (its objects collected and owned by a single person).

Figure 8.14   Sacred Pipes.

Figure 8.15   Medicine Bundles (left to right): Great Plains Style, Algonquin Beaded, Otter Pelt.

In some tribes, certain objects bear a standardized meaning. Among the Crow [Great Plains], horsehair signifies a desire for fine horses, elk teeth or beads imply wealth, and a piece of otter skin carries the healing power of water because otters are considered the kings of water animals. However, each object in a bundle is frequently invested with meanings known only to the bundle's owner. Such could be the case of a collection that included a tuft of grass wrapped in cotton cloth, a grey powder in a buckskin purse, three flint arrow points, a short length of braided hair, sage in a cloth bag, an oddly shaped red stone, seeds in a pouch, an eagle's claw, pieces of root tied together, and a chip from a buffalo horn.

Some bundle objects are not collected directly by their owner but are bought from a shaman, a renowned warrior, or a chief in the belief that such items will convey some of their original owner's power and wisdom to the purchaser.

The significance of a bundle does not consist solely of objects in a pouch but, rather, includes also chants, ritual manipulations, rules about when bundles are opened (often at seasonal junctures), how bundles are stored, offerings to the bundle's spirits, and mental attitudes of awe, trust, and respect.

The bundle is ceremoniously opened when supplicants wish to gain spiritual power or blessing in a time of need. Each object is reverently displayed by a priest who has been trained in the ritual, and then the priest and assistants sing prayers invoking the spirit symbolized by the object (Kehoe 1981, 299).

SHIELDS

Leather shields not only served to protect warriors' bodies during battle but also to protect their spiritual selves during any of life's emergencies. Thus, shields have been carried on many noncombat occasions, attached to an individual's horse, mounted on posts of honor, or displayed on lodge or teepee walls. Because shields are believed to safeguard a person's innermost self, they continue to be valued today even though they no longer serve as instruments of battle.

The decorations on shields are intended to symbolize components of the shield bearer's identity. For instance, upon returning from a vision quest, a youth would often add to his shield a design representing a momentous incident experienced during the quest, such as an encounter with a guardian spirit. In Figure 8.16, the Thunderbird on the Crow shield and the bison on the Cheyenne shield represent the shield owners' guardians.

MASKS

Although wearing masks in ceremonies has been widespread in North America, the use of masks has varied considerably from one region to another. In the past, the variety of masks and their frequency were far greater among the Pueblo [Southwest], Iroquois [Great Lakes], and tribes of the Northwest than among Great Plains and Southeast bands. In the Great Plains, mask wearers were limited to such groups as the Mandans' Bull Dancers, who donned buffalo heads for their performances, and members of the Assiniboins' Fool Society, who clowned about in grotesque disguises.

Masks have been fashioned from diverse materials. For the Buffalo dances of the Pueblo, a simulated buffalo head has frequently been created from bear hair and cow horns, then slipped over the performer's head, with the hood resting on the shoulders and a black beard falling down over the breast. "The tips of the swaying horns carry eagle down; and more down is stuck to the shaking heads, like snow. The bodies of the dancers are bare save for the usual dance kirtles [tunics] and moccasins" (Waters 1950, 269).

Along the Northwest Coast—from the State of Washington, through Canada, to Alaska—the carving and painting of cedar-wood masks (see Figure 8.17) has been a highly developed art. These wooden disguises—frequently

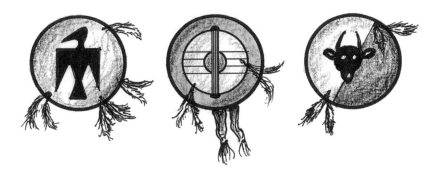

Figure 8.16   Great Plains Shields—Crow, Kiowa, Cheyenne

Figure 8.17   Cedar-Wood Mask.

adorned with feathers and straw hair—have served as properties both in ceremonies and in storytelling sessions. A fanciful mask, along with a costume depicting an animal spirit, completely converts a familiar member of a Kawkiutl community into a convincing specter from the spirit world.

> Bearskins might be sewn so that the dancer really appeared to be a bear with a head transformed into a beautiful, stylized, yet terrible spirit bear's face. For another, eagle feathers might be sewn so closely over a suit that the dancer truly seemed a great bird with an overarching beak.
>
> (Kehoe 1981, 411)

Some masks have been created for the rituals of such secret organizations as a shaman society, a war society, or the society that initiates youths into the tribe.

DOLLS

Dolls as instruments of religious rituals appear in numerous Indian rites. An example is the Arapaho [Great Plains] *Tai-me* ceremonial doll carved from wood and clad in ribbons and furs. However, the most famous North American dolls have been the Hopi and Zuñi [Southwest] kachina (*katsina*) figures designed as icons of deities (Figure 8.18).

In Hopi culture, katchinas are supernatural beings with the power to control the weather, aid villagers in many daily activities, punish people who breach ceremonial or social customs, and serve as messengers between mortals and the gods. The dolls, carved from cottonwood roots and painted to represent religious beliefs, are statues of those mystical beings. The purpose of adults giving dolls to children is to teach each new generation the nature of the kachina spirits, how kachinas affect people's destinies, and how to behave in order to court the favor of the deities.

Figure 8.18   Kachina Dolls.

MUSICAL INSTRUMENTS

Most Native American religious rites have been accompanied by chants and by rhythms and melodies played on a variety of instruments (Figure 8.19). Percussion instruments have been the most prominent—drums, rattles consisting of pebbles inside a container (gourd, animal-hide bag, buffalo or cow horn), two sticks tapped together, and flat wooden clappers.

> [For tribes on the Great Plains] drums played such a vital part in every healing ceremony that it is important to understand why they were used. The round form usually represented the entire universe, and its steady beat was its pulsing heart. It was as the voice of the Great Spirit, which stirred men and helped them to understand the mystery and power of all things; it soothed the tortured mind, and brought healing to the suffering body.
>
> (Mails 2002, 21)

A typical drum was constructed on a wooden frame or on a carved, hollowed-out log, with tanned buckskin or elkskin stretched across the opening to form a drumhead that was held taut by sinew thongs.

The traditional drum that accompanied dancers and chanters in ceremonies was large, with a drumhead two or three feet across. Several drummers surrounded the instrument to pound out the rhythms. Smaller, flatter drums with painted designs on the drumheads were played by individuals rather than by a group.

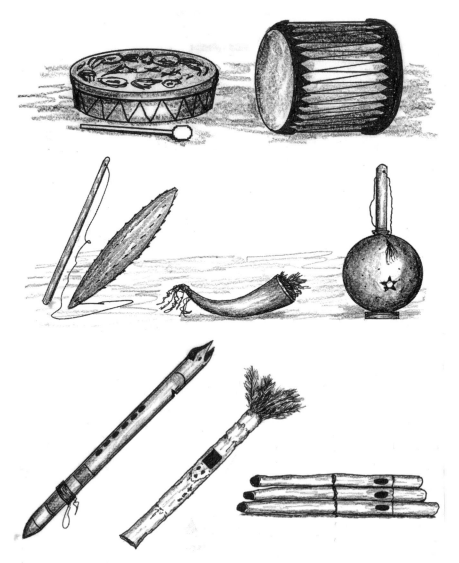

Figure 8.19   Native American Musical Instruments: Shallow Drum, Most Popular Drum Style, Bull Roarer, Horn Rattle, Gourd Rattle, Flute, Bone Whistle, Whistles Shaped as a Pan Pipe

Indian flutes have been second only in popularity to the percussion instruments. Flutes were played not only during ceremonies but also were important in rituals for healing, meditation, and spiritual renewal. When used in courtship they were referred to as *love flutes*. Tribes continue to revere flutes today as proper instruments for sending prayers to deities. Unlike flutes in other cultures, those in Native American tradition have two air chambers rather than only one. The two chambers are separated by a wall inside the instrument. The long lower chamber has whistles and finger holes for changing the tones; a hole at the bottom of the upper chamber enables that section to function as a secondary resonator. This double-chamber arrangement accounts for Indian flutes' distinctive sound.

> The traditional flute of the Native American people was made as per the measurements of the human body. The flute's length was the distance from armpit to wrist, whereas the length of the top air chamber and the distance between the whistle and the first hole were both one fist-width. The distance between the holes was one thumb width whereas that from the last hole to the end was the width of one fist. [Most] Native American flutes contain five or six holes and they are played on minor pentatonic scales. However, there can be seven to nine holes as well as no holes at all.
>
> (Native American flute 2007)

Most Indian flutes have been carved from such soft woods as juniper and redwood for brightness of tone and aroma. Or they are fashioned from such hard woods as walnut and cherry for tonal richness.

Bird-bone whistles are akin to flutes, with such tribes as the Chumash [California] binding several whistles together to form a type of panpipe made from bird or deer bones or from elderberry branches.

Another instrument is the bull roarer, which consists of a wooden handle connected by a long thong to a fish-shaped wooden slat. Twirling the slat around in the air produces a humming or howling sound that is sometimes interpreted as being the voice of the gods. The smaller the bull roarer and the faster it is twirled, the higher the pitch of its buzz or whine.

TRADITIONS COMPARED

The following comparison opens with likenesses between the two religious traditions, then continues with differences.

Similarities

Both Christianity and Native American religions include symbols and sacred relics in their belief systems.

The symbols in each tradition assume oral and graphic forms. The oral symbolism appears in songs, chants, prayers, and stories—and sometimes in sacred numerals. The graphic symbols include drawings, paintings, carvings, sculptures, and writings. Although Indian cultures lacked a writing system that matched the structure of spoken language, some tribes used pictograms to convey religious concepts.

Sacred objects in both traditions include items related to significant religious events and experiences, such as the Christians' crucifix, chalice, shroud, and vestments used in holy services and Native Americans' vision quests and medical treatments.

Differences

Contrasts between Indian religions and Christian culture include their (a) diversity of focus, (b) use of animals, and (c) types and significance of musical instruments.

The expression *diversity of focus* refers to the variety of beings or concepts to which symbols and sacred relics refer. The focus in Christianity is far more restricted than in Indian worldviews. Most important Christian symbols and relics are related to Jesus—the crucifix, chalices, shroud, and images of his mother, Mary. Second only to Jesus are Christian saints, whose pictures and statuettes are revered. In contrast, Indian symbols and relics relate to a wide variety of spirits, usually in the form of animals, such as those encountered during vision quests or ones important in religious lore.

Indian symbolism includes far more animals than does Christian imagery, especially because Indian belief systems assign power and influence to animals, whereas Christianity does not. In the Bible, the creature most obviously assigned a personality trait is the lamb, believed to symbolize innocence and purity. Thus, in the Old Testament, lambs are sacrificed to symbolically honor God. And in the New Testament, Jesus is referred to as "the lamb of God" (John 1:29), on the belief that his dying on the cross was the perfect sacrifice to convince God to forgive Christians' sins (Romans 8:3; Hebrews 10). But the lamb had no power to be shared with humans. However, in Indian religions, animals display personality traits and powers that people would be wise to respect and that might be transferred by those animals to selected humans —physical strength, wisdom, foresight, persuasiveness, avarice, deviousness, and more. A person, by treasuring an icon of such an animal, could attempt to encourage the creature to share its envied power or trait with the appreciative human.

Indian religions and Christianity also differ in their conceptions of instruments suitable for playing religious music. Most instruments employed in Native American religious performances feature rhythms. Such is the case with drums, rattles, and clappers. In contrast, most instruments used for Christian performances feature melodies, as do organs, harps, lyres as well as string and brass instruments. Indian religions and Christianity both assign an important role to woodwinds, such as flutes.

Apparently adherents of Indian religions have often attributed sacred characteristics to musical instruments and have regarded the instruments themselves with reverence. Consequently, the sound of a drum, bull roarer, flute, or whistle might be interpreted by a Native American as the actual voice of an ethereal spirit, so that the instrument is treated as if it contained a soul. Christians, on the other hand, would cherish the message of the music played on an organ or violin, and they might think the rendition of a tune was spiritually inspired, but they seldom would claim that the instrument itself embodied a spirit.

Religious Societies

The expression *religious societies* identifies organizations that promote the aims of the religions with which the organizations are associated. Both American Indian and Christian sects have maintained such societies. However, typical functions of societies in Indian tradition have tended to differ from the functions in Christian tradition. Indian societies have focused inward, concerning themselves with the authentic conduct of established rituals. In other words, Indian societies have performed essential roles in the religion and have guarded the authenticity of those roles. In contrast, Christian societies have more often focused outward, aiming at recruiting more adherents into the faith.

CHRISTIAN SOCIETIES

Three prominent forms of Christian organizations are missionary societies, fraternal associations, and youth groups.

Missionary Societies

The charter granted by the king of England to the Pilgrims who established the Massachusetts Bay colony in 1620 instructed the colonists to "wynn and invite the Natives...[to] the onlie God and Saviour of Mankinde." Thus, from the outset the European immigrants' intent in the New World included bringing North America's native peoples into the Christian community. This commission was taken seriously by such ministers as John Eliot who learned the

Massachusetts' tribal language and by 1646 was preaching to Indians in the towns of Dorchester Mills and Newton. He thought Christian Indians should be segregated from their tribes and settled into towns of *Praying Indians* where they could be instructed in Christian practices. Natick was the first praying town, established in 1651, followed by fourteen more towns of Praying Indians that had a total population of four thousand by 1674. Indians were taught English, agriculture, domestic crafts, Bible reading, and devotional literature (Hummon 2006).

However, Eliot's effort and that of others were individual ventures associated with a single minister or church. Not until missionary societies were formed did the attempt to proselytize among the Native Americans become a major social movement. The first British missionary societies were created early in the eighteenth century, with the Society for the Propagation of the Gospel working in India beginning in 1710. By the middle of the century British missionaries were also operating in North America. The American colonies' own mission boards did not appear in significant numbers until the early nineteenth century when individual societies began to unite in order to mount massive evangelical campaigns. For example, the Young Men's Missionary Society of New York (1815) joined the New York Evangelical Missionary Society (1816) and other small mission groups to form the United Domestic Missionary Society (1822). In 1826, representatives from Congregational, Presbyterian, and Reformed churches created the American Missionary Society, with the United Domestic Missionary Society as one of its members (Records of the American Home Missionary Society 2001).

The task of missionary societies in North America was to add new Christians to church rolls and persuade backsliders to return to the faith. The objects of missionaries' attention were both European settlers and Indians. Although the height of missionary activities with Indians has now long passed, missionary societies in the twenty-first century are still active in some American Indian communities.

Fraternal Societies

Fraternal societies are collections of like-minded individuals who enjoy each other's company, subscribe to a set of ethical and self-improvement ideals, and include social-service projects among their activities.

KNIGHTS OF COLUMBUS

An example of a Roman Catholic fraternal organization is the Order of the Knights of Columbus, a society launched in New Haven, Connecticut, in 1882 by a group of Catholic laymen who sought strength in solidarity and security through unity of purpose and devotion to a holy cause: they vowed to be defenders of their country, their families, and their faith. These men were bound together by the ideal of Christopher Columbus, the discoverer of the

Americas, the one whose hand brought Christianity to the New World. The Order has been called "the strong right arm of the Church," and has been praised by popes, presidents and other world leaders, for support of the Church, programs of evangelization and Catholic education, civic involvement and aid to those in need. (Knights of Columbus 2006).

The Order was destined to become the largest Catholic charitable organization in the world.

YMCA/YWCA

A Protestant society with a fraternal and philanthropic intent is the Young Men's Christian Association (YMCA), along with its female counterpart, the Young Women's Christian Association (YWCA). The YMCA (see the YMCA logo in Figure 9.1) originated in London in 1844 to counteract distressing social conditions among youths who had come to big cities near the end of the Industrial Revolution. Seven years later, YMCA branches were founded in North America—Montreal on November 25 and Boston on December 29. The Boston society owed its start to a sea captain and missionary, Thomas Sullivan, who was inspired by the early success of the London YMCA that had expanded to 24 sites by 1851. In the United States, YMCA's grew to 50 by 1855 and 1,379 by 1900. According to the organization's historical account, one out of three Americans reports being a YMCA member at some point in life. The YMCA develops character by demonstrating and teaching the core values of caring, honesty, respect, and responsibility. These values, derived from Christian teachings but embraced by all the worlds' major religions, form a blueprint for decision making and a moral and ethical foundation for life. The "Y" has been concerned with character development for more than 150 years. Methods have changed—from evangelical Christianity in the organization's early years to "values clarification" in the 1960s and 1970s—but the organization's commitment to Christian principles has not. (South Shore YMCA, 2006).

The society takes credit for a host of contributions, including

YMCAs invented basketball (1891) and volleyball (1895). YMCAs pioneered camping (1885), public libraries (1852), night schools (1878), and teaching English as a second language (1856). YMCAs introduced the world's first indoor pool (1885) and group swim lessons (1907), [then] offered after-school childcare long before "latchkey kids" had been given

Figure 9.1   YMCA.

a name. . . . The Boy Scouts of America, Camp Fire Girls, Negro National Baseball League, Gideons, Toastmasters, racquetball, and Father's Day all got their starts at YMCAs.

(Brief history 2006)

In 2005, the YMCA's U.S. headquarters announced that the total membership in the nation's 2,594 branches exceeded 20.1 million, half of them children. "For the first time ever, more Americans belong to a YMCA than the combined population of the top five U.S. cities" (YMCA membership 2005).

The Young Women's Christian Society also started in London shortly after the first YMCA, then followed the YMCA to North America in 1858 where it initially bore the title Ladies' Christian Association. Since then, the YWCA has continued to promote fellowship among Christian women and girls through activities "combining religious fervor with practical social action" (Philips 1999). By 2000, the YWCA advertised itself as the oldest and largest women's membership movement in America, with branches in 123 countries working to empower women, improve their economic status, and eliminate racism.

In addition to unquestionably Christian societies like the Knights of Columbus and YMCA/YWCA, there are also fraternal organizations whose religious status is controversial, with some people calling them Christian and others calling them non-Christian or even anti-Christian. Two such groups are the Masons and the Ku Klux Klan.

MASONS

The origins of the order of Free and Accepted Masons are quite obscure. Some historians trace the beginnings of Free Masonry to ancient Egypt and to the stonemasons who built pyramids, temples, and the sphinx. Other historians credit the society's origin to the Middle Ages' guilds of masons who constructed the era's palaces, castles, and cathedrals. Whereas debate continues over when and where the society began, there is no question that it was founded on concepts from the masonry craft, as reflected in the logo (Figure 9.2) featuring a mason's square and compass. The "G" in the logo perhaps stands for *God,* because one requirement for membership is that each

Figure 9.2   Masons.

candidate must acknowledge that the universe was created by, and continues to be supervised by, a supreme being.

Free Masonry in its present-day form first appeared in the British Isles during the early eighteenth century and was soon carried to the American colonies by English and Scotch immigrants. The first branch in North America was established in 1731 as The Grand Lodge of Pennsylvania, and over the following century the influence of Masonry grew rapidly.

> Of the fifty-six signatories of the Declaration of Independence, only nine can definitely be identified as Freemasons, while ten others may possibly have been. Of the general officers in the Continental Army, there were so far as documentation can establish, 33 Freemasons out of 74. [Masons who signed the declaration included] George Washington, Benjamin Franklin, and John Hancock.
>
> (Masonic foundations 2006)

Since the eighteenth century, Free Masonry has been criticized by doctrinaire Christians as a belief system antagonistic to Christianity. In 1738 the Catholic pope issued a proclamation denouncing Free Masonry, with that bulletin followed in 1751 and 1884 by similar papal censures. Not until 1974 did the Vatican rescind those statements and display a more tolerant view of Masonry.

Typical of Masonry's modern-day critics are fundamentalist Christian groups that object to Free Masonry's

- Requiring all members to express a belief in a supreme being but allowing them to decide what that deity is like. Consequently, Masonry's members can swear fealty either to the Bible's God or to the dominant deity of another faith—American Indian, Islamic, Buddhist, Hindu, Baha'i, or the like.

- Insisting that people go to heaven for doing good works and engaging in self-improvement while on earth, rather than for having confessed that Jesus died to atone for humans' sins and for depending on the "grace of the Lord" to determine whether they are worthy of entering heaven.

- Classifying the Bible as a useful guide to morality, but it is only one of many good books and not the direct word of God nor a revelation of God to mankind.

- Ranking Jesus on the same level as other religious leaders. Because in Free Masonry there is no trinity (God, Jesus, Holy Spirit), Masons do not pray "in the name of Jesus Christ."

In effect, fundamentalist Christians officially reject Free Masonry as a form of Christian faith. Nevertheless, evangelical Christian groups that subscribe to a literal interpretation of the Bible often include substantial numbers of Masons among their congregants. One of the severest critics of Masonry, James L. Holly—a Baptist medical doctor who condemned Free Masonry as *secular humanism*—estimated that in the early 1990s between 500,000 and 1.3 million members of the Southern Baptist Convention were Masons, including 14 percent of Baptist pastors and 18 percent of Baptist deacons (Christian Research Institute 1994). Furthermore, there were masons among the luminaries in Baptist American history. For example, not only was Robert E. Baylor one of eight Masons who petitioned for a charter for Baylor University in 1845, but since then every president of that prestigious Baptist institution has been a Mason (Maddox 2006).

Thus, by the twenty-first century conflict continued in the ranks of evangelical Christians over the status of the Masonic Lodge. What appears to be a compromise position is the somewhat conciliatory position expressed by sponsors of a fundamentalist Christian web site.

> We are not claiming that all who are involved in Free Masonry are cultists. What we are saying is this—Free Masonry at its core is not a Christian organization. There are many Christians who have left Free Masonry after discovering what it is truly all about. [However,] there are also good and godly men, true believers in Christ, who are Free Masons.
>
> (What is Free Masonry 2006)

KU KLUX KLAN

The Ku Klux Klan was created in 1866 by six Confederate Civil War veterans. As black slaves were now free and the South was suffering radical social change, lower-class whites who saw their former economic advantage slipping away joined the Klan so as to attack people they saw as oppressors who were robbing whites of their "inalienable rights" as evangelical Christians. Those "oppressors" included blacks, judges, and politicians (who sought to carry out emancipation laws), white teachers from the North (who came to educate the former slaves), and all sorts of Northern "carpetbaggers." The Klan's methods included intimidating, harassing, torturing, and lynching their foes. One frightening tactic was that of sending night riders in white robes and hoods to burn crosses in front of their victims' homes.

Over the past 140 years, the size and influence of the Klan has waxed and waned. In the xenophobic social climate of the early twentieth century, when waves of European immigrants entered America, the Klan's targets expanded to include Catholics and Jews. At the close of World War I, the ranks of the Klan suddenly swelled when publicists launched a campaign to defend America against "Niggers, Catholics, Jews...dope, bootlegging, graft, nightclubs and road houses, violation of the Sabbath, unfair business dealings, sex, and scandalous behavior" (Anti-Defamation League 2005).

By 1921, the Klan numbered almost 100,000 members and money flooded into its coffers. At its peak in 1924, 40,000 uniformed Klansmen paraded through the streets of Washington, DC, during the Democratic National Convention. Like a modern political lobby, the group was so influential that many politicians felt compelled to court it or even to join, particularly in the Midwestern states.

(Anti-Defamation League 2005)

Throughout the Klan's history, the organization has periodically split into competing factions, with some groups committing such blatant atrocities that public opinion would turn against the entire body. In addition, economic prosperity, such as that of the post–World War II era, dampened the Klan's appeal. As a result, by the twenty-first century, there was no centralized Ku Klux Klan. Instead, there were three separate coalitions, each containing a number of individual Klan chapters (*Klaverns*). There were also numerous independent Klaverns. Estimates place the present-day membership in the 110 or so existing Klaverns at no more than a few thousand Klansmen and Klanswomen (Anti-Defamation League 2005).

Over the decades, Klan members have consistently identified themselves as devoted Christians with strong white supremacist convictions. The Klan insignia (Figure 9.3) is a cross with the image of a red drop of blood in the center, intended to signify Jesus shedding his blood for the white Aryan race.

The web site of the one of the three Klan coalitions, the American Knights of the Ku Klux Klan, advertises the group's creed as:

We, the Ku Klux Klan, reverently acknowledge the majesty and supremacy of Jesus Christ, and recognize his goodness and divine providence. Furthermore, we recognize our relationship to him as his sons and daughters of the living God.

(American knights 2006)

However, virtually all mainstream Christian groups have condemned the Klan, its policies, and tactics.

Although American Indians were never primary targets of the Klan, after the mid-twentieth century, when Indians gained political strength and rights,

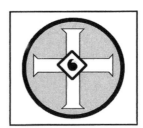

Figure 9.3   KKK.

they occasionally came into conflict with Klansmen. In 1958, after a series of Klan cross-burnings in Robeson County, North Carolina, several hundred Lumbee Indians broke up a publicly advertised Klan rally at a local field.

> The Indian men confronted the Klansmen, and after heated words were exchanged, shots were fired and the only light bulb knocked out, leaving the field in darkness. The Klansmen apparently disappeared quickly into the night, abandoning their fallen flag, cross, and other items for the safety of the woods. The Indian community, and no doubt the Black community, and the county's progressive Whites, celebrated.
>
> (Museum of the Native American Resource Center 2006)

Youth Groups

Christian denominations often sponsor clubs for adolescents that function as religious societies, conducting activities intended to promote a particular religious faith and to foster the welfare of the faith's adherents. The club's aims usually include the goal of attracting converts to the sect. Formal or informal instruction in the religion's doctrine and rituals is typically part of club activities.

Prior to the 1980s, religious clubs operated only outside of public school systems. However, in 1984 the U.S. Congress passed the Equal Access Act (EAA), primarily because conservative Christians pressed for legislation that would permit the establishment of Bible-study, fellowship, and prayer clubs in public high schools. As a result of the act, the number of Christian Bible clubs in public schools rose from around 100 in 1980 to an estimated 15,000 by 1995 (Robinson, 2003). Two representative youth groups that function internationally are *Young Life* and *Youth for Christ*, which advertise their programs in the following manner.

> *Young Life* operates out of Colorado Springs (Colorado) as "a non-profit, non-denominational Christian organization reaching out to teens with programs in more than 800 communities in the United States and Canada and more than 45 countries overseas. More than 100,000 kids are involved in Young Life weekly, with more than 1 million kids participating in Young Life throughout the year."
>
> ("About Young Life" 2006)

The aim of *Youth for Christ,* based in Denver (Colorado), is "to share the Good News about Jesus in a way that is relevant to [youth]." The organization lists "ministries in over 200 cities throughout the USA and over 100 countries around the world. The young people in every city and every country have needs that are somewhat unique to them. For that reason, local YFC ministries vary from location to location." *Youth for Christ* conducts two sets of programs titled *Campus Life* (for high-school students) and *Campus Life-M* (for middle-school and junior-high students). The high school version is designed "to help senior-high young people make good choices, establish a solid foundation for life, and positively impact their schools. Like every ministry of YFC, *Campus Life* seeks to engage these young people wherever they are found as life-long followers of Jesus Christ....A *Campus Life* club generally meets in various homes each week, hosted by students. In some cities, *Campus Life* may own a building they use to host club meetings, or have access to a school gym, cafeteria or classroom, or, less frequently, churches." (Youth for Christ 2006)

INDIAN SOCIETIES

Organizations within a tribe qualify as religious societies if they maintain belief in supernatural spirits that have power to influence events in the world. Virtually all Native American nations have included such societies among their social institutions. Although most societies have been well-known throughout a tribe and usually have conducted some form of public activities, they have been "secret" in the sense that members of the general public are excluded from societies' meetings and are not privy to the groups' sacrosanct doctrines. Each society has had its code of behavior, insignia, modes of dress, chants, dances, and medicine bundles.

One convenient way to view religious societies is in terms of their types, functions, membership, structure, and status.

Types and Functions

The two most prominent types of societies have been healing associations and warrior brotherhoods. Other types have included ones assigned to protect and propagate religious lore, keep historical records, maintain sacred objects, initiate youths into adult status, serve as a vocational guilds, conduct dances and ceremonies, dramatize myths, and amaze the populace.

HEALING SOCIETIES

Virtually all Native American bands have maintained one or more medicine societies.

Typical practices of Indian healers can be illustrated with the Iroquois [Great Lakes] False Face Society. If an ill or injured individual saw a strange face during a dream, that vision was interpreted as an omen prompting the sufferer to summon the False Face Society to conduct a curing ceremony that involved society members appearing at the patient's dwelling wearing fantastic masks. To cure any sort of ailment, the False Face practitioners circled the patient, danced to the rhythm of rattles, scooped hot coals from a fire, and blew the ashes over the sufferer. Patients who recovered were then obliged to join the society and create their own masks, usually disguises resembling faces seen in their original dreams (Reader's Digest 1978, 132).

The Sioux [Great Plains] had multiple Holy Medicine Lodges, each with its particular nostrums and songs. Whenever a lodge member died, a novitiate would be inducted into the order, taught the sacred curative treatments, and issued a set of commands to guide his life—such commands as: frequently prepare a holy feast for the Supreme Being, never spill the blood of fellow tribe members, and do not steal others' belongings (Eastman 1894 in Clements 1986, 215).

WARRIOR SOCIETIES

Every Great Plains tribe maintained several military societies that guarded the community against intertribal raids, fought at the forefront of battles during a war, maintained order on buffalo hunts, engaged in contests of strength and endurance, sponsored dances and feasts, celebrated historical events with chants and stories, and displayed their intended identities by wearing distinctive costumes.

In modern times, older military societies have often been revived, no longer to engage in warfare but, rather, to sponsor community-service activities and powwows, with the powwows taking the form of gatherings at which participants sing, dance, socialize, and generally have a good time. Among the Comanches [Great Plains], the Little Pony Society was reconstituted in 1972 to honor tribe members who had fought in Vietnam. In like manner, the Black Knife Society of the Yamparika branch of the Comanche nation was restored in 1976. The four traditional Southern Cheyenne (*Tsetschestahase*) [Great Plains] men's societies (Kit Fox, Elk Horn Scraper, Red Shield, and Dog Men) were renewed as the Bowstrings, Elk Horn, Kit Foxes, and Dog Soldiers.

An example of a modern-day insignia for a Native American religious fraternity is this flag of the Mohawk Warrior Society (Figure 9.4).

Some societies have been a combination of warriors and healers. Such was the case of the Kiowa [Great Plains] Buffalo-Men brotherhood. One or more Buffalo Men joined each raiding party. Whenever a brave was injured, the Buffalo men would shake their rattles and buffalo tails while singing a chant soliciting supernatural aid in healing the warrior's wounds (Mails 2002, 20).

MORE SPECIALIZED SOCIETIES

The following are additional associations, often unique to an individual tribe or to a cluster of Indian nations.

Figure 9.4 Mohawk Warrior Society.

In many bands, a particular group was assigned to conduct rites of passage that celebrated children's advance into adulthood. An example is the practice of the Northern Pomo [California] that required all young adolescent boys and girls from upper-social-class families to be schooled in tribal history, morals, and spiritual dogma. The instructors, disguised as ghosts, also pierced their young students' ears and septums so they could wear ornaments signifying their entrance to adult status. In contrast to upper-class youth,

> [the] common boys and girls excluded from the school were marked by their lack of earrings and nose ornaments, as unlikely to achieve mastery of any craft or office, and were relegated to the humdrum chores of getting subsistence and making only utilitarian objects.
>
> (Kehoe 1981, 381)

An instance of a highly specialized society among the Omaha [Great Plains] was the Thunder Order, whose members were assigned to guard the tribe's pair of sacred pipes. There was also a Plains society dedicated to willing people to death, a fellowship of "big-bellied men," and a Cheyenne brotherhood of firewalkers (Blair 1911, 224).

The Crow [Great Plains] believed that tobacco was a form of medicine, a gift from benevolent spirits, worthy of having its own society whose members were responsible for planting and harvesting the crops. Both men and women of the Tobacco Order conducted ceremonies in which dances and songs were usually of a secret nature. The prestige associated with being a member of the order encouraged prospective novices to pay heavy initiation fees to a sponsor who would then give the newcomers seeds and instruct them in proper crop-cultivation methods.

The Wichita [Great Plains] maintained a series of dance societies—as many as 14 during the early twentieth century, three of which were for women. Each fellowship's dances were intended to furnish particular services for the tribe. For instance, the Calumet Pipe Sticks Dance accompanied the presentation of feathered pipe stems to a prominent person or neighboring band. The Rain Bundle ceremonies were designed to promote the maturation of the corn crop. The Surround-Fire and Small-Robes rituals featured chants to attract the supernatural powers of revered animals, while the aim of another dance was to foster the safe return of war parties (Newcomb 1961, 273–274).

Frequently, individuals who had been visited by a bear, buffalo, elk, or hare during a vision quest would form societies dedicated to that guardian spirit, and society members would then dress in the manner of their admired animal during dance and song rituals.

Clown societies—sometimes referred to as *mirth-makers*—have been found in nearly all North American Indian nations, but particularly among Plains Indians who believed that everything in nature often contained its own opposite polarity, hence the expected existence of such contraries as women warriors, *berdaches* (homosexuals)...[and] *heyoka* or sacred clowns who displayed wisdom through seemingly foolhardy action. [The peculiar behavior of clown-society members] revolved around a few basic themes or attributes: burlesque, mocking the sacred, playing pranks or practical jokes, making obscene jokes or gestures, caricature of others, exhibiting gross gluttony or extreme appetite, strange acts of self-mortification or self-deprecation, and taunting of enemies or strangers.

(Mizrach 2007)

Some clown brotherhoods were composed of "crazy" warriors who did everything backwards—even riding their steeds backwards—and were known to be "reckless and extraordinarily brave" (Newcomb 1961, 185).

Other societies consisted of conjurers who amazed audiences with sleight-of-hand tricks. A typical stunt of the Omaha tribe's Bear Dreamers was that of swallowing long sticks.

Membership

The rules governing how an individual might join a religious society could differ from one tribe to another. For example, any member of the Witchita nation [Great Plains] would be accepted into one of the semi-secret tribal orders. However, the Kiowa's [Great Plains] order of the Principal Dogs was limited to ten members renowned as the most daring men in the tribe.

The Principal Dog leader was recognized as the bravest of the brave. He wore a long sash hanging from his shoulders to the ground. In battle he dismounted in the thick of the fray and anchored himself to the ground by driving his lance through the end of his sash. As he stood rooted to the ground, as a target for scores of arrows, he urged his warriors on.

(Reader's Digest 1978, 185)

The act of joining a society typically involved an initiation ceremony. In the Kwakiutl [Northwest] Shamans Society, members were assigned roles to play during the ritual that accompanied the induction of new recruits, with the members wearing costumes that conveyed the status and personality traits of the spirits they portrayed. The masked person in the role of *Hamatsu* (Cannibal Spirit) wore a cedarbark necklace signifying his exalted rank. *Hamatsu's* retinue included such bloodthirsty birdlike creatures as Crooked Beak of Heaven (enjoyed eating human flesh), Raven (plucked out the eyes of *Hamatsu's* victims), *Hoxhok* (cracked skulls and sucked out brains), and Grizzly Bear (disemboweled humans with a swipe of his claws). Other participants in Kwakiutl initiation rites were less frightening—a woman symbolizing the weather and a goat representing mountain-climbing skill (Reader's Digest 1978, 313).

The Caddo [Great Plains] medicine guilds (Beaver, Mescal-bean, Yuko) initiated new members during public ceremonies in which the shamans required the prospective practitioners to imbibe drinks made from herbs and tobacco that cast the drinkers into an unconscious state for twenty-four hours. When the novitiates wakened, they sang at length of their dream experiences and of the journeys their souls had taken under the spell of the herbal brew (Newcomb 1961, 311).

Each society maintained a code of conduct that members were compelled to obey. For example, individuals in Hopi and Navajo [Southwest] kachina cults were required to remain sexually continent, avoid quarreling, cherish good thoughts, and stay away from non-Indians (Waters 1950, 279).

Origins

Most societies apparently originated from visions in which spirits directed recipients to organize a particular kind of group, with the spirits also describing the sorts of songs, dances, emblems, and equipment to use.

To account for the beginning of the Midewiwin healing society, Ojibwa [Great Lakes] lore tells of the Good Spirit's servant, Great Rabbit, pitying "the original people" (Ojibwa tribe members) who were helplessly suffering from hunger and disease. Great Rabbit sought to help the victims by communicating with the Ojibwa through Otter, who would later become the sacred spirit of the Midewiwin. It was Otter who carried to the tribe the healing instruments provided by Great Rabbit—a chant, sacred drum, rattle, tobacco, and the Midewiwin secret formulas for curing illness. The chant told of the Good Spirit's desire to have the original people free from hunger and disease so they could live long and happy lives. Midewiwin medicine bundles thereafter would be made from otter pelts (Reader's Digest 1978, 141).

A Maidu [California] myth explains that the need for a safe and predictable social system for the Maidu people prompted the Creator (*Wónommi*) to decree the establishment of a male secret society. The Creator had stimulated ancient Maidu leaders to action with this admonition:

> Until now you have let all your boys grow up like a wild tree in the mountains; you have taught them nothing; they have gone their own way. Henceforth you must bring every youth, at a proper age, into your assembly house, and cause him to be initiated into the ways and knowledge of manhood. You shall teach him to worship me, and to observe the sacred dances which I shall ordain in my honor....Never neglect my rites and my honors....Then shall your hills be full of acorns and nuts; your valleys shall yield plenty of grass and herbs; your rivers shall be full of salmon, and your hearts shall be rejoiced.
>
> (Loeb 1933, 165)

Structure and Status

Some societies have been age-graded, with individuals moving to a higher-level group as they grew older. The Arapaho [Great Plains] age-structure was very strict, more so than the Kiowa [Great Plains] war societies in which the Rabbits fellowship was for boys ages six to around 12. Then, during adolescence, Kiowa youths usually advanced to the Herders or the Gourd Dancers. Ultimately—if they proved extremely brave in battle—Kiowa warriors might be accepted into the select Crazy Dog Society (Marriott & Rachlin 1975, 38).

The organizations within an Indian nation have varied in their comparative prestige as determined by which kinds of activities were most important for the community's welfare. For instance, Pueblo peoples [Southwest] in the past had medicine, warrior, hunt, kachina, and clown associations. The tribes in the arid western region assigned the highest esteem to rain-bringing kachina and medicine societies. In contrast, the Tanoan-speaking tribes to the east, whose fields were adequately irrigated by rivers, vested greater prestige in war societies which protected the clans from attack by Apaches, Plains Indians, and Spaniards (Kehoe 1981, 129).

The several societies of the same type within a tribe could also differ in comparative prestige. Thus, warrior groups were arranged in status hierarchies among the Mandan, Hidatsa, Arapaho, and Gros Ventre [Great Plains]. However, there were few if any status distinctions among military societies in such bands as the Sioux, Crow, Omaha, Cheyenne, and Assiniboine, where "a young man joined whichever society took his fancy or became a member by invitation; often a vision told him which society to join" (Reader's Digest 1978, 185).

In warrior societies, an individual's status was usually based on how brave and daring he proved in battle. Among the Comanche [Great Plains], the most impressive soldiers were war chiefs dressed in flowing feathered war bonnets. They were expected to direct attacks, be the first to help comrades, and be the last to retreat. A step lower than war leaders on the prestige scale were warriors in buffalo-scalp headwear. Less spectacular battle performances were expected of them than of the war chiefs (Newcomb 1961, 185).

TRADITIONS COMPARED

The following paragraphs identify ways that Indian religions and Christian culture have been alike and different.

Similarities

In both Amerindian and Christian cultures, religious societies have served as influential, long-lasting social institutions. And in both cultures, membership in a society has offered individuals not only the pleasure of working with like-minded fellows but also a sense of pride for contributing to a respected cause. In addition, societies in both traditions have been noted for a series several similar features—a secret creed, membership rules, initiation rites, codes of behavior, insignia, mottos, and songs. Furthermore, both Native American and Christian societies have included physical and mental healing as an important social service, offered by the Indians through their medical societies and by the Christians in their missionary work.

Differences

The intended functions of Indian religious societies have been remarkably different from the functions of Christian societies. The aim of Indian religious orders has been to promote the practice of orthodox religion within the tribe. Such has been the purpose of such societies' concern with war, healing, maintaining religious history, protecting sacred objects, conducting rites of passage, and more. In contrast, the dual aim of most Christian societies has been (a) to recruit new believers into the faith and reform backsliders (recall wayward sheep that had strayed from the fold) and (b) to provide philanthropic service —*good works*—for humankind.

Native American and Christian cultures have also differed dramatically in the number and variety of their religious organizations, with Indian societies far outstripping Christian groups in their quantity and diversity of functions. Numerous roles assigned to societies in Indian tribes (conducting rites of passage, preserving sacred objects, propagating religious history, and more) have been regular duties borne by the clergy—priests, ministers, deacons, monks, nuns—in Christian denominations.

Among the practices distinguishing Indian societies from Christian groups has been the important role of dancing in most Amerindian bands. Whereas dancing is nearly ubiquitous in Indian societies, rarely if ever has it been part of Christian groups' activities—with some present-day youth societies a possible exception.

Finally, the importance of warrior societies in Amerindian religious history has not had a significant counterpart in Christian culture since the time of the Crusades to the holy land in the Middle Ages (1066–1291). Until the early twentieth century, Indian war societies continued to invoke the support of deities for success in battle. Whereas Christian nations typically still claim that God is on their side in wars, and nations' leaders and the populace pray for God's aid in achieving victory, such activity is not the responsibility of warrior societies as it has been in Indian cultures.

PART II

HISTORY'S PATH

To chart the evolving pattern of interaction between American Indian religions and Christian culture over the past four centuries, Part II sketches significant developments over three eras.

The Colonies—1600–1775
The New Nations—1776–1876
The Growing Nations—1877–1949

· 10 ·

The Colonies—1600–1775

Within hardly more than two decades—1598–1620—European colonists arrived on the East Coast of North America and in the Southwest of what would eventually become the United States. In the East, immigrants from England founded the Virginia colony in 1607. One year later, the first French colony was established in Canadian territory at Quebec City. English Puritans settled Plymouth in Massachusetts in 1620. And out west, a caravan of Spanish colonists in 1598 traveled north from Mexico to cross the Rio Grande River into the region that is now New Mexico and parts of adjacent states.

Throughout the modern history of North America, colonization from the east would be far more important than from the west, since the great majority of the territory that now makes up Canada and the United States would be populated by ever-increasing waves of European immigrants who arrived on the continent's eastern shores. In the west, the Spanish pursued two separate colonizing efforts. The late sixteenth-century move into the New Mexico region would be followed 170 years later with the founding of missions up the coast of California from San Diego to Sonoma, north of San Francisco.

Because colonization from the east established the dominant culture of both Canada and the United States, the following description of events from 1600 to 1775 begins with east-to-west colonization, then turns to the efforts of the Spanish in the Southwest.

INVADERS FROM THE EAST

The account of the westward movement begins with the sociopolitical relationships that evolved between the Indians and colonists, then closes with the place of religion in those relationships.

Sociopolitical Developments

Throughout the seventeenth century, a variety of communities were established along the Atlantic coast of North America by groups from European countries—Britain, France, the Netherlands, Germany, Belgium, Sweden, Finland, and Spain. However, the largest number of immigrants were from England, principally members of the middle class—farmers, artisans, tradesmen—along with unskilled laborers who came as indentured servants to settle in New England and Virginia. As the decades advanced, the immigrants spread west and south, gradually forming the 13 colonies that created the United States of America near the end of the eighteenth century. During the same era, both French and British settlers founded communities in the eastern sector of what would eventually become Canada.

To the European immigrants, the New World represented a marvelous opportunity—millions of acres of free open land along with the land's riches to enjoy. There were vast forests to provide lumber for buildings and ships, beaver and bear to kill for their hides, tobacco to harvest, fertile soil for growing crops, and—it was hoped—massive gold and silver deposits. To the Indians, the pale-faced newcomers were at first a curiosity, but soon were recognized as a threat to the Indians' way of life—their homes, their hunting territory, and a culture that placed religion at its core.

SOCIETAL CONDITIONS

The two cultures—Native American and European—were so vastly different that both Indians and immigrants were bound to be amazed at the style of life of their new acquaintances. Most of the Europeans judged the indigenous peoples to be uncivilized, illiterate, pagan savages living a primitive sort of existence. The Indians, on their part, were astonished at the newcomers' manner of dress, written language, technology (sailing ships, guns, metal tools), religious practices, horses, and concepts of property. This last matter—concepts of property—would become the object of bitter conflict between the Indians and immigrants, a conflict continuing into the twenty-first century.

Before the arrival of European settlers, American Indians' claim to land was founded on occupation and conquest. *Occupation* refers to who is living on a portion of land at a given time. And *living* means both residing at a location and using territory that is not immediately inhabited at the time. So not only did an Iroquois [Northeast, Great Lakes] longhouse qualify land as being occupied but so also did the fields the Iroquois tilled and woodlands in which they hunted, fished, and gathered berries. Among the Cheyenne and other Great Plains tribes, *occupation* meant the entire region within which they periodically moved their teepee villages and where they hunted buffalo. Sometimes the borders of the occupied land would be fairly well marked by streams or mountains, but other times the borders were quite vague, with the territory of one tribe overlapping that of another.

Conquest refers to one band conquering and then holding the land of another band by means of warfare. For example, in the mid-seventeenth century when the French were expanding their territory,

> The Huron [Great Lakes] lived under constant threat of attack by the other Iroquois tribes dwelling south and east of Lake Ontario. Suddenly, in 1648, the Iroquois launched their final invasion of Huronia. Several brave Jesuit priests died as martyrs, and within a year both the Hurons and the missionaries had been either wiped out or driven elsewhere.
>
> (History of Canada 2006)

In vivid contrast to the Indians' notion of land rights was the custom of the immigrant Europeans. For the colonists, property ownership was proven by land deeds—legal documents on file with the government specifying property boundaries (established by surveyors) and providing a record of who previously owned that piece of land. Property owners could also build fences and stonewalls to define the borders of their holdings. Because the Native Americans had no documents and no fences, colonists could easily convince themselves that attractive lands were up for grabs, available to anyone who staked a claim.

GOVERNMENT POLICIES AND PRACTICES

To the colonists, the term *government* referred, first, to the British and French monarchies that claimed the colonial territories as their own and, second, to the local representatives of the monarchies, such as the Jamestown, Plymouth, and Quebec governments. England and France publicly recognized the American Indian tribes as sovereign nations and, therefore, did not openly condone the European settlers taking those nations' land by force. But the same aim of acquiring Indian property could be achieved "legally" through charters, treaties, and land cessions.

Charters served as the British and French monarchs' permission for delegated representatives to govern territories claimed by Britain and France. And under the charter umbrella, treaties were the instruments colonists used to wrest the lands from Indians in the form of purchases or forced sales. Such contracts were often negotiated after colonists had been at war with the Indians. Often too, wars were started when colonists illegally settled on Indian land and the treaties were used to legally justify settlers seizing the land. How such a system worked can be illustrated with the way colonization extended south from Virginia's Jamestown.

As the population grew [through increasing immigration from Europe and rising birth rates], there started a migration to the south and in 1653, the first settlers from Virginia occupied a section of land north of Albemarle Sound (now in North Carolina). The [British] King's Charter for Carolina was issued in 1665, with Carolina being split into North and South in 1723. By the 1750s, white settlement had entered southwest Virginia, and North Carolina's "western lands" (Tennessee) were just a step away. It was the Virginians who took that first step, yet it is North Carolina who maintained the land records. Later, the treaties appear, and slowly Indian land was consumed; the land speculators, along with the vast number of settlers guaranteed it. The last Tennessee treaties of the 1830s required Tennessee's First People [the region's Indians] to remove out of the state, and on to the country west of the Mississippi River.

(Colonial Period 2006)

Treaties in Canada began in 1701 when the British Crown pressed formal agreements on First Nations (Indian bands) to encourage peaceful relations between the indigenous peoples and non-natives. The treaties defined, among other things, the respective rights of Native North Americans and the European governments to "use and enjoy lands that Aboriginal people traditionally occupied" (Department of Indian Affairs, 2006). The treaty system became more formal with the enactment of the British Royal Proclamation of 1763 that prohibited the purchase of First Nation lands by any party other than the Crown. The Crown could purchase land from a First Nation group that had agreed to the sale at a public meeting of the group.

SETTLERS' ACTIONS

In 1620, there was an estimated population of 500 immigrant settlers in what would become the United States (Virginia 400, Plymouth 100). Over the ensuing decades, as more newcomers arrived from a greater variety of European countries (English, Scotch-Irish, Germans, Dutch, Irish, Welsh, French, Swedes), the regions of the Atlantic seaboard and inland were gradually filled with colonists. But with the advancing years, the greater cause of population growth was not new immigration; instead, the reason was a substantially higher birth rate than death rate among settlers, particularly in the northern colonies where cold winters destroyed mosquitoes and other disease-carrying insects. Population increase in southern agricultural areas was slowed by malaria, yellow fever, and other diseases as well as by warfare with the Indians. Present-day estimates place the American population of non-Indians at 26,600 in 1640, at 151,500 in 1680, at 250,900 in 1700, and 1,593.600 in 1760. Throughout the seventeenth and eighteenth centuries, the British Isles continued to be the dominant source of colonists. In the southern plantation states, black slaves made up 40 percent of the non-Indian populace by 1760 (Immigration to the United States 2006).

As the numbers of colonists grew, their need—or at least their desire—for more land rose at an accelerating pace. More settlers moved into neighboring Indian lands and pushed the frontier ever-farther west. Even when the British and French governments sought to honor Indian nations' rights as sovereign nations, there was little they could do to prevent aggressive gun-wielding trappers, traders, gold seekers, and settlers from encroaching on Indian properties. As a consequence, wars continued to break out along the frontier between whites and Indians.

The problem of warfare was exacerbated by the competition between Britain and France over regions of the New World. Both nations courted the favor of Indian tribes, eliciting their help in the territorial struggle. An example is the French and Indian War (1954–1763). The disputed area was around the Great Lakes and the Ohio, Missouri, and Mississippi Rivers, to which the French laid claim. The French buttressed their claim by building a series of forts to defend their right to the region. The British then moved to destroy the forts. In the ensuing battles, both sides included Iroquois warriors in their armies, with the ultimate victory going to the British, to whom the French granted the disputed lands south of the Great Lakes. Thus, "Perennially short of resources, governors in wartime relied (or, rather, hoped to rely) on Native American allies to do most of the fighting against imperial rivals" (Richter 2001, 182).

So it was that colonists were in continual conflict with Indians over land, with the most active confrontations occurring along the western frontier rather than in the eastern regions where the Europeans and African slaves had become well established. Two reasons for the reduction of conflicts in the earlier settlements were that Indians in those areas had usually accepted their subservient status and, in some places, had adopted features of European culture, including religion, and European diseases killed off vast numbers of the native population. For example, the New England settlements were largely cleared of Indians by major outbreaks of measles, small pox, the plague, and other deadly illnesses, starting in about 1618.

Earlier—from the middle 1500s into the early 1600s—sailors on fishing ships from Europe that visited the Americas had infected Indian populations with sicknesses for which the indigenous tribes had no immunity. The imported diseases included smallpox, measles, chickenpox, typhus, typhoid fever, dysentery, scarlet fever, diphtheria, bubonic plague, cholera, and malaria. In terms of the number of Indians killed, the most devastating of the infectious maladies was smallpox. A smallpox epidemic would engulf a region, slaying thousands, then lay dormant for a period of years before breaking out again, as illustrated by incidents from Porterfield's chronology (2006):

> 1617–1619: A disease thought to be smallpox sweeps through what is now the Massachusetts Bay. Nine out of ten [Native Americans] die. The disease [was apparently] brought by a fishing crew or the crew of Thomas Hunt's slaving expedition in 1615. Because they are so few

in number, the Indian people cannot stop the Mayflower from landing in 1620.

1619: By now 90 percent to 95 percent of the [Central American] Indians alive in 1519 have been killed by European diseases. The bubonic plague that began in Florida has spread to New England.

1635–1640: Nearly half of the Huron people of what is now Canada die from European diseases brought by fur traders and missionaries.

1738: Smallpox kills half of the Cherokee Indians of the Southeast.

1750–1752: A wave of smallpox stretches from what is now Texas to the Great Lakes.

1775–1783: A smallpox epidemic sweeps across the North American continent from Mexico to Canada.

Epidemics were more disastrous for densely populated island-based bands than for tribes in such thinly populated regions as the Great Plains. Hence, the Caribs and Arawaks of the Caribbean islands were nearly annihilated, as were the Beothuks of Newfoundland. The Cheyenne and Sioux [Great Plains] were far less affected.

In summary, the two actions by Europeans that wrought the greatest damage to indigenous Americans' lives were the occupation of Indian lands, an action often accompanied by wars over the lands, and the spread of diseases that decimated the Indian population. A third contribution that the European immigrants made toward the indigenous peoples' welfare was the introduction of alcohol, a legacy extending into the twenty-first century when the incidence of alcoholism among Indians in the United States was three times higher than the national average, and the Native American death rate for ages 15–24 was 11.4 times higher than for other Americans. In the mid-1990s, the Indian Health Service reported that "The excess death of younger people is attributed to higher rates for homicide, suicide, accidents, and death attributable to alcoholism" (Newhouse 1999).

INDIANS' RESPONSES

Native peoples reacted in several ways to the settlers' encroachment on their territories. Some Indians sold portions of their land to the colonists. Others, intimidated by the Europeans, retreated from their traditional home sites to nearby sparsely populated locations or to the west beyond the frontier. Still others engaged the intruders in battle. Those who died in epidemics had no need to decide what to do about their properties, which could now be taken over by other Indians or by whites eager for land.

An unplanned outcome of the spread of Euro-Americans across North America was the birth of a new self-awareness within a portion of the Indian populace. As Native American tribes were devastated, pushed about, dispersed, and intermixed by the whites, some observant Indians began to see themselves as not just members of a band (Choctaw, Iroquois, Kwakiutl, and the like) but as a broader type of people—Indians or Redmen—in contrast to whites and blacks. Particularly after the 1730s, this new awareness was promoted by such native visionaries as "the Delaware Prophet" Neolin, who attracted a wide following during the 1760s.

> Prophets called for the revival or invention of ceremonies that would restore the balance of forces between human and other-than-human persons [such as Manitou and Orenda] and symbolically purge Indian communities of European corruption. Converts ritually ingested the "black drink," an herbal emetic that caused them to vomit out foreign contamination. They threw away their alcohol as the most vile contaminant, but also their fiddles, their fondness for gender-mixed dancing in the European style, and anything else that assaulted the newly clarified Native and spiritual order.
>
> (Richter 2001, 180–181)

Included in this movement was the belief that the Bible's version of the world's creation and of human salvation was limited to the whites, and that legendary Indian accounts of such matters were equally valid for Indians. Thus, Euro-Americans had no right to consider the native peoples inferior in any way to whites.

> In the same period that diverse colonists of varied European backgrounds were discovering in North America their first glimmerings of a "White" racial identity, nativist Indians perhaps even more compellingly discovered that they were "Red." Indeed, Indians appear to have used that color term earlier and more consistently than did Euro-Americans, who continued to describe Native Americans' complexion as being only slightly more "tawny" than their own.
>
> (Richter 2001, 181)

This sense of unity among Indians—though certainly not held by all—would surface periodically over the ensuing decades and become the spirit energizing the Native American movement in the twentieth and twenty-first centuries.

With the foregoing discussion as a background, we turn now to the impact of Christian culture and formal schooling on aboriginal Americans during colonial times.

Religious Matters

When the earliest English colonists left Europe, there was little doubt that a key assignment for their life in North America would be to Christianize the native peoples. In June 1606, Britain's King James I granted a charter to a

group of London entrepreneurs (the Virginia Company) to establish Jamestown as a English settlement in the Chesapeake region of the New World. In
a preamble to the letters of authority given to the leaders of the venture, the
British sovereign wrote:

> We are greatly commending, and graciously accepting of, [the Virginia
> Company's] desires for the furtherance of so noble a work, which may,
> by the providence of Almighty God, hereafter tend to the glory of his
> divine Majesty, in propagating of Christian religion to such people, as
> yet live in darkness and miserable ignorance of the true knowledge and
> worship of God, and may in time bring the infidels and savages, living
> in those parts, to human civility, and to a settled and quiet government.
> (Shifflett 1998)

On May 14, 1607, the Virginia Company's 108 settlers arrived in North
America to establish the first permanent English colony on the banks of the
James River, 60 miles from the mouth of the Chesapeake Bay. The colonists'
official religious denomination was Anglican—the Church of England.
Although, as the decades advanced, Jamestown's faithful grudgingly tolerated
the arrival of Baptists, Puritans, and Quakers, the settlers could not bear the
Indians' religions, condemning such beliefs and practices as irrational and an
offense to God. Motivated by such contempt, the colonists made only fitful,
reluctant efforts to attract native peoples into the Anglican Church. The Algonquin Indians, on their part, were usually unwilling recruits. Most of them
resisted attempts to transform them into Christians.

As explained earlier, the second permanent English colony was established
in 1620 at Plymouth on Cape Cod Bay, 460 miles north of Jamestown. There
was no question about the religious nature of the Plymouth voyage to North
America, for the settlers were Pilgrims who had separated from the Church
of England and thereby incurred the displeasure of King James I and the
Anglican establishment. The Pilgrims left England to escape religious persecu-
tion and establish their own community in the New World. The 102 adventurers embarked from Plymouth, England, on the ship Mayflower in
September 1620, landing 65 days later on the North American shores at Cape
Cod Bay, where they named their new settlement after the English city from
which they had sailed.

The dominant Indian tribe in the Cape Cod region was known as both the
Pokanoket nation (Place of the Cleared Land) and Wampanoag nation (People
of the Dawn). From the outset, relationships between the Indians and settlers
were usually cordial, symbolized by the First Thanksgiving in 1621, which
brought together the native people and colonists in a celebration of good will.
For most of the next half century, those genial relationships continued until
destroyed by the eleven-year King Phillips War between Indians and colonists,
a conflict identified by the English name of *Metacomet* (Phillip), who was the
current high chief of the Wampanoags.

Christianity and the Wampanoag religion differed in important ways. Christians viewed the passing of time as a linear function—day after day, year after year. In contrast, the Wampanoags saw time as cyclical—the sun's repetitive daily trip, the phases of the moon, and the reoccurring seasonal progression of spring, summer, autumn, and winter. Indian religious celebrations that related to those events (Planting Ceremony, Green-Corn Harvest Ceremony) differed from the ones Christians commemorated (Christmas, Maundy Thursday, Palm Sunday, Good Friday, Easter). In addition, the Wampanoags observed a Four-Directions ceremony, a Sweat-Lodge ceremony, and a Color ceremony.

The most aggressive efforts to Christianize Massachusetts' Indians was launched in the mid-1600s by John Eliot of Harvard University, who translated the Bible into the Algonquin language and established Praying Towns for Indian converts. In subsequent years, the entire Bible would be translated into five other North-American Indian tongues as well. However, as in most Indian communities, the New England converts were often selective in adopting Christian doctrine, choosing only those convictions and practices that would fit in with traditional Indian worldviews. The result was a syncretic combination of Christianity and Native American beliefs (Native Traditions 2006).

In Canada, the French who settled Quebec were likewise bent on Christianizing the aboriginals. French fur trappers and traders were accompanied by Jesuit priests who pursued their mission of recruiting Indian and Inuit bands into the Catholic fold.

The Europeans peopled the New World with diverse Christian sects. The newcomers included Anglicans, Independents, Puritans, and Quakers. There were French Catholics and Huguenots, Spanish Catholics, Swedish Lutherans, and Dutch Calvinists. Non-Christians included Spanish Jews and Africans (mainly slaves on southern plantations) who retained tribal practices (Cremin 1970, 148).

In colonial North America, the principal governing unit consisted of a village or town and its surrounding countryside. Although the New England colonies were officially under the jurisdiction of the British government, daily affairs were supervised by a village's or town's council or board of selectmen chosen by the citizens. As time passed, towns that comprised a colony elected legislatures that adopted regulations promoting such Christian interests as teaching the Bible.

The colonial church cared for the inhabitants' spiritual needs and provided the moral foundation for towns' and villages' secular responsibilities—establishing laws governing people's personal behavior, maintaining civil order, settling property disputes, providing roads, directing commerce, and the like. Thus, any separation of church and state was only in the functions of the two institutions, not in their philosophies or goals. Both were dedicated to promoting a prosperous community of dedicated Christians.

THE ROLE OF SCHOOLING

Education in colonial New England was not separate from religion. Quite the opposite. Education was designed primarily to further Christian goals and was conducted by the faithful in home, church, and school. The most fundamental educational unit was the home. Parents were expected to teach their offspring Christian precepts from the Bible and how to read and write. The ability to read was dictated by the Protestant conviction that people should be directly in touch with God and with God's word rather than their requiring an intermediary, such as a priest, who was qualified to understand—and to communicate with—the Lord. The colonists' enthusiasm for reading would contribute not only to a lively business of importing books from "the old country" but also to the growth of print shops, publishers, and libraries throughout the seventeenth and eighteenth centuries.

At church on Sunday, the minister preached a sermon intended to inform the congregation of the contents of the Bible and how to apply scripture in everyday living. Before or after the sermon, the minister or a teacher could instruct the young in church doctrine, often by means of the official set of questions and answers about life and religion that formed the sect's catechism.

In Britain and France over previous centuries, schools had been founded at an increasing rate, usually by religious bodies. Thus, colonists brought to the Americas a tradition of schooling that focused on Christian doctrine and skills useful in vocations—reading, writing, and ciphering. Various colonial locations served as schools, including homes (kitchens or parlors), churches, ministers' dwellings (manses), meetinghouses, shops, barns, and schoolhouses. Frequently a mother in her home would not only instruct her own children but teach the children of neighbors as well, thereby creating the popular institution known as the *dame school.*

> Pupils were taught by anyone and everyone, not only by schoolmasters, but by parents, tutors, clergymen, lay readers, precentors [choir directors], physicians, lawyers, artisans, and shopkeepers.... The content and sequence of learning remained fairly well defined, and each student progressed from textbook to textbook at his own pace.
>
> (Cremin 1970, 193)

The materials of instruction in home and school typically included a *hornbook,* which was not a book in the usual sense but, rather, was a board (3-by-4 inches in size) on which was attached a sheet of paper covered with a transparent sheet of horn. The reading matter printed on the paper included the alphabet, a few common syllables, and a passage from the Bible, such as the Lord's Prayer, or the Apostles' Creed.

The hornbook would typically be supplemented by a primer, which would prepare the young to read the Bible itself. For example, *The New England Primer,* a tiny volume hardly longer or broader than a young child's hand, is estimated to have sold six million copies, or an average of 40,000 a year, between 1687 and the mid-1800s in a still sparsely settled America (Morison 1936, 79). Two assumptions undergirded a Puritan view of child development: children are born evil, bound to sin if not guided away from their natural state and children are born with a capacity to learn. The first of these assumptions was founded on religious doctrine, the second apparently on common sense. Crucial to Puritan doctrine was the idea that the sin of disobedience to God that Adam and Eve committed when they ate the forbidden fruit in the Garden of Eden was a sin carried down through all generations. The newborn child was the recipient of this original sin and would be condemned to hell after death if not redeemed. *The New England Primer* introduced children to the first letter of the alphabet with a verse that made this premise clear (*New England Primer* 1836, 11).

"A = In Adam's fall we sinned all."

The letter *B* appeared beside a drawing of the Bible.

"B = Thy life to mend, this *Book* attend."

The *Primer* explained at length that, because of innate sin, untutored children would naturally frolic "and take delight among young folk who spend their days in joy and mirth," thereby passing their time in idleness, disobeying parents and others in authority, lying and cursing and stealing, ignoring their studies, playing truant from school, fighting with brothers and sisters and schoolmates, refusing to pray or attend church, failing to read the Bible, disobeying the Ten Commandments, and declining to accept or follow Christ (*The New England Primer* 1836, 10–64). The verse accompanying letters *F* and *U* in the alphabet described the consequences of such waywardness (15–16).

"F = The idle *Fool* is whipt at school.

"U = *U*pon the wicked, God will rain a horrible tempest."

In effect, schooling in the colonies proceeded throughout the seventeenth century and beyond with a strong Christian bent. Thus, the limited number of Indian children who were permitted to attend school (permitted by both the colonists and the children's parents) were served a hearty menu of Christianity. The most successful attempts to provide schooling for Indians appeared in New England, where missionaries made special efforts to enroll native youths in English-language schools (Cremin 1970, 194–195).

A critical event in 1647 would significantly affect the course of public schooling in what would become the United States. The Massachusetts legislature issued a school act that compelled every community of 50 householders or more to establish a school that all students would attend, with the aim of foiling the scheme of "that old deluder, Satan, to keep men from the knowledge of the Scriptures." The school would be financed by "the parents or masters of such children or by the inhabitants in general" (Vaughn 1972, 237). This step toward ensuring that all children and youths would become literate was soon taken by other colonies as well, so that publicly supported schooling for the general populace was on its way.

As noted earlier, over the decades leading to the American Revolution, births in colonial families combined with immigration to increase the density and geographical spread of the population. Such growth was accompanied by three developments that affected education in the colonies.

First, separate villages and towns became politically organized under overarching governing bodies, thereby forming provinces that would, in the final decades of the century, become the first 13 United States. Decisions about education made by provincial legislatures would apply to all villages and towns within the province, thus encouraging greater uniformity among a colony's schools.

Second, population growth added diversity in educational opportunities as more types of schools and kinds of apprenticeship became available. The rate of increase in school enrollment exceeded the rate of general population growth as the citizenry saw formal education and training as increasingly important for getting ahead in the world. However, the expansion of schooling was limited mostly to whites. Indians and blacks who attended school were few in number.

Third, immigration from abroad, along with travel within the colonies, added greater religious, ethnic, and cultural diversity to communities so that people were obliged to be more tolerant of neighbors whose lifestyles and belief systems differed from their own.

To summarize, in seventeenth-century North America—and especially in New England and Quebec—state, church, and school were not institutions isolated from each other and pursuing separate goals. Instead, they were a trinity guided by, and dedicated to, promoting a combination of Christianity and worldly prosperity for the colonists. In New England, Christianity represented the Puritan part of colonial culture; worldly prosperity represented the Yankee part.

INDIANS' EDUCATION

How, then, did the schooling offered to Native North Americans by the Christian colonists compare with Indians' customary teaching aims and methods? First, note Coleman's assessment of the missionaries' efforts, then consider the educational methods embedded in Indian cultures.

Unlike the more tolerant and adaptive Jesuit missionaries in French North America, almost all missionary efforts in the English colonies, overwhelmingly Protestant, engaged in both deculturation and enculturation of an extraordinarily absolute kind. They generally accepted

Indian potential for "uplift," but sought the utter extirpation of the tribal culture and the inculcation of English ideas of religion and "civility," down to the smallest details of appearance and behavior.

(Coleman 1993, 37)

In contrast to the Europeans' instructional methods were the Indians' traditional means of transmitting their culture to succeeding generations. Rather than attending a formal school, Indian children learned their band's language and customs by copying the people they interacted with during the routine of community life. Parents, siblings, and neighbors advised the young about proper behavior, encouraging compliance by punishment for infractions. The tribe's religion and history were taught by means of legends and stories of past events retold by elders in the evening around a campfire or in a longhouse, wigwam, or teepee. Youths acquired occupational skills as apprentices working alongside their parents, older siblings, and neighbors in the daily activities of making a living.

On the Columbia River plateau boys learned to fish the rivers crowded with salmon each spring; in the fall they hunted for bear, deer, and elk. Girls smoked salmon, gathered roots and berries, wove baskets, and sewed clothing and moccasins. Both went on vision quests. In the high-desert Southwest, Anasazi boys learned to raise corn, beans, and squash in an arid land, to hunt and to weave cotton, and to understand the nature of their spiritual role. Girls cared for the home, ground corn and cooked, and participated in the seasonal ceremonies. Both learned that the village was of greater importance than the individual. Since native groups...relied exclusively on oral learning, storytelling was ubiquitous.

(Szasz 2006)

Summary

Among the important early influences of European immigration on the native peoples' lives in eastern North America were the newcomers'

- taking Indian lands through occupation, warfare, treaties, and purchase,
- bringing disastrous diseases for which aboriginal peoples had no immunity,
- imposing political structures and educational practices founded on Christian tradition,
- holding Indian religions in contempt, and
- making a partial effort to "civilize" the natives by teaching them a European way of life with emphasis on Christian beliefs and practices.

INVADERS FROM THE WEST

As in the account of invaders from the East, the following discussion first addresses sociopolitical developments in the Southwest (societal conditions, government policies and practices, settlers' actions, Indians' responses) and then turns to religious and educational matters.

Sociopolitical Developments

SOCIETAL CONDITIONS

In 1519, a scheming, bold conquistador, Hernán Cortés, moored 11 Spanish galleons in the harbor of San Juan de Ulúa Island off the east coast of Mexico. Aboard were 550 sailors and soldiers along with 16 horses, which were the first steeds to set foot on the North American continent. Within two years, Cortés would conquer the region's powerful Aztec (Mexica) empire. In 1522 he was appointed Governor and Captain General of *Nueva España* (New Spain) by the Spanish king, Carlos V. To provide headquarters for this new Spanish colony, Cortés destroyed the magnificent Aztec capital of Tenochtitlán and erected on that site *Ciudad de Mexico* (Mexico City), a European-style colonial center built from rubble of ruined Aztec pyramids, temples, and palaces. That act launched three centuries of Spanish control over Central America.

As the decades advanced, a social-caste structure evolved in the colony. In terms of power and prestige, pure-blood Spanish from the mother country were at the pinnacle of the system, with persons of aristocratic heritage ranked above ordinary Spaniards. On a step below those from Spain were *criollos*, Mexico-born children of Spanish parents. One step lower were the *mestizos.*

> The dearth of Spanish women at the start of the Colonial era led to numerous unions between Indian women and Spaniards. An immediate consequence was the birth of many mixed-blood—mostly illegitimate— offspring. These so-called *mestizos* made up a rapidly growing socioeconomic class that, for the most part, were considered inferior by pure-blood Spaniards. *Mestizos*—who today make up the vast majority of Mexico's population—were to remain poor and uneducated for many generations.
>
> (Palfrey 1998a)

The bottom of the caste system was occupied by Native Americans.

> Scarcely looked upon as human beings, hundreds of thousands of Indians were literally worked to death. Others succumbed to new diseases introduced by the Spaniards: smallpox, measles, plague, tuberculosis, and even the common cold. At the time of the Conquest, about nine million

indigenous people inhabited Mexico's central plateau. By 1600 they numbered a scant two and a half million.

(Palfrey 1998a)

GOVERNMENT POLICIES AND PRACTICES

In 1535 the Spanish sovereign appointed Antonio de Mendoza as the first of 61 viceroys who would govern New Spain over the next 300 years. Under Mendoza's fifteen-year rule, explorers spread south and north to claim new lands for the Spanish crown. The aim of their travels was to further the Spanish government's tripartite goal in the New World—accumulate riches (primarily gold and silver), force more territory under Spanish rule, and convert America's native peoples to Catholicism. Expeditions north of the Rio Grande would range as far east as present-day New Orleans, as far north as Kansas, and as far west as the Grand Canyon.

The general tone of the Spanish *conquistadores'* intended relationship with North American Indians was reflected in Francisco Vázquez de Coronado's standard exhortation to native peoples when he and his troop of explorers entered the Zuñi [Southwest] village of Hawikuh in 1540. Coronado had arrived during the Indians' summer religious festivals, and he announced to the villagers that they were henceforth required to "acknowledge the [Catholic] Church as the ruler and superior of the whole world, and the high priest called Pope, and in his name the King and Queen" of Spain. If the Zuñi failed to obey the newcomers' orders, "with the help of God we shall forcefully ...make war against you...take you and your wives and children, and shall make slaves of them" (Public Broadcasting System, 2001).

Although Coronado and his men failed in their search for the mythical gold-laden Seven Cities of Cibola, their reports about the geography and peoples of a great portion of the territory north of the Rio Grande would be useful a half century later when the Spanish sought to establish permanent colonies in the Southwest.

The impetus for colonizing the area was King Philip of Spain's order in 1583 that a man be selected to lead such a conquest,

> a man who was not only wealthy, devout, and of good repute but could be depended upon to obey the laws controlling colonization and the conversion of Indians, and who had demonstrated his ability to serve as the first governor of the new province, which would be called New Mexico.

(Terrell 1979, 39)

Church authorities in Mexico City who were responsible for selecting that man engaged in "such prolonged deliberations, were so extremely cautious, and argued so much among themselves, that nothing at all was accomplished for twelve years. At last, in 1595, the appointment was awarded to a man of wealth, distinguished lineage, and the nature of a beast—Don Juan de Oñate from Zacatecas" (Terrell 1979, 39–40).

After three years' preparation, Oñate led his caravan of colonizers across the Rio Grande to the Indian pueblos of the region that would become New Mexico (*Nuevo Mejico*). The massive entourage consisted of nearly 100 fully loaded wagons, 130 families, 270 single men, 11 Franciscan friars, dozens of Mexican Indian and Negro servants, troops of horsemen, and a herd of 7,000 animals.

At each pueblo, crowds of Indians were collected to hear Oñate's announcement of the sort of future they could expect. Spanish troopers—with loaded guns, swords, and lances at the ready—surrounded the assemblage. A Spanish notary, Juan Perez de Donis, who witnessed the occasion, wrote the following account of the event at which Oñate explained that he had been sent to the Indians

by the most powerful king and ruler in the world, who desired especially to serve God our Lord and to bring about the salvation of their souls, but wished also to have them as his subjects and to protect and bring justice to them, as he was doing for other natives in the East and West Indies. To this end [King Philip I] had sent the Spaniards from such distant lands to theirs at enormous expense and great effort. Since, therefore, the governor had come with this purpose, as they could see, it was greatly to their advantage that, of their own free will and in their own names and in those of their pueblos and republics, and their captains, they render obedience and submission to the king, and become his subjects and his vassals.... By so doing they would live in peace, justice, and orderliness, protected from their enemies, and benefited in their arts and trades and in their crops and cattle. [The Indians], after deliberation, spontaneously agreed to become vassals of the most Christian king, our lord, and as such they immediately rendered their obedience and submission. The governor explained to them that they should realize that by rendering obedience and vassalage to the king, our lord, they would be subject to his will, orders, and laws, and that, if they did not observe [the orders], they would be severely punished as transgressors of the commands of their king and master, and that, therefore, they should reflect on what they wished to do and what to answer. They replied that they understood and they wanted to submit to his majesty and become his vassals. [Oñate then suggested that since the Indians] were rendering obedience and vassalage to him of their own free will...they should fall to their knees as a demonstration that the Spaniards and they were now all one people.
(de Donis in Terrell 1979, 40–41)

The governor also explained the religious nature of his expedition.

The main reason which had moved the king to send him to this land was the salvation of their souls, because they should know that their bodies had also souls which did not die even through their bodies did. But if they were baptized and became good Christians, they would go to heaven to enjoy and eternal life of great bliss in the presence of God. If they did not become Christians, they would go to hell to suffer cruel and everlasting torment. [Oñate] told them that this religion would be explained to them more at length by the most reverend father commissary and the friars, who were present and who came in the name of his Holiness, the only universal pastor and head of the church, the Holy Father at Rome...therefore it was important that they should acknowledge God and his vicar on earth...and kiss the hand of the father commissary.

(de Donis in Terrell 1979, 41–42)

The notary, in closing his account of the incident, wrote that the Indians declared that they understood all that Oñate had said to them. But John Terrell, in his modern-day interpretation of the occasions, observed that if the Indians did comprehend Oñate's Spanish-language oration, then "surely a miracle of linguistic communications had occurred" (Terrell 1979, 42)

As the colonists settled in New Mexico, Oñate divided the territory into seven mission districts with a priest in charge of each. The districts were of imprecise size and lacked exact borders, particularly on the north. Thus, the Spanish had only a vague idea of how many Indian tribes there were within each district or what the tribes' names and characteristics might be.

The initial, moderately amicable relations between the Spaniards and Indians were short-lived. As Oñate began exploring the region to find treasure, he placed one of his nephews, Juan de Zaldivar, in command of a search party. Zaldivar prepared for his trek by visiting the Indian pueblo of Acoma, located atop a tableland, and demanding that the residents furnish supplies he needed—maize, fowls, robes, blankets, and other items. Because the villagers had already given those supplies to Oñate himself, they turned down Zaldivar's demand. In response, Zaldivar ordered his soldiers to take the supplies by force. In the ensuing battle, Zaldivar and ten soldiers were slain. Oñate retaliated against the Keres tribe in Acoma by sending armed troops to kill over 800 and arrest another 500 men, women, and children whose punishment he then decreed.

One foot was cut off of all males over the age of 25, and they were sentenced to 20 years of slavery. Males between the ages of 12 and 25 were not maimed but received a sentence of similar length in personal servitude. The right hands of two Hopi Indians who happened to be in Acoma at the time of the battle were amputated, and they were sent to their people as living examples of what Indians who defied Spaniards might expect to suffer.

(Terrell 1979, 47)

In summary, at the outset of Spanish colonization in the Southwest, the government policies required indigenous residents to yield meekly to the conquerors' control. Failing to do so invited daunting consequences.

SETTLERS' ACTIONS

A key structural feature of Spanish colonies throughout the New World was the *encomienda* (trusteeship) system. Under this arrangement, the Spanish crown controlled all of the territories but would entrust individuals with the management of large estates that comprised a colony. Ostensibly, land ownership remained with the Indians who lived on the land, but the Spanish king could assign a trustee or *encomendero* the responsibility of managing an estate. The *encomendero* was typically an upper-class Spaniard, authorized to tax the people living on the estate and summon them for mandatory labor. The *encomendero* was also obligated to maintain order through military force and to teach Catholicism to the natives. However, authorities in far-off Spain faced an impossible task of monitoring the *encomienda* system, so *encomenderos* were able to conduct business pretty much as they wished. Typically, the Indians on an estate were ruthlessly exploited by both the *encomenderos* and the landowners of adjacent plantations who sought to "seize more lands from the natives, increase taxes, and ultimately force the natives into slavery. [The Spanish] reasoned that riches were wasted on pagans and more properly bestowed upon Christian subjects of the Spanish king. . . . The conquistadors regarded plunder, slaves, and tribute as the just rewards for men who forced pagans to accept Christianity and Spanish rule" (Encomienda 2006).

The activities pursued on estates consisted mainly of farming (multiple varieties of corn, beans, and squash, plus fruits from European stock), of herding (cattle, sheep, horses, oxen, goats, and mules brought from Spain), and of mining (silver, gold, copper).

INDIANS' RESPONSES

The Southwest's native peoples reacted to Spanish rule in several ways, as influenced by such conditions as (a) how close they were to the concentration of Spanish power, (b) the Indians' traditional lifestyles, (c) their treatment by the *encomendero* who governed the estate on which they were located, (d) the influence of the Catholic friars in the region, and (e) how much they valued the worldly goods that the Spanish brought to the region.

The territory encompassed by the *Nuevo Mejico* of colonial times included today's state of New Mexico and substantial portions of Arizona, Texas, the Oklahoma panhandle, Utah, Colorado, and Kansas. The greatest concentration of Spanish power was in the south, the area closest to Mexico. The New Mexico colony was, in effect, a buffer state protecting the Spanish in Mexico from wild tribes to the north, west, and east—Apaches, Camanches, Utes, Caddoans—and from the trappers, traders, miners, and settlers that came from North America's East Coast. But the farther the Spanish extended their activities away from the Mexican border, the weaker their influence over the Indians. The conquistadors' ability to control remote tribes was hampered by long distances to travel, uncharted wilderness, and the Spanish crown's unwillingness to provide the funds and military strength needed to make effective forays into the wilds.

Indian bands differed in their lifestyles. Some were more placid than others. The Hopi, Zuñi, and semi-nomad Coahuiltecans were among the less warlike groups, in contrast to Apache marauders along the western border and Comanches and Utes to the north. As a consequence, Indians who were known to be fierce warriors were more likely to be spared a life on a Spanish estate than were members of less belligerent bands.

Encomendores were not all alike in their treatment of the Indians living on their *encomiendas*. Some overlords were harsher than others in treating their vassals. According to regulations from Spain, Indians who tilled an *encomendore's* fields and labored in his mines were to be paid a fair wage for their efforts. But rarely did overlords honor the regulation, as greed usually triumphed over compassion. Some of the native peoples not only labored without pay but were also literally worked to death. Hence, those who were fortunate enough to be under the charge of a humane overlord would be less distressed with their lot than those destined to live under a tyrant.

The Franciscan priests were often at odds with Spanish civil authorities and landholders—not only over money but also over treatment of the Indians. Particularly in the seventeenth century, the mendicant friars responsible for Christianizing their pagan wards would express sincere concern for the Indians' plight by confronting estate holders about ill treatment of the Indians. Priests, by holding the threat of divine damnation over the *economendores*, could sometimes effect a change in how landlords dealt with the indigenous peoples.

Then there were the many thousands of Indians whose unintended response to colonization was that of suffering and dying from epidemic diseases the conquistadores had brought from Europe. In 1638 Fray Juan de Parada reported that "the 60,000 natives who had been baptized in New Mexico had been reduced to around 40,000 because of 'the very active prevalence these last years of smallpox'" (Reff 1987, 704).

Finally, among the wondrous objects that the Spanish imported to the New World, the one that Indians most enthusiastically and profitably embraced was the horse. Oñate's 1598 cavalcade that brought brood mares and jennies to the Southwest led to the spread of horses throughout the West, as some of the colonists' animals escaped from their pastures, others were bartered to Indians, and still others were stolen. Horses dramatically transformed the culture of many Indian bands, particularly those of the Great Plains, Southwest, and Northwest. With horses, Indians could far more efficiently hunt large game (buffalo, deer, elk, moose), battle enemies, and quickly travel long distances. Early in the Spanish colonial era, Indians became skilled riders and breeders, with some tribes creating their own equine strains. For example, in the

Northwest, the Cayuse pony was developed by the Cayuse band, and the Appaloosa breed was developed by the Palouse branch of the Nez Perce. The Spanish item that Indians likely ranked second to the horse in popularity was the rifle, which greatly enhanced Indian braves' effectiveness as hunters and warriors.

Religious Matters

The mission system in the New World was designed to provide a setting in which indigenous peoples could (a) live safely, protected from both hostile Indian tribes and abuse by Spanish soldiers, civil authorities, and overly aggressive settlers, (b) be converted to Catholicism, and (c) acquire features of European culture that the Spanish particularly valued. Each mission was a self-sustaining community organized around a church that was usually of adobe construction.

Missions were operated by religious orders. The first and always the most numerous missionaries were Franciscans, later joined by Jesuits. The two orders founded hundreds of missions in Mexico and the Southwest. When the Jesuits were expelled from *Nueva España* by the Spanish government in 1767, Franciscans and Dominicans took over the Jesuit holdings.

Spanish colonial authorities had the right of decision over ecclesiastical matters, a right granted to the Spanish crown by the pope in Rome. Thus, civil authorities decided where and when missions would be founded or closed, what administrative policies missions would adopt, who could be missionaries, how many missionaries could be assigned to each location, and how many soldiers would be stationed at a mission to enforce the law and protect the residents from attack. The colonial government also paid the costs of founding a mission, the missionaries' overseas travel, and the missionaries' salaries.

The ideal of the missionaries themselves, supported by royal decrees, was to establish autonomous Christian towns with communal property, labor, worship, political life, and social relations all supervised by the missionaries and insulated from the possible negative influences of other Indian groups and Spaniards themselves. Daily life was to follow a highly organized routine of prayer, work, training, meals, and relaxation, punctuated by frequent religious holidays and celebrations. In this closely supervised setting the Indians were expected to mature in Christianity and Spanish political and economic practices until they would no longer require special mission status. Then their communities could be incorporated as such into ordinary colonial society, albeit with all its racial and class distinctions. This transition from official mission status to ordinary Spanish society, when it occurred in an official manner, was called "secularization." (Wright 2001)

How successful Spanish priests were in converting Southwest Indians to Catholicism continues to be a subject of debate. Palfrey (1998b) has stated that most of the Southwest's Indians were Christianized during the seventeenth century by the early wave of Franciscan friars who "took responsibility for the basic education of the Indians, an effort greatly enhanced by their assiduous study of Indian languages. They established schools where youngsters learned to read and write and were introduced to European music and the arts. Adults were trained to practice agriculture and trades, learning European methods in masonry, carpentry, ironwork, weaving, dying, and ceramics."

In contrast to Palfrey's optimistic description of the friars' proselytizing success is Terrell's (1979, 62–64) charge that the missionaries, in letters sent to Spain, painted a much exaggerated picture of how enthusiastically the Indians embraced Catholicism. Consider, for example, a passage from Fray Alonso de Benavides' report to King Philip IV in the 1620s.

> When we ring the bell for Mass and the teaching of the Doctrine, [the Indians] all come with the greatest cleanliness and neatness that they can, and enter the church to pray, as if they were Christians of very long standing....And all make confession in their own tongue....If the missionaries go passing along the roads, and the Indians see us from their pueblos or fields, they all come forth to meet us with very great joy, saying "Praised be our Lord Jesus Christ! Praised be the most holy Sacrament."
>
> (Benavides in Terrell 1979, 64–65)

However, according to Eggan (1950), "The Pueblo [Indians] have managed to retain their cultural independence in the face of almost overwhelming political and religious pressures....They became nominal Catholics, but they took their own religion underground and have maintained it to the present day, guarding their ceremonies and their inner life against the outside world." The Indians' habit of retaining long-established religious rituals led to frequent conflict between the Spanish and the tribes. For example, the Hopi were forced by Spanish soldiers to tolerate Christianity. But when ordered to cease all kachina worship, the Hopi rebelled and joined the Rio Grande Pueblos in the Pueblo Rebellion of 1680 that resulted in the destruction of the region's missions (Waldman 1999, 91).

Some missionaries were very strict in demanding that the Indians completely abandon indigenous religious practices, but others tolerated an admixture of Christian and Indian traditions, including such native rituals as *matachine* dances and *mitotes* (native celebrations with dancing and perhaps peyote), whenever the friars judged those activities to be relatively free of features unacceptable in Christianity (Wright 2001).

As most Indians under Spanish colonial rule had become Christians (at least in name) by 1700, Catholic clerics subsequently focused greater attention on "the spiritual needs of wealthy Spanish settlers, many of whom in turn bequeathed their worldly goods to the Church. By the end of the eighteenth century over half of New Spain's land and close to two thirds of the money in circulation had fallen into the hands of the Church" (Palfrey 1998b).

CONCLUSION

Around the beginning of the seventeenth century, permanent colonies of European settlers were founded on North America's East Coast and in the Southwest of what would eventually become the United States. The English established Jamestown in 1607 and Plymouth in 1620. The French created Quebec City in 1608, and the Spanish launched their Southwest colonies with a caravan of settlers in 1598. The two main goals of each colony were to furnish a profitable living for the settlers (land, mineral wealth) and promote the Christian religion among both settlers themselves and the Native Americans whose lands the Europeans would seize. This goal of Christianizing Indians was pursued with somewhat greater vigor and consistency by the Spanish Catholic friars in the Southwest's missions and by the French Jesuit missionaries in Canada than by the Protestants who settled the U.S. East Coast and then trekked west.

Amerindians responded in various ways to the colonists' proselytizing efforts. Some adopted Christianity in full and abandoned all vestiges of their tribe's traditional beliefs and practices. Others proved extremely hostile, not only rejecting the missionaries' overtures but also meeting the settlers' advances with armed attacks. Still others (perhaps the majority with whom the colonists came into extended contact) became partial converts, adopting portions of Christian belief and practice while retaining such features of native religions as animal guardian spirits, vision quests, dances, chants, stories, amulets, sweat baths, and secret societies.

· 11 ·

The New Nations—1776–1876

This chapter is built around a series of events that significantly influenced Indian religions' interactions with Christian culture throughout the first century of the newly founded United States of America. The tale begins with the final 24 years of the eighteenth century (1776–1800), then continues with the 60 years until the Civil War (1801–1860), and ends with the late war years and postwar period (1861–1876). During this era, Canada continued to be a British colony, periodically accorded increasing self-governance responsibility by the British crown.

THE EARLY YEARS—1776–1800

The closing quarter of the eighteenth century featured thirteen American colonies in armed revolt against the British crown, then winning their independence and struggling to establish a new form of democratic government that would accommodate both Christian tradition and a version of secularism derived from the recent European Enlightenment movement. In Canada, Britain had acquired the former French colonies in 1763 by defeating France in the Seven Years War, then in the final quarter of the century concentrated on consolidating British holdings north of the United States. Events from the era that are reviewed in the following pages include (a) the founding of the U.S. Government through the interaction of Christian tradition and secularism that led to the U.S. Constitution, and (b) the evolution of the Canadian Constitution and its implications for the First Nations and their religions.

The New Republic's Foundation

In the beginning stages of the American Revolution against British rule (1775–1784), the colonists issued a Declaration of Independence (1776) which set the tone for the new republic's operating principles that would be spelled out in the U.S. Constitution (1789). The dominant ideology of the Constitution was a version of secularism that contrasted with a traditional Christian world-view. Ever since that time, secularism and Christianity in both U.S. and Canadian cultures have advanced side-by-side in tension, conflict, and compromise. That conflict has critically affected Amerindian-Christian relationships until the present day. The following brief sketch of the two contrasting worldviews illustrates the nature of their confrontation.

CHRISTIAN TRADITION

Christianity, at its outset two thousand years ago, was a minor religion, limited principally to churches around the Mediterranean Sea. The number of adherents grew slowly until Roman Emperor Constantine in the fourth century CE converted to the faith and declared Christianity the empire's official religion. Thereafter, Christianity was widely adopted throughout Europe and the Middle East. The faith periodically split into new factions, but all sects still maintained a core of common beliefs, including the conviction that (a) a single God had created the universe and continued to operate it, (b) Jesus was God's son on earth and Jesus died to atone for believers' sins, (c) people were obligated to obey God's commandments, and (d) peoples' souls lived on after physical death to spend eternity in either heavenly bliss or hellish misery, with each person's destiny determined by God.

A particularly important split among Christians was launched in 1517 when a German monk, Martin Luther, posted on a church door a list of 95 theses protesting the way the Roman Catholic Church network was being run. That act marked the birth of Protestantism, which would thereafter contend with Roman Catholicism for devotees. Subsequently, Protestantism itself would divide into factions that disagreed with each other over details of church doctrine or over how churches were organized and administered. Hence, when the first European settlers arrived on the eastern shores of North America in the seventeenth century they represented multiple Christian Protestant denominations —Anglican, Puritan, Congregational, Baptist, Presbyterian, Methodist, Quaker, Dutch Reformed, and more. Catholics also arrived but formed only a minority of the colonists except in what would become French Canada. In North America's Southwest, the religion imported by Europeans would be a Spanish variety of Catholicism.

Therefore, from the outset of European colonization in North America, the overwhelming worldview of settlers was Christian, and that belief system has continued at the core of North American culture ever since. Surveys in the early twenty-first century reported that between 77 percent and 82 percent of

U.S. residents identified themselves as Christians—52 percent as Protestants and 24.5 percent as Roman Catholics (Adherents, 2005). The Canadian census of 2001 found the proportion of self-identified Christians to be 72 percent, of which 43 percent were Roman Catholics and 29 percent Protestants (Atlas of Canada 2007).

However, across the decades since the founding of the United States and Canada, Christian culture has been obliged to compete for citizens' allegiance with the Enlightenment movement's secularism.

ENLIGHTENMENT'S SECULARISM

A nascent philosophical innovation known as *The Enlightenment*, which had sprouted in Europe, came to fruition in the eighteenth century and greatly impressed influential colonists, including the founders of the United States of America. The Enlightenment was grounded in the conviction that "human reason could be used to combat ignorance, superstition, and tyranny, and to build a better world" (Brians 2000). Enlightenment thinkers' principal targets were religion and the domination of society by a hereditary aristocracy. Such French philosophical luminaries as Voltaire (1694–1778) pursued the movement's goals by attacking the fundamentals of Christian belief: that the Bible was the inspired word of God, that Jesus was an earthly version of God, and that non-believers in Christian doctrine were destined to roast in hell.

Rather than trusting holy books written by the ancients as the source of truth, Enlightenment's proponents trusted human reason—logical deductions based on careful observations of events. When conclusions found in holy scriptures clashed with conclusions drawn from empirical observations and logic, people should prefer the latter. Reason should win out over religious dogma.

This Enlightenment worldview would become the foundation for both modern science and secular, democratic political structures. It would furnish a "framework for the American [1776] and French [1789] Revolutions, the [nineteenth-century] Latin American independence movement, the Polish Constitution [1791] [and would lead to] the rise of capitalism and the birth of socialism" (Age of Enlightenment 2005).

Thus, the 1700s generated the second of the two major belief systems that would participate in the founding of the U.S. republic. That second system was Enlightenment's secularism which vied with the existing religious belief system for determining the place of religion in public life.

So, on the brink of the American Revolution, colonists' strong Christian tradition would be challenged by the Enlightenment's emphasis on using humans' reasoning powers to arrive at judgments about the universe and about proper relationships among people. That challenge was epitomized in Thomas Paine's (1737–1809) essay *Common Sense* (1776) that helped inspire the leaders of the Revolution. In his tract, Paine applied reason in assessing the colonies' relationship with Britain, portraying the colonists as victims of exploitation, shown by a recently imposed stamp tax.

> We have boasted the protection of Great Britain, without considering
> that her motive was *interest* not *attachment;* that she did not protect us
> from *our enemies* on *our account,* but from *her enemies* on *her own*
> *account,* from those who had no quarrel with us on any *other account,*
> and who will always be our enemies on the *same account.*
>
> (Paine 1776)

Common Sense ended with a description of the ideal government, a description that closely resembled the government the colonists actually would create
after their military victory over the British. In 1794 Paine wrote *The Age of*
Reason, in which he reflected the convictions of a person who held to the tradition of believing in God and life after death but who was a secularist in founding conclusions about daily life on his ability to reason—on his skill at adducing
a line of logic.

> I believe in one God, and no more; and I hope for happiness beyond this
> life. I believe in the equality of man; and I believe that religious duties
> consist in doing justice, loving mercy, and endeavoring to make our
> fellow-creatures happy....
>   I do not believe in the creed professed by the Jewish church, by the
> Roman church, by the Greek church, by the Turkish church, by the Prot-
> estant church, nor by any church that I know of. My own mind is my own
> church. All national institutions of churches, whether Jewish, Christian,
> or Turkish, appear to me no other than human inventions, set up to ter-
> rify and enslave mankind, and monopolize power and profit.
>   I do not mean by this declaration to condemn those who believe oth-
> erwise; they have the same right to their belief as I have to mine. But it
> is necessary to the happiness of man that he be mentally faithful to him-
> self. Infidelity does not consist in believing, or in disbelieving; it consists
> in professing to believe what he does not believe.
>
> (Paine 1794, part I)

Paine's expressed beliefs appeared typical of most of the founding fathers—
beliefs portraying a bold democratic-secularism edifice erected atop a stratum
of lingering Christian tradition. Such a worldview would be expressed in the
Constitution that the nation's founders would adopt in 1789.

THE U.S. CONSTITUTION

The U.S. Constitution is obviously a product of the Enlightenment rather
than of Christian faith. Neither the original Constitution nor any of its amendments include such words as *God, Jesus Christ,* or *Christian.* Furthermore, the
Constitution declined to privilege one religion over any other, and it permitted
individuals to follow, without prejudice, whatever belief system they wished.
The document's first amendment stated, "Congress shall make no law respecting an establishment of religion, or prohibiting the free exercise thereof."

Whereas Christian tradition had always portrayed Christians as God's chosen people, superior to believers in other faiths, the Declaration of Independence that preceded the writing of the Constitution maintained that "We hold these truths to be self-evident, that all men are created equal, that they are endowed by their Creator [who was not identified as the Christian God] with certain unalienable rights, that among these are life, liberty, and the pursuit of happiness."

Furthermore, the new republic's structure, as established in the Constitution, differed significantly from that of European monarchies and Judeo-Christian tradition. In the United States, decision-making power was not to be vested in a hereditary king or emperor but, rather, in the citizens and their elected representatives. And rules about how people should behave would not be dictated as commandments by either a monarch, a religious authority (such as a pope), or a God but, instead, by laws passed by the citizens' representatives. Finally, there would be no officially established upper-social-class—a royalty or aristocracy—that was accorded privileges not available to commoners.

But despite the founding fathers' enthusiasm for the Enlightenment's secularism, they could not entirely shed their religious upbringing, which included a belief in the Bible's Old Testament (especially the Jewish Torah).

> When it came time to design a seal for the new nation, it is said that [Benjamin] Franklin wanted it to portray Moses bringing down the waters upon Pharoah, while Jefferson would have preferred a rendering of the children of Israel in the wilderness, with a cloud leading them by day and a pillar of fire by night. Neither of these prevailed, however, and the Great Seal that finally issued from the hands of Charles Thomson and William Barton showed the familiar eagle holding the olive branch and arrows, and on the obverse a pyramid watched over by the eye of Providence, with the mottoes *Annuit coeptis* (He [God] has favored our undertaking) and *Novus ordo seclorum* (A new order of the ages has begun).
>
> (Cremin 1980, 17)

Nor could the founders, in their own behavior, shake off the gender and social-caste distinctions inherited from a European background in which women, blacks, and Indians were not equal to white men. Such key founders as George Washington and Thomas Jefferson had black slaves, American Indians lacked the status of citizens, and women lacked the vote and the chance to hold office. Therefore, the new nation's basic principles (freedom-of-religion, all-created-equal, unalienable-rights, no-officially-privileged-social-class) were ideals to be pursued, not descriptions of the reality of the times.

What significance, then, did the principles of the Declaration of Independence and the Constitution hold for Amerindians? In the earliest years of the new republic, those principles exerted virtually no influence over the way

Indians and their cultures were treated. But in the long run, the principles proved important, for they are the values that Amerindians and their support-ers—particularly in modern times—have used to successfully press their case for fair treatment. Equal-rights advocates have been able to convince legisla-tors and the courts that past treatment of Indians and their religions offended the Constitution and the Declaration of Independence. Those advocates' appeals would not have been feasible if the commitment to equal-rights-and-freedoms had been absent from the nation's most fundamental documents.

The Southwest and Far West

During the closing years of the eighteenth century and well into the nine-teenth, the Spanish colonies of the Southwest continued intact, with Indians working small plots of land within the Spanish overlords' haciendas. Catholic priests were successful in converting a large portion of the native population to Christianity, but with the Indians often retaining indigenous religious beliefs and practices alongside their newly acquired Catholicism.

It was during this period that the Spanish extended their colonizing north-ward from Mexico up the California coast. Between 1769 and 1823, Spanish padres established 21 missions from San Diego in the south to Sonoma in the north. Each mission station consisted of a church and its surrounding commu-nity that was occupied by Spanish civil and military authorities, Catholic priests, and Indians. One effect of missionaries' success in Christianizing native peoples was that tribes vanished as distinct political and cultural units, "their members absorbed into the dominant white culture, usually at the bottom, as in the case of the California Mission Indians, who lived a serf-like existence in the Spanish feudal order" (Waldman 1985, 58). An estimated 68,000 Indians from at least 23 identifiable tribes lived in the region affected by the string of missions (Terrell 1979, 136). Ostensibly the Indians were willing members of the mission communities. However, if any chose to leave a mission station and return to their tribe, Spanish soldiers from the mission's garrison would usually recapture them and return them to the mission.

By the early nineteenth century, the Spanish were in secure control of New Spain, which consisted of Central America, Southwestern North America, and the California coast. By 1810, there were an estimated six million inhabitants in New Spain, of which 60,000 were Spanish born in Spain, 940,000 were Spanish born in the territories, 3.5 million were indigenous Mexicans and 1.5 million were Mestizos of mixed Spanish and Indian blood (Mexico's history 2006).

Canada in the Late Eighteenth Century

By the mid-eighteenth century, control of the eastern territory of what is now Canada was divided between France and Great Britain. The struggles between the two colonial powers for dominance led to the French and Indian War (1754–1763), which ended with the defeat of the French. The Treaty of

Paris in 1763 awarded the British all of French North America east of the Mississippi River. What had been known as New France now became the British colony of Quebec, populated by 70,000 French inhabitants plus Indians and a few hundred British subjects. This new amalgamation of Canadian territories under the British was first governed under a Royal Proclamation (1763), with that original plan periodically replaced by subsequent legislation in the British Parliament to accommodate changing conditions in the Canadian colony. Each new piece of legislation shifted increasing self-governing power to the colony, but ultimate decisions were always made in England. Not until the final decades of the twentieth century would Canada truly be self-governed under its own constitution.

CANADA'S CONSTITUTION AND CHARTER OF RIGHTS

The U.S. Constitution was issued at a single time, 1789, and later expanded with occasional amendments. The first amendment, which was added as part of a bill of rights in 1791, focused not only on religion but on other rights as well:

Congress shall make no law respecting an establishment of religion, or prohibiting the free exercise thereof; or abridging the freedom of speech, or of the press; or the right of the people peaceably to assemble, and to petition the Government for a redress of grievances.

In contrast to the method of creating the U.S. Constitution, Canada's Constitution and Charter of Rights and Freedoms developed in a very different manner. The Canadian Constitution—in the form of the 1982 Constitution Act—was an accumulation of earlier codified acts and of non-codified conventions. The codified sources included such documents as the British Royal Proclamation of 1763, the Constitutional Act of 1791, the British North American Act of 1867, the Statute of Westminister of 1931, and the Canada Act of 1982 as passed by the British Parliament. The Canadian Constitution, unlike its U.S. counterpart, included unwritten doctrines and customs (Constitution of Canada 2007).

Canada lacked a formal statement of citizens' rights until the Charter of Rights and Freedoms was adopted in 1981. In 1982 it became part of the Constitution Act. The charter had been preceded in 1960 by a non-constitutional statute titled *Canadian Bill of Rights*. In its final form, the Charter began with a preamble followed by an extensive series of rights and eight *fundamental freedoms.* The preamble ("Whereas Canada is founded upon principles that recognize the supremacy of God and the rule of law") was followed by freedoms of conscience, religion, thought, belief, expression, the press, peaceful assembly, and association. What exactly freedom of religion, thought, and belief meant was not specified in the Charter, so those provisions' practical meanings have continued to be spelled out in case law. That is, as cases involving religion, thought, and belief have come into courts, the decisions in the separate cases have served as the guides to what precise sorts of religion, thought, and belief are permitted and under what circumstances (Canadian Charter 1982).

Some critics have noted a conflict between the freedom-of-religion provision and the portion of the preamble that reads "the supremacy of God." Is that phrase not a commitment to a religion—perhaps to the Judeo-Christian tradition? Could that God be the First Nations' Manitou or Glooskap or Wakan Tanka or Gitche-Manedo? And what about Indian bands that have multiple deities? Thus, some observers have suggested that in order to reflect a true commitment to freedom of religion, thought, and belief, the reference to God should be eliminated from any rights charter of an ostensibly secular nation.

So, how has the Canadian Charter affected the nation's Native Peoples? Because in the eighteenth century there was no such statement of rights, members of the First Nations had no commitment on the part of the British colonial government to treat the colonies' original residents as equals who officially deserved rights. Only in recent decades has the Canadian Charter enabled promoters of fair opportunities for Amerindians, Inuits, and Métis to argue that any present-day maltreatment of the bands is unconstitutional and must be corrected. Also, in the spirit of the Charter, human-rights advocates have insisted that past maltreatment warrants generous reparations for the victims (see Chapter 15).

THE MIDDLE YEARS—1801–1860

A problem that European colonists had faced in the eighteenth century continued in Canada and intensified in the United States during the nineteenth century. It was the problem of what the European colonizers should do about North America's original peoples. Which mode of treating the Indians would be best—mutual respect, assimilation, isolation/restriction, or elimination? The following analysis of the middle years is organized around that question. The discussion begins with a definition of the four modes, then continues with a description of the settlers' western movement and schooling for Amerindians.

Modes of Interaction

Four ways that the European intruders could relate to North America's native inhabitants were to (a) live beside the Indians and Inuits in mutual respect, (b) assimilate the Native Peoples into European Christian culture, (c) isolate and restrict the Native Peoples, or (d) eliminate Amerindians.

The mutual-respect option would mean that any property the European immigrants acquired would be on terms that the Indians found entirely acceptable, with those terms also judged to be fair by impartial observers. In addition, mutual respect would mean that Indian culture would be neither damaged nor denigrated. Amerindian religious beliefs, objects, and practices would be honored. The European immigrants would neither attempt to change those beliefs nor try to entice or force Indians to abandon their traditional faiths.

Assimilation would consist of Indians adopting European culture completely or partially, with the adoption either voluntary on the Indians' part or
forced on the Indians by the Euro-Americans and Euro-Canadians. In the
realm of religion, complete assimilation would involve the native peoples
accepting the entire array of Christian beliefs and practices while discarding
all vestiges of Amerindian religions. Partial assimilation would mean that
Native Americans accepted certain aspects of Christianity while retaining
aspects of tribal faiths.

The term *isolation/restriction* refers to confining Indians to special locations, mainly places known as reservations.

An elimination mode of Indian/European interaction would involve the
Europeans getting rid of Indians, either by moving them out of territories the
European settlers wished to occupy or by killing the Indians off through dis-
ease or warfare.

During the nineteenth century, each of those modes of interaction—mutual
respect, assimilation, isolation/restriction, and elimination—was practiced in
North America during some times and in some places.

Westward Ho

Increasing immigration from Europe and high birth rates among the citizens of the fledgling United States and Canada combined to swell the number
of settlers who sought to own property. At the time of the first federal census in
1790, the population of the United States was 3,929,214. Over the next
60 years, the number of residents grew by 35 percent each decade. Thus,
between 1800 and 1850, the population would almost quadruple—from
5,308,483 to 23,191,876. Two ways that the federal government might cope
with the citizens' demands for property were those of acquiring more territory
and of moving Indians out of areas that settlers wished to occupy. The first of
these strategies was effected by the Louisiana Purchase, the second by removal
legislation.

THE LOUISIANA PURCHASE

By 1801, when Thomas Jefferson became the third president of the United
States, the nation consisted of 16 states and several territories, all east of the
Mississippi River. Virtually all land west of the Mississippi was claimed by
Spain. Before 1762, France had putative title to an immense region that
extended north from New Orleans, up the western side of the Mississippi,
and northwest through lands surrounding the Missouri River. That region
was known as the Louisiana Territory. In 1762, Spain had acquired it from
France, but in 1802 returned it to French control.

Jefferson recognized that France was in serious financial trouble and could
not afford to govern its American colony, so Jefferson sent James Monroe in
January 1803 to Paris as *minister extraordinary*, authorized to offer up to

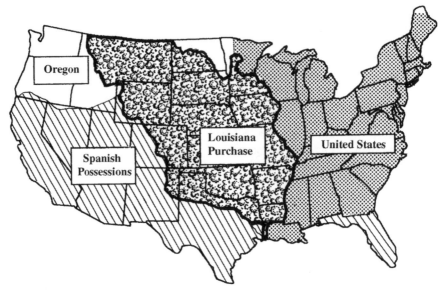

Map 11.1   The Louisiana Purchase—1803.

$10-million for the Louisiana territory. In April, the French emperor, Napo-
leon Bonaparte, agreed on a negotiated price of $15 million. As shown in
Map 11.1, the Louisiana Purchase added 827,000 square miles to the United
States, doubling the nation's size at a cost of three cents per acre. (The white
areas on the map were territories whose ownership was in dispute. For instance, the Oregon country was claimed by Spain, Great Britain, Russia, and
the United States.)

Even before the United States owned the Louisiana Territory, Congress in
January 1803 endorsed Jefferson's plan for a Corps of Discovery that would
explore the region's terrain, wildlife, Indian tribes, and economic potential.
The expedition would be led over a two-and-one-half-year period (1804–
1806) by two former army officers, Meriweather Lewis and William Clark.
The journey carried the explorers as far as the Oregon country and the Pacific
Ocean. Upon its completion, the expedition was deemed an enormous success.
It furnished maps and descriptions of a vast territory, information about 48
Indian tribes, and the first scientific records of 177 plant species and 124 ani-
mals and birds (Lewis & Clark, 2007). The results of the expedition further
whetted the appetite of trappers, miners, adventurers, and settlers to seek their
fortunes out west.

However, from the Indians' perspective, the Corps of Discovery proved to
be disastrous. What is apparently a typical present-day Amerindian assessment
of the Lewis and Clark expedition is reflected in the remarks of Gerard Baker,
a Mandan-Hidatsa Indian and superintendent of the National Park Service's
Lewis and Clark National Historical Trail.

We [Indians] started going from a dependency on the environment, on the spiritualism of the land, to a dependency on the traders and the military and everything else that came after Lewis and Clark. So we essentially lost....It was a good time for that year, for 1804–1805, but there's been a lot of negative changes after that....[Lewis and Clark] didn't know it was going to be that way, I guess, for the future.

(Baker 2007)

White settlers took advantage of the Louisiana Purchase by moving rapidly into the vast prairie country between the Appalachian Mountains in the east and the Rocky Mountains in the west. But travel to territories beyond the Rocky Mountains proved too difficult for all but the hardiest. Jefferson had hoped the Corps of Discovery would find a convenient water passage to the Pacific Ocean via rivers beyond the Missouri. That hope was shattered as Lewis and Clark's route had taken them across the most treacherous section of the Rocky Mountains. Not until three decades later did other explorers find a reasonable gap in the Rockies—South Pass—in what is now western Wyoming. That discovery made the 2,000-mile Oregon Trail possible, as its route coursed through South Pass, allowing wagon loads of migrants and their goods to reach California and the Northwest. Large numbers of settlers moving on the trail did not begin until 1843, when about 1,000 pioneers made the journey. Then, over the next 25 years more than a half million people went west on the trail, some to California's gold fields and others to Oregon for farmland. Peace treaties were signed with the Cheyenne [Great Plains] in 1851 to help ensure the safety of trekkers. But after whites violated the treaties, travelers were again subject to Indian attacks.

In summary, the Louisiana Purchase, Corps of Discovery, and Oregon Trail led to a mass westward invasion of Indian territories by fur trappers, land speculators, farmers, Christian missionaries, soldiers, and would-be miners. Nearly all held Native American cultures in contempt, including Indian religions.

U.S. TREATIES

As noted in Chapter 10, a crucial method used by the European colonists to capture Indians' lands and control the native population was to negotiate treaties. In the new U.S. republic, that practice was greatly expanded until finally abandoned in 1871. According to Charles Kapplar's compilation of treaties (1904), nearly 700 pacts had been signed with tribes between 1784 and 1868.

Ostensibly, the U.S. federal and state governments wished to interact with Indian tribes in a spirit of mutual respect—sovereign nations living side by side, equal in rights, opportunities, and prosperity. Treaties would be the devices that legally cemented this reciprocal relationship. But in fact, the treaties were designed to rob the Indians of property, freedom of movement, prosperity, and—quite frequently—cultural heritage. The spirit in which treaties should be negotiated by the U.S. Government was expressed by President Jefferson in a secret letter he sent in February 1803 to William H. Harrison, then governor of the Indiana territory, a region that included the present-day states of Illinois, Indiana, Wisconsin, and parts of Minnesota. Jefferson's plan to get tribal lands at little cost consisted of enticing Indians into debt through their buying goods at government trading posts, with the Indians then forced to repay the debt by ceding vast properties to the government. Any armed resistance by the Indians would result in their lands being confiscated and the Indians driven away. Thus, Jefferson's mode of whites' interaction with Amerindians would be a combination of deceitful exploitation, isolation/ restriction, and—if necessary—elimination. In his advice to Harrison, the president wrote:

> Our system is to live in perpetual peace with the Indians, . . . To promote this disposition to exchange lands, which they have to spare and we want, for necessaries [manufactured goods], which we have to spare and they want, we shall push our trading uses, and be glad to see the good and influential individuals among them run in debt, because we observe that when these debts get beyond what the individuals can pay, they become willing to lop them off by a cession of lands. At our trading houses, too, we mean to sell so low as merely to repay us cost and charges, . . . In this way our settlements [of white immigrants] will gradually circum- scribe and approach the Indians, and they [the Indians] will in time either incorporate with us as citizens of the United States, or remove beyond the Mississippi. . . . Should any tribe be foolhardy enough to take up the hatchet at any time, the seizing of the whole of that tribe, and driving them across the Mississippi as the only condition of peace, would be an example to others, and a furtherance of our final consolidation.
>
> (Garman 1998)

A Georgia governor expressed the rationale behind the treaty system in words that apparently reflected the attitudes of many of his countrymen.

> Treaties were expedients by which ignorant, intractable, and savage peo- ple were induced without bloodshed to yield up what civilized people had the right to possess by virtue of that command of the Creator deliv- ered to man upon his formation—be fruitful, multiply, and replenish the earth, and subdue it.
>
> (Utley 1984, 36)

Usually the land transferred via treaties went to the federal or state government, which could then do what it wished with the property, such as sell it to individuals. In other cases, treaties transferred the acreage directly to pri- vate citizens. Such was the case in an 1823 pact by which Seneca lands in New York State were sold to a John Greig and a Henry B. Gibson. The total area consisted of 17,927 acres, of which 16,642 would go to Greig and Gibson (at a cost of 26 cents per acre), while the Seneca tribe would retain 1,280 acres or 7 percent of the total as a living area (Gorham 1823).

Some treaties were not primarily intended to deprive Amerindians of their land but, rather, were designed to establish peaceful relations between a tribe's warriors and the white settlers. For example, the main purpose of an 1852 federal treaty with the Apaches [Southwest] was to ensure that

> hostilities between the contracting parties shall forever cease, and per-petual peace and amity shall forever exist between said Indians and the Government and people of the United States; the said nation, or tribe of Indians, hereby binding themselves most solemnly never to associate with or give countenance or aid to any tribe or band of Indians, or other persons or powers, who may be at any time at war or enmity with the government or people of said United States.
>
> (Kappler 1904)

A secondary purpose that was not delineated precisely in the agreement was that of restricting the Apaches to a confined region—a reservation, in effect, but not identified as such. The wording of the document cast the U.S. Government in the guise of a benevolent, fair, and generous patron.

> Relying confidently upon the justice and the liberality of the aforesaid government, and anxious to remove every possible cause that might dis-turb their peace and quiet, it is agreed by the aforesaid Apaches that the government of the United States shall at its earliest convenience des-ignate, settle, and adjust their territorial boundaries, and pass and execute in their territory such laws as may be deemed conducive to the prosperity and happiness of said Indians.
>
> (Kappler 1904)

Another purpose included in some treaties was that of assimilating Indians into Christian culture, a process that was expected to eradicate native religions. To accomplish such an end, treaties required schools that taught an English—meaning a Christian-based—curriculum. For instance, a treaty signed with the Northern Cheyenne and Arapaho [Great Plains] in 1868 required parents

> to compel their children, male and female, between the ages of six and sixteen years, to attend school;...and the United States agrees that for every thirty children, between said ages, who can be induced or com-pelled to attend school, a house shall be provided, and a teacher, compe-tent to teach the elementary branches of an English education, shall be furnished.
>
> (Kappler 1904)

By the mid-1850s, the government was implementing a reservation policy designed to acculturate Indians into a Christian Euro-American worldview and lifestyle. To explain this forced-isolation-and-assimilation policy, Commissioner of Indian affairs Francis A. Walker said,

> The reservation system...shall place all members of this race under strict reformatory control by the agents of the Government. Especially it is essential that the right of the Government to keep the Indians upon the reservations signed to them, and to arrest and return them whenever they wander away, should be placed beyond dispute.
>
> (Wilkins 2002, 108)

In summary, treaties served as devices by which the European settlers of the United States could, via their federal and state governments, divest Amerindians of their lands and hasten the demise of tribes' cultures, including tribes' religions.

CANADIAN TREATIES

Beginning in 1701, the British government negotiated a succession of treaties in Canada that were intended to (a) encourage peaceful relations between the country's original inhabitants and the European immigrants and (b) define how the aboriginal North Americans and the immigrants would use the lands that the First Nations had traditionally occupied. The number of Canadian treaties—hardly more than two dozen—was miniscule compared to the hundreds negotiated in the United States.

Under several Upper Canada Treaties (1764–1862) and Vancouver Island Treaties (1850–1854), First Nations surrendered lands in Ontario and British Columbia in exchange for the same sorts of returns found in typical U.S. treaties—money, reservations on which to live, and rights to hunt and fish in the surrendered areas. Eleven treaties signed between 1871 and 1921 ceded huge territories in Western and Northern Canada to the government in exchange for "reserve lands and other benefits like agricultural equipment and livestock, annuities, ammunition, gratuities, clothing, and certain rights to hunt and fish. The Crown also made some promises regarding the maintenance of schools on reserves, or the provision of teachers, or educational assistance to the First Nation parties to the treaties" (Department of Indian Affairs 2000).

For the First Nations, the consequences of the treaties were similar to those experienced by Amerindians in the United States—the loss of lands, limits on where and how Indians could live, and a deterioration of traditional cultures, including First Nations' religions.

U.S. REMOVALS

By the time the new U.S. republic was formed, five Indian nations in the southeastern states had become known as *The Civilized Tribes*. The Cherokee, Creek, Choctaw, Chickasaw, and Seminole nations were identified as "civilized" by white settlers because the five had adopted a variety of

Anglo-American customs—style of dress, large-scale farming, Western education, and slaveholding. Each tribe had a written constitution, a judiciary system, a legislature, an executive branch, and a school system. But the whites of the region yearned for the tribes' extensive lands and thus pressed their representatives in Congress to rid the area of Indians, whose properties could then be converted to plantations owned by whites.

On December 8, 1830, U.S. President Andrew Jackson promoted the whites' cause by urging Congress to pass an Indian Removal Act. He cloaked the government's land-grab in self-righteous compassion, while bluntly denigrating Native Americans' lifestyles and religions.

> It gives me pleasure to announce to Congress that the benevolent policy of the Government, steadily pursued for nearly thirty years, in relation to the removal of the Indians beyond the white settlements is approaching to a happy consummation. Two important tribes [Choctaw, Chickasaw] have accepted the provision made for their removal [to west of the Mississippi River]...and it is believed that their example will induce the remaining tribes also to seek the same obvious advantages.
>
> The consequences of a speedy removal will be important to the United States, to individual states, and to the Indians themselves.... [The policy] puts an end to all possible danger of collision between the authorities of the general and state governments on account of the Indians. It will place a dense and civilized population in large tracts of country now occupied by a few savage hunters. It will relieve the whole State of Mississippi and the western part of Alabama of Indian occupancy, and enable those States to advance rapidly in population, wealth, and power. It will separate the Indians from immediate contact with settlements of whites;...enable them to pursue happiness in their own way and under their own rude institutions;...and perhaps cause them gradually...to cast off their savage habits and become an interesting, civilized, and Christian community.
>
> Toward the aborigines of the country no one can indulge a more friendly feeling than myself, or would go further in attempting to reclaim them from their wandering habits and make them a happy, prosperous people. The Choctaw and the Chickasaw tribes have with great unanimity determined to avail themselves of the liberal offers presented by the act of Congress, and have agreed to remove beyond the Mississippi River.
>
> (Jackson 1830)

In a spirit of humanitarianism, a minority of congressmen and public officials thought the Indians should not be deprived of their properties. However, the majority supported Jackson's position, and the Removal Act became law. The putative intent of the legislation was to make removal voluntary, as stipulated in treaties the tribes were obliged to sign. However, over the next quarter century, the eviction of the nations from their homelands in Florida, Georgia, Alabama, and Mississippi would be forced.

> By 1837, the Jackson administration had removed 46,000 Native American people from their land east of the Mississippi, and had secured treaties which led to the removal of a slightly larger number. Most members of the five southeastern nations had been relocated west, opening 25 million acres of land to white settlement and to slavery.
>
> (Public Broadcasting System 2007)

At least 60,000 Indians eventually relocated in the West, mainly in the Oklahoma and Kansas territories, a region popularly referred to as the Great American Desert. In 1838 Cherokees had been compelled to travel almost 1,300 miles without sufficient food, water, or medicine. Four thousand Cherokees —over one quarter of the total—died along the way, and the journey became known as the Trail of Tears. The removal policy was also applied to bands other than the five tribes. Potawatomies traveling to the Indiana territory suffered similar loses on their Trail of Death.

In summary, the Five Civilized Tribes were originally an example of voluntary assimilation. On their own initiative—with the Anglo-Americans' approval —members of the five nations had taken on the accouterments of European culture. But the whites' envy and greed would outweigh their admiration for the natives' transformation and would produce the tragic removal act—the federal government's attempt to eliminate them.

Schooling for Amerindians

The schooling provided for North America's native peoples in colonial times was followed by new provisions in both the United States and Canada throughout the nineteenth century, with schools serving as devices for Christianizing Amerindian children and youths.

SCHOOLING IN THE UNITED STATES AND CANADA

Even before the new U.S. republic had adopted a constitution, the Continental Congress in 1787 had enacted the Northwest Ordinance that promised Christian education for the nation's Indians: "Religion, morality, and knowledge, being necessary to good government and the happiness of mankind, schools, and the means of education shall forever be encouraged. The utmost good faith shall always be observed toward the Indians" (DeJong 1993, 34).

An important step toward "good faith" was taken in 1810 with the founding of the first American foreign missionary society by Presbyterians and Congregationalists under the title American Board for Commissioners for Foreign Missions (ABCFM). In addition to sending missionaries overseas (Africa, China, Hawaii, India, the Middle East), the board placed ministers with Indian nations, particularly with the Civilized Tribes of the Southeast. By the late 1820s, prior to Andrew Jackson's Removal Act, the board operated eight schools for the Cherokees (Coleman 1993, 40).

A further act of "good faith" was demonstrated when the U.S. Congress in 1819 abandoned the U.S. Constitution's mandated separation of church and state by endorsing a partnership between the federal government and church organizations through the Indian Civilization Fund Act. The legislation provided federal dollars for "benevolent societies" to instruct Indians in reading, writing, arithmetic, and agriculture (Szasz 2006). Presbyterians, Congregationalists, Methodists, Baptists, Moravians, Quakers, and Episcopalians could then officially ply their trade in tribal areas, endeavoring to civilize Indians. Although the act called for a $10,000 per year federal grant to support such schools, in practice the amount was less than 10 percent of that sum, so Christian denominations and the tribes themselves were obliged to raise funds, with the Indians bearing the greater cost. Around one-fourth of the treaties that the U.S. Government would sign with tribes included federal promises of schools for Indians (Indian education 2007). By 1824, there were thirty-two missionary schools enrolling more than 900 Indian pupils (Coleman 1993, 39). Over the next half century, schooling for Native Americans would be provided almost exclusively by Protestant and Catholic groups.

An example of a mission school is the one established in the Kansas territory in 1839 by the Methodists. It was a central boarding school on a branch of the Santa Fe Trail that passed through Shawnee Indian lands, intended to serve such tribes as the Shawnee, Kansa, Munsee, Delaware, Ottawa, Chippewa, Otoe, Osage, Cherokee, Peoria, Kickapoo, Potawatomi, Wea, Gros Ventres, Omaha, and Wyandot. The learning fare included basic academic studies—English language, arithmetic, history, geography, Christian religion—along with manual arts and agriculture. At the peak of the school's growth, the establishment consisted of 2,000 acres, 16 buildings, and nearly 200 Indian boys and girls ages five to 23.

> Classes were held six hours each day except Saturday and Sunday. On Saturday teaching was limited to three hours. The boys worked in the shop or on the farm, usually for five hours a day. The girls helped with the sewing, washing, and cooking. The students, as a rule, went to bed at 8:00 P.M. and rose at 4:00 A.M.
>
> (Shawnee Indian Mission 2006)

Although residential schools conducted by white missionaries became the most common form of European education for Indian youths, some tribes maintained their own day schools and Sunday Schools that Amerindians attended. In 1860, Choctaws, who had been removed from the Southeast to the Oklahoma territory, operated 22 neighborhood day schools that enrolled around 500 students. By that year, literacy in the Choctaw language had become widespread (Baird, 1985, 26).

In Canada, the early history of schooling for the native peoples was similar to the history of schooling in the United States. Beginning in 1620, three Catholic orders—Recollets, Jesuits, and Ursulines—had conducted boarding schools for Indian youths until that experiment ended in 1680 because of very limited success in convincing Indians to enroll their children. Later, during the 1820–1940 period, Anglicans, Methodists, and Catholics would found residential schools. And in 1847, a colonial-government-sponsored study by Egerton Ryerson set the model for future Aboriginal schooling by stressing domestic and agricultural skills, the locale's dominant European language (English or French), and Christian religion, for "nothing can be done to improve and elevate [Indians'] character and condition without the aid of religious feeling" (Indian residential schools 2007). The schools would continue to be operated by religious sects, but the government would periodically inspect the schools and would grant funds on the basis of the inspectors' reports.

In both the United States and Canada, the education that missionaries typically offered Indians was divided between academic studies and vocational skills. The academic portion consisted of the same subjects taught in Euro-American schools—English (or French) language, arithmetic, history, geography, and the religious doctrine of the Christian sect that operated the particular school. In the vocational portion, Indian boys were taught blacksmithing, woodworking, and European-style farming. Girls learned European forms of cooking, sewing, and "domestic arts."

Attending a mission school could be a bewildering experience for Indian children, because the educational diet offered by Protestant ministers and Catholic "Black Robes" was so radically different from the content and teaching methods of traditional Amerindian education. As noted in Chapter 10, Indians had no formal schools but, rather, learned skills from family members and neighbors—tracking game, growing corn, grinding acorns into meal, sewing buckskin garments, constructing teepees and longhouses, making pottery, painting and tattooing their bodies, fighting battles, surviving snowstorms, and enduring hardships without complaint. Indian children were steeped in tribal lore through hearing stories and witnessing religious ceremonies. They acquired their names and life ambitions through visions and dreams.

One example of the nature of Indian education is DeJong's description of advice given an Indian youth by an experienced hunter in the tribe.

When you have any difficulty with a bear or a wildcat—that is, if the creature shows signs of attacking you—you must make him fully understand that you have seen him and are aware of his intentions. If you are not well equipped for a pitched battle, the only way to make him retreat is to take a long sharp pointed pole for a spear and rush toward him. No wild beast will face this unless he is cornered and already wounded. These fierce beasts are generally afraid of the common weapon of the larger animals

—the horns, and if these are very long and sharp, they dare not risk an open fight.

(DeJong 1993, 8)

Learning from such advice was a far cry from a missionary school's tasks of memorizing the answers to questions in a Christian catechism, reciting the arithmetic times tables, or conjugating English or French verbs. Consequently, for typical Indian youths, Euro-American schooling was a perplexing experience that could alienate them from the traditional culture of their tribe, including their tribe's religion.

THE EPOCH'S FINAL YEARS—1861–1876

Interactions between Euro-Americans and Native Americans were significantly affected over the 1861–1875 period by the Civil War and its aftermath in the United States and by the British North American Act in Canada.

U.S. Grant's Peace Policy

Not long after the Civil War of 1861–1865, Ulysses S. Grant—the general who had commanded U.S. Government troops to victory in the final year of the war—was elected president of the nation for two terms (1869–1877). When Grant assumed office, relations between white settlers and Indians were very bad indeed, particularly in the Great Plains where Indians waged guerilla warfare that U.S. Government troops were ill-prepared to combat.

At the outset of his presidency, Grant adopted a Peace Policy with the motto "It's cheaper to give rations to the Indians than to conquer them." In his inaugural address, he committed the government to encouraging Indians toward "civilization and ultimate citizenship." He then astonished the nation by appointing an Indian and former army officer, Ely S. Parker, as commissioner of Indian affairs. On the belief that Indians could not become properly civilized until they were first Christianized, a newly created Board of Indian Commissioners appointed missionaries as Indian agents who were assigned to mediate disputes between tribes and Euro-Americans, to supply teachers, and to settle Indians on reservations where they would form agricultural communities. Congress authorized more than $1 million each year to educate Indian children, with nearly half of that sum contracted to missionaries (Yazzie 2002). Thus, Indians were to be assimilated into Euro-American culture by abandoning their religion and their way of life in favor of a mode of Christian living envisioned by white reformers.

How well the Peace Policy worked is reflected in a report filed in 1869 by a Major General Stanley, who had been assigned to survey conditions among the Sioux in Dakota territory.

At the agencies established for the Sioux, there is one class of Indians which has been friendly for four or five years and are nearly residents, only leaving from time to time to hunt or pick wild fruit. With this class there is no trouble. There is another class passing half its time at these agencies and half in the hostile camps. They abuse the agents, threaten their lives, kill their cattle at night and do anything they can to oppose the civilizing movement, but eat all the provisions they can get, and thus far have taken no lives. During the winter for the past two years, almost the entire hostile Sioux have camped together in one big camp on the Rosebud, near the Yellowstone. In the summer time they break up and spread over the prairies, either to hunt, plunder, or come into the posts to beg.

(Peace Policy 2007)

By the end of Grant's second term, the Peace Policy had disintegrated as Christian denominations continued to bicker, Indians were unwilling to surrender their traditional lifestyles, settlers encroached on properties allotted to Indians in treaties, and corruption was rampant in the U.S. Interior Department's supervision of Indian reservations. Furthermore, Indians not on reservations were the responsibility of the U.S. Army, whose personnel were still furious over the massacre of General George A. Custer's forces that had gone to the Little Big Horn River in Montana to subdue the Sioux and Cheyenne in 1876.

Although the major provisions of the Peace Policy had crumbled away, the schooling plans that had been accumulating over the decades not only remained but would expand significantly at the nation entered a new era after 1876.

British North America Act

Canada, as a colonial possession within the British Empire, achieved a new status of self-governance in 1867 when the Parliament in England passed the British North America Act. Canadian leaders could then declare their territories in the eastern region to be a kingdom in its own right. But Parliament balked at such a title and substituted the term *dominion* for *kingdom*. In this new arrangement, the provinces of Quebec, Ontario, New Brunswick, and Nova Scotia formed a federation, which would be joined in 1870–1871 by Manitoba, Prince Edward Island, and British Columbia. Not until 1905 did Alberta and Saskatchewan become dominion members.

Under the North American Act, the education of Indians became the responsibility of the new federation, with Indian day schools governed by treaty provisions of the 1850s. The Act also set the stage for the 1876 Indian Act that gave control of Indian education to the dominion's minister of the Department of Indian Affairs whose decisions would determine the forms of Indian schooling from that time forward.

CONCLUSION

During the final quarter of the eighteenth century, neither the U.S. Government nor the British Government that controlled the Canadian territories had an intentional, consistent policy about how to treat the cultures of North America's native peoples, including how to view Indians' religions. Should the Euro-Americans and Native Americas interact as members of sovereign nations that respected each other's ways of life? Or should the Euro-Americans attempt to replace Indians' traditional cultures with European lifestyles and belief systems—including the elimination of native religions in favor of Christianity?

By 1876, the issue of how to treat the Aboriginal population had been settled. The governments of both the United States and Canada were then firmly committed to an assimilation policy. Indians were to become "civilized" by abandoning tribal traditions and by adopting Euro-American and Euro-Canadian ways in language (English, or French in parts of Canada), modes of dress, occupations, housing, dietary practices, schooling, and the Christian religion.

The U.S. and Canadian governments would vigorously apply their assimilation policies in the next historical period—1877–1949.

·

· **12** ·

·

The Growing Nations—1877–1949

This chapter is presented in two parts. The first part identifies political events that significantly affected relationships between Amerindians and the U.S. and Canadian governments' Christian tradition. The second part recounts the development of government-financed schooling for Native American children and youths—schooling that bore serious consequences for indigenous cultures and their religious components .

INFLUENTIAL POLITICAL EVENTS—UNITED STATES

As noted in Chapter 11, after the American Civil War, the governments and the European-heritage peoples in both the United States and Canada puzzled over what to do about the Native Americans. While the general sentiment seemed to favor assimilating Indians into Euro-American culture, how to achieve that goal was far from clear. Should Indians remain on reservations, or should they be dispersed throughout the general populace? Should tribes be considered sovereign nations governed by their traditional customs? And now that the buffalo-hunting livelihood of Great Plains Indians was eliminated by the whites killing off the herds, could former hunting peoples be converted into farmers successfully? Who should control the vast lands that still belonged to indigenous bands? And what should be done about treaties that had been signed with Indian nations over the past two centuries?

Attempts to resolve such issues took the form of legislation over the coming decades. The general effect of lawmaking in the late 1800s was to drastically reduce Indians' traditional land holdings and to vigorously pursue the aim of assimilating Native Americans into Euro-American and Euro-Canadian culture. In the United States, an 1887 law broke up reservations and tribal communities, a 1924 act awarded Indians U.S. citizenship, and a 1934 law permitted Indian communities to restore tribal governments that had been declining.

Each of these events sparked debate among government officials and Indian leaders about whether the changes increased or diminished Indians' wellbeing.

The nature of the changes in the United States can be illustrated with the aftermath of Grant's Peace Policy, the Dawes Act, the Sun Dance ban, the General Citizenship Act, the Indian Reorganization Act, and treaties signed at earlier times.

Grant's Peace Policy Aftermath

A key feature of President Grant's Peace Policy was the formation of a Board of Indian Commissioners to monitor the activities of the federal Bureau of Indian Affairs. The board was composed entirely of prominent Protestant laymen. Distressed Catholic clergymen charged that the commissioners would favor their own denominations in determining which church groups would be assigned control over agencies on Indian reservations.

> By [the Catholics'] own calculation—on the basis of missions established and priority in mission work—the Catholics expected to get 38 agencies [but] they received only seven. The Methodists, who had relatively little mission work to their credit, were assigned 14. The Orthodox Friends received 10, the Presbyterians nine, and so on down the line through Episcopalians, Hicksite Friends, Reformed Dutch, Baptists, Congregationalists, Lutherans, and Unitarians.
>
> (Prucha 1979, 2)

Whereas it appeared that the Catholics had been squeezed out of a significant role in conducting Indian schools, that impression was put to rest as Catholics took advantage of the federal government's offering mission schools contracts paying a given sum per student. The Catholic Bureau of Indian Missions pursued such contracts with such success that the Catholic Missions and Sisters' two boarding schools and five day schools in 1874 (with $8,000 in federal funds) expanded to 18 boarding schools (with $54,000) by 1883 and to an income of $431,933 by 1889. That was by far the largest amount of federal monies awarded to any group, and Catholics became the dominant sect conducting Indian education until the contract system ended in 1900 (Prucha 1979, 3–4, 26–27).

Hence, competition continued among denominations to determine which sect would assimilate more Indian souls into its brand of Christianity.

The Dawes Act—1887

Numbers of humanitarians—both Native American and Euro-American—
believed that placing Indians on reservations meant keeping them forever in
bondage, never free to determine their own destinies. An attempt to solve this
problem assumed the form of the federal General Allotment Act of 1887, usually called the Dawes Act after its sponsor, U.S. Senator Henry L. Dawes of
Massachusetts.

According to the legislation, Native-American tribal land would be surveyed
and the arable portion divided into allotments for individual Indians, with each
head of a household receiving 160 acres, each single person over age 17 getting
80 acres, and each minor awarded 40 acres. To protect Indians from fraudulent
land speculators, the Secretary of the Interior Department was authorized to
hold the allotments "in trust" for 25 years, after which the land title would
belong to the allotment holder or to the holder's heirs. But after the allotments
were distributed, there still would be vast areas of Indian lands which the federal
government could sell to non-Indians on "terms and conditions as shall be considered just and equitable between the United States and said tribe of Indians."
When the transfer process was complete, Indians who had received allotments
would become U.S. citizens (Dawes Act, 1887). From 1887 to 1900, the federal
government certified 53,168 allotments totaling nearly 5 million acres (Fixico,
1986, xi–xii). In the 45 years following the Dawes Act, 60 million acres of land
—nearly half the total belonging to Indians under treaties—was opened by the
government to non-Indian settlers and venture capitalists.

What supposedly was intended as an act of kindness turned out to be disastrous for most Native American tribes and their members. The legislation
served simultaneously to assimilate Indians into the general population and
to remove them from lands that European immigrants yearned to own. Not
only were tribes deprived of immense territories, but most of the Indians were
poorly equipped to prosper as small-plot holders in the nation's capitalistic
economic system.

The Sun Dance Ban—1904

In Chapter 6, the Sun Dance was portrayed as a widely celebrated ritual
among Great Plains nations, a ceremony that publicly tested warriors' bravery,
endurance, and ability to bear physical pain. This annual rite had assumed a
key role in indigenous societies that were constantly engaged in warfare—
defending one's tribe against attack, raiding other tribes, and warding off
armed intrusions by Euro-American settlers and soldiers. However, by the
opening of the twentieth century, conditions of life for plains Indians had
changed drastically, as most Amerindians were relegated to reservations,
inter-tribal warfare had ceased, and the U.S. Army was in control of potentially
unruly bands. Thus, the time had passed when warriors served as tribal leaders, and the federal government took steps to quell religious ceremonies that
Indians considered legitimate modes of Native-American spirituality.

The more visible expressions of the Indian spiritual world drew direct government fire when the Indian Bureau issued its "list of Indian Offences" in 1883. Now a medicine man could be hauled before the Court of Indian Offenses for providing his people with spiritual counsel or for practicing the rituals and incantations of his calling. One by one the old-time shamans died without passing their lore to apprentices.

But the hardest blow came with the ban on the Sun Dance. Once the centerpience of the social and religious fabric of the Sioux, the Sun Dance provided an annual forum for spiritual communication and comfort. No other institution afforded so pervading a sense of religious security. No other event so strengthened the values and institutions of society. Of all the voids that settled into Sioux life in the early reservation years, this emotional void was the worst (Utley 1884, 243).

In effect, under the new societal conditions of the late 1800s, Christian Euro-Americans deemed the Sun Dance a heathen ceremony in which the Sun was worshipped in ways that included self-torture, so the U.S. Government banned the dance in 1904, a prohibition that lasted until 1935. Outlawing the Sun Dance removed the plains bands' most treasured rite of religious renewal. Today, in a more tolerant twenty-first century, the Sun Dance continues to be celebrated, often with the flesh-tearing feature eliminated.

The General Citizenship Act—1924

Some Amerindians became U.S. citizens as a result of the Dawes Act, and others became citizens by serving in the nation's military during World War I. However, the entire Native-American population did not receive citizenship until June 1924 when Congress passed the General Citizenship Act that served as a further step toward assimilating Indians into the dominant American society. Under the act, Amerindians could be citizens of both the United States and their traditional tribes.

The Indian Reorganization Act—1934

The next landmark congressional decision was the Indian Reorganization Act that reversed the direction of the Dawes Act. In contrast to the Dawes Acts' disposing of reservation lands by selling them to non-Indians, the Reorganization Act (also known as the Howard-Wheeler Act after its congressional sponsors) stressed the retention, conservation, and development of Indian properties.

The Secretary of the Interior is hereby authorized to restore to tribal ownership the remaining surplus lands of any Indian reservation heretofore opened, or authorized to be opened, to sale.... The Secretary [is] to acquire through purchase, relinquishment, gift, exchange, or assignment, any interest in lands, water rights, or surface rights to lands...for the purpose of providing lands for Indians.

(Indian Reorganization Act 1934)

The Howard-Wheeler bill also reconstituted and strengthened tribal governments that had seriously declined while the Dawes Act was in effect.

Any Indian tribe, or tribes, residing on the same reservation, shall have the right to organize for its common welfare, and may adopt an appropriate constitution and bylaws, which shall become effective when ratified by a majority vote of the adult members of the tribe, or of the adult Indians residing on such reservation, as the case may be, at a special election authorized by the Secretary of the Interior under such rules and regulations as he may prescribe. Such constitution and bylaws when ratified as aforesaid and approved by the Secretary of the Interior shall be revocable by an election open to the same voters and conducted in the same manner as hereinabove provided. Amendments to the constitution and bylaws may be ratified and approved by the Secretary in the same manner as the original constitution and bylaws....[The constitution shall provide] the tribal council [the right]...to prevent the sale, disposition, lease, or encumbrance of tribal lands, interests in lands, or other tribal assets without the consent of the tribe; and to negotiate with the Federal, State, and local Governments.

(Indian Reorganization Act 1943)

Furthermore, the Howard-Wheeler legislation offered tribes the opportunity to form business organizations and credit systems, to provide vocational education for students, and to restore native arts and crafts. (Fixico 1986, xiii).

In summary, the Reorganization Act recognized Indian nations' rights over remaining hereditary lands and over tribal governments. However, the act did not include any recognition by the U.S. Government of the legitimacy of Indian religions or sacred ceremonies.

The Effect of U.S. Treaties

The hundreds of treaties the U.S. Government had signed with Indian nations in the past could, in the twentieth century, serve as legal ammunition for Amerindians as they sought to protect their current lands and to reclaim lands and self-governance rights that had suffered erosion throughout the 1800s. Across the decades, Euro-American settlers, cattlemen, and mining companies had breached treaty agreements by encroaching on Indian properties, often abetted by unscrupulous federal and state authorities.

Although the federal government had stopped negotiating treaties in 1871, the existing agreements had no termination dates. In other words, treaty provisions were in perpetuity, intended to last forever. Therefore, treaties' conditions continued in effect even as new legislation—the Dawes Act, the Indian Reconstruction Act—became law. When disputes over land ownership and use came before the courts, decisions often were rendered in favor of the Indians' claims under the treaties. The Supreme Court never found any part of any treaty unconstitutional.

As the middle of the twentieth century approached, the legal status of Indian tribes and their members was rather absurd. During colonial days treaties had been arranged between *independent nations*—between an Indian band and the British Crown. Then, under the newly established United States, tribes were dubbed *domestic dependent nations* subject to U.S. laws. And with the adoption of the 1924 General Citizenship Act, all Native Americans became citizens of both the United States and their traditional tribe (domestic dependent nation). So, to what rights and powers were Indians entitled in twentieth-century America? With what power and authority did treaties actually provide Indians? This became an increasingly troublesome public issue as the century advanced, and it still continued to rankle in the twenty-first century.

INFLUENTIAL POLITICAL EVENTS—CANADA

Canadian legislation and government practices that significantly affected First Nations' rights and political status during the late nineteenth and early twentieth centuries included the Indian Act, Sun Dance ban, and treaties.

The Indian Act—1876

After the British Parliament passed the British North American Act of 1867, the newly empowered Canadian Government issued the Indian Act of 1876 which defined who qualified as an Indian and essentially made Indians wards of the state—ostensibly not competent to lead their own lives responsibly. The act applied only to Indians, not to Inuits. The Minister of Indian Affairs and Northern Development was given broad powers in deciding how to administer the law. After its inception, the legislation was periodically revised, with the updated act remaining in effect today. Although first conceived as a device for assimilating First-Nation peoples into Euro-Canadian society, the act and regulations for implementing it often had the opposite effect.

Historically, the Act evolved to protect the small share of Canada's land base which remained to our original peoples.... Statutes dating back to the middle of the last century created the concept of "status" to separate those who were entitled to reside on Indian lands and use their resources from those who were forbidden to do so. Status soon came to have other implications. Status Indians were denied the right to vote, they did not sit on juries, and they were exempt from conscription in time of war (although the percentage of volunteers was higher among Indians than any other group). The attitude that others were the better judges of Indian interests turned the statute into a grab-bag of social engineering over the years. When the Potlatch and Sun Dance were seen as uncivilized, the *Indian Act* was used to ban them. Possession of liquor, on or off the reserve, was punished more harshly under the Act than by general laws. Loitering in pool rooms was forbidden. Indian children were removed from their homes, under the Minister's authority to educate them, and sent to residential schools. Children who were habitually absent from school were "deemed" to be juvenile delinquents.

(Henderson 1996)

Sun Dance Ban

The Sun Dance in Canada received the same treatment as in the United States. From 1882 until the 1940s, agents of the Department of Indian Affairs officially persecuted Sun Dance participants, and in 1895 the flesh-rending and gift-giving aspects of the ritual were outlawed by an amendment to the Indian Act. Nevertheless, such nations as the Plains Cree, Saulteaux, and Blackfoot continued secretly to hold Sun Dances, usually without the prohibited features. In 1951, the government dropped the Indian Act passages that forbade the dance's flesh-tearing and gift-giving features so that the ceremony could be openly celebrated.

The Effect of Canadian Treaties

Whereas the U.S. Government stopped signing treaties with Indian tribes in 1871, the Canadian Government continued negotiating treaties, even as recently as 2000 (Backgrounder 2001).

As the twentieth century advanced, a growing sense of guilt for having exploited the country's aboriginal peoples caused the government and supportive citizens to adopt a far more conciliatory attitude toward First Nations' claims than had been true in the past. This evolving sense of compassion and fairness would be illustrated in the manner courts adjudicated cases involving Indians' rights. By the mid-twentieth century and beyond, jurists adopted a set of principles to serve as guidelines for ruling on treaty issues.

The treaty should be given a fair, large, and liberal interpretation in favor of the Indians. Treaties must be read not according to the technical meaning of their words, but in the sense that they would be naturally understood by the Indians. As the honor of the Crown is always involved, no appearance of "sharp dealings" should be sanctioned. Any ambiguity in the wording should be interpreted as against the drafters and should not be interpreted to the prejudice of the Indians if another interpretation is reasonably possible.

(Backgrounder 2001)

Summary

During the 1876–1949 era the Canadian Government sought to solve "the Indian problem" by assimilating Native Americans into the nation's Euro-Canadian society. Indians and Inuits would be eliminated, but not by killing them off or shipping them elsewhere. Instead, the native peoples would be transformed into "regular Canadians" by eliminating their culture—tribal governments, religious practices, languages, modes of dress, living quarters, and more. But at the same time that aboriginals were supposed to be assimilating, restrictions were imposed on where they lived and how they behaved, so they felt they were being treated as incompetent chattels. In addition, new treaties continued to transfer more Indians' and Inuits' lands to non-Indians. But as the twentieth century progressed, a growing humanitarian concern on the part of the government and general population began to accord the Aboriginal peoples freedoms and rights equal to those enjoyed by non-native Canadians. This pattern of evolving policies was reflected in changes to the Indian Act over the decades and in the increasingly generous interpretation of treaties.

SCHOOLING FOR AMERINDIANS—1877–1920s

As illustrated in Chapter 11, among the devices the U.S. and Canadian governments attempted for assimilating Amerindians into Euro-North-American society, the most drastic was the schooling provided for Native-American children and youths. Policy makers recognized that adult Indians and Inuits were so steeped in their traditional beliefs and ways of life that transforming them into proper Americans and Canadians would be an extremely difficult task, perhaps impossible. Hence, the preferred way of fashioning Indians into acceptable specimens of European culture would be to mold them when they were young, before they had become thoroughly acculturated as Indians. That goal could most readily be accomplished if the young were immersed in a European lifestyle without interference from Amerindian traditions. Thus, removing learners from their home communities and placing them in European-style environments would increase the efficiency of the enculturation effort. Such conversion could best be accomplished in boarding schools, especially ones distant from the students' homes. However, locating children in boarding schools was not always feasible, so other educational settings would also be needed to accomplish the governments' aims. Those additional settings would include reservation day schools and boarding schools, regular public schools, and some remaining mission schools. Because the development of Indian education in the United States was similar to that in Canada, the two nations are discussed together in the following section.

In both the United States and Canada, nearly all educational provisions for Indians and Inuits had four aims: (a) to equip Native Americans with the rudimentary academic abilities of reading, writing, and speaking English, (b) to encourage individualism by weaning Indian youths away from their primary allegiance to the tribe and turning them into workers with the skills of a trade—farmer, carpenter, blacksmith, woodsman, seamstress, and the like—(c) to convert them to Christianity, and (d) to assimilate them into the dominant Euro-American culture (Adams 1995, 21–27).

The task of teaching Christian piety was especially arduous because many of the personal behaviors regarded as vices in Christendom were not viewed as such in Native-American cultures. "In particular, Indian children needed to be taught the moral ideals of charity, chastity, monogamy, respect for the Sabbath, temperance, honesty, self-sacrifice, the importance of pure thoughts and speech—indeed, an almost endless array of personal characteristics important to the formation of 'character'" (Adams 1995, 168).

Off-Reservation Boarding Schools

Off-reservation residential schools housed Indian children and youths in facilities far from their homes so that for months or years the students might not visit their reservations or see family members. The Canadian schools were operated by church denominations, both Protestant and Catholic, and financed by the federal government. Many U.S. Indian boarding schools were also conducted by Christian orders on government funds, and those that were not directly administered by churches usually included a strong measure of Christian teachings.

The model for what would become the standard U.S. Bureau of Indian Affairs' off-reservation boarding school was set by an army officer, Captain Richard H. Pratt, when he established the Carlisle Indian School in November 1878 at an abandoned military post in Pennsylvania.

Pratt's total-immersion curriculum was designed to civilize Amerindians by means of half-day vocational training, half-day English-language academic studies, uniforms, military discipline, mandatory church attendance, and an "outing system" that had students living among farming families in nearby communities. To recruit students for his Carlisle experiment, Pratt traveled to reservations where he urged tribal leaders to permit Indian children to enroll. He met with considerable success, but his endeavor did not gain universal approval among the Indians.

[Pratt left the Sioux reservation] with 60 boys and 24 girls—and left behind parents anguished over the parting and fearful for their children's fate in a far-off place peopled only by whites. [An Indian leader named] Spotted Tail visited Carlisle a few months later and had his worst fears confirmed: his own children, locks shorn, Indian garb discarded in favor of tightly buttoned military dress, engaged in chores no Indian had ever done before. After an angry scene with Pratt, he stormed out with his children and thereafter set his influence against Carlisle.

(Utley 1984, 245)

During Pratt's 25 years at Carlisle, the school enrolled a total of over 5,000 students from a wide variety of tribes. Officials in the U.S. Bureau of Indian Affairs judged the Carlisle model to be such a success that the school became the template for federal off-reservation boarding institutions throughout the early decades of the twentieth century.

After Thomas Jefferson Morgan became commissioner of Indian Affairs in 1889, he made clear that the boarding schools were intended to assimilate and Christianize young Indians.

> When we speak of education of the Indians, we mean that comprehensive system of training and instruction which will convert them into American citizens, put within their reach the blessings which the rest of us enjoy, and enable them to compete successfully with the white man on his own ground and with his own methods.
>
> (Clark Historical Library 2007)

By the 1890s the Bureau of Indian Affairs was ordering pupils in government schools "to attend the churches and Sunday-schools of their respective denominations." Morgan assumed that by staying eight years in a boarding school, Indian youths would receive two years of intensive English language training plus other studies that would equip learners with the equivalent of a sixth-grade public-school education. In 1892, a ninth year was added to boarding school, plus kindergarten classes. Morgan's rules provided for "Sunday morning, afternoon, and evening services, daily morning and evening prayers, and a special Wednesday evening prayer meeting. As for the content of religious instruction, teachers were encouraged to emphasize the Ten Commandments, the beatitudes, and prominent psalms" (Adams 1995, 167–168).

The effectiveness of the Indians' religious education is questionable because of the students' insecure command of English and, in particular, because they were unacquainted with the esoteric meanings of ministers' and priests' verbiage. One Indian woman's recollection of her years of Christian teaching was perhaps typical of most students.

> I remember one preacher especially, although they were all about the same. I couldn't understand a thing he was talking about but had to sit and listen to a long sermon. I hated them and felt like crying. If I nodded my head going to sleep, a teacher would poke me and tell me to be good. It seemed as if this preacher would talk all night. He put a great deal of emotion into his sermons. He would work himself up to a climax talking loud and strong, and then calm down to a whisper, and I would think, "Now he is going to stop." But no, he would start all over and go on and on.
>
> (Helen Sekaquaptewa in Adams 1995, 171)

On one occasion at the Carlisle school, Pratt used an assembly period to collect evidence about how well the school was attracting students to the Christian faith. When he asked how many youths were already Christians, 34 stood up. When he asked how many were "trying" to become Christians, 72 rose. Adams (1995, 172) has noted that "this account was presented as evidence that the school's missionary program was rapidly winning converts. But it is also an indication of the number who remained skeptical of the Christian message; the vast majority had remained seated."

In 1900 there were 25 off-reservation boarding schools in 15 states with a total enrollment of more than 6,000 (Szasz 1999, 10). By the mid-twentieth century, more than 100,000 Indians had attended the 500 off- boarding schools the government had founded (Porterfield 2001).

In Canada, serious efforts to establish permanent residential schools for Indians began during the mid-1800s after the Gradual Civilization Act of 1857 enabled the Canadian Government to finance schools that would teach Euro-Canadian culture, including religion. All such schools were operated by Christian churches—Anglican, Presbyterian, Roman Catholic, and United Church of Canada. The number of schools grew from 54 in 1898 to 81 by 1946. (A detailed account of this era in Canadian history is offered in Chapter 14.)

The total immersion into Euro-American and Euro-Canadian culture, as practiced in residential schools, was intended to assimilate Indians into that culture as thoroughly and quickly as possible. To accomplish this aim, the school staff punished students for displaying any semblance of Indian life. Using a tribal language, even during non-class hours, was forbidden, as were rituals—dances, songs, and quests for visions. The schools' sponsors hoped that the "reformed" youths would return to their villages as emissaries, promoting the assimilation of tribe members into a European-style of life. But too often the result was quite the opposite. The returnees' school experience had alienated too many of the young from their heritage, rendering them unsuitable for either Indian society or Euro-American and Euro-Canadian society.

Reservation Day Schools

Even before the advent of off-reservation schools, day schools on the outskirts of Indian villages had been introduced in the United States. By the 1860s there were already 48 day schools operating in different parts of the country. Parents often preferred a day school to a boarding school, because the day school permitted children to spend their out-of-class hours at home where they participated in traditional tribal life. Thus, day-school pupils could maintain and expand their indigenous language skills and could participate in tribal ceremonies.

Day schools offered only a minimal primary-level education, so that graduates who sought more advanced studies were transferred to boarding schools. Day schools were favored by the government because they were more economical than boarding schools. However, the fact that pupils spent nonschool hours following traditional village lifestyles diminished the likelihood that the young would assimilate into a European version of culture. One government agent in charge of a reservation complained in 1878,

> It must be manifest to all practical minds that to place these wild children under a teacher's care but four or five hours a day, and permit them to spend the other nineteen in the filth and degradation of the village, makes the attempt to educate and civilize them a mere farce.
>
> (Adams 1995, 29)

Ensuring that children enrolled in day schools and attended class regularly was not an easy task. Reservation agents often suspended the distribution of the food and clothing rations to families (as promised in treaties) until the classrooms were filled.

In Canada, church denominations conducted day schools on First Nations reserves. For example, Methodists operated such schools at Berens River, Cross Lake, Oxford House, and Nelson House in Northern Manitoba province from 1867 until 1925. The missionaries' efforts were founded on the assimilationist conviction that "If the government was to build Canadian citizens (or, at least, citizens coming as close to the Euro-Canadian ideal as such 'savages' could come) one of the best ways to begin was with a good solid English Canadian education in the schools" (Gray 1995). Thus, the curriculum consisted of such English schooling subjects as reading, spelling, arithmetic, grammar, history, geography, music, singing, and drawing. In addition, some schools offered advanced students Christian catechism, dictation, mental arithmetic, composition, and Bible scripture. Over the years, great emphasis was placed on Christian religion. After 1900, more stress was placed on hygiene studies, boys were taught agriculture, and girls were instructed in Euro-Canadian domestic science.

Day schools in Canada suffered from the same problems as those in the United States. What was taught in school was at odds with the culture to which pupils returned during out-of-school hours. In addition, attendance was erratic. Schools' annual reports cited a variety of causes of poor attendance—low quality of teaching, students preferring their "wild untutored home life" to the restricted routine of a day school, and children accompanying their parents on hunting and fishing trips.

In both the United States and Canada, missionaries and government officials alike decided that boarding schools accomplished the assimilation task far more efficiently than did day schools.

Reservation Boarding Schools

After founding off-reservation schools, the federal government established similar residential schools on reservations. These institutions were conducted in much the same fashion as the off-reservation facilities—guided by the same aims, teaching the same academic and vocational subject matter, and following the same rules of dress and behavior. Many Indian parents preferred the nearby reservation schools over the distant off-reservation institutions, because tribe members could then easily visit the students. In some cases, families moved their teepees close to the school site so as to be near their children. Before long, Indian-Affairs officials were emphasizing on-reservation education at the expense of the financially hard-pressed off-reservation boarding schools.

Public Schools

Some Indian children had already been attending public schools on their own volition in the 1870s and 1880s, but only in 1891 did the U.S. government attempt to promote that option by contracting with school systems to accept Indian students at $10 per capita. Over its first decade or so, the public-school initiative achieved no more than "indifferent results." But gradually more children enrolled. By 1930, of all the Indian children in schools, 53 percent attended public schools, 39 percent were in federal schools, and 9 percent in private institutions. That trend continued over the next 40 years. By 1970, public schooling for Indians had tripled "from 38,000 in 1930 to 129,000, which meant that 65 percent of all Indian children in school were attending public school. Those who attended federal schools in 1970 accounted for only 26 percent of Indian children in school, or a total of about 51,000" (Szasz 1999, 89).

It is true that public schools did not impose on students the amount of Christian doctrine and practices found in boarding and day schools operated by church denominations. However, Indian children were still exposed to the vestiges of Christian practices found in virtually all U.S. and Canadian public schools, such as daily opening exercises that featured prayers and Bible readings, the Ten Commandments and other Bible verses posted in classrooms, prayers blessing graduation exercises and athletic events, hymns sung on solemn occasions, pictures of Jesus or the Madonna in the hallways, and pageants at Christmas and Easter. Furthermore, Indian pupils were urged—if not outrightly ordered—to avoid tribal language and speak only English.

Lingering Mission Schools

By the early years of the twentieth century, the church-sponsored mission schools, which had preceded government-financed boarding and day schools, were still found in small numbers on some reservations. Such schools remained, even as boarding and public schools expanded, because they were long-established institutions that had won the respect of tribe members, many of whom had attended them during their youth. Some missionary schools continued to receive federal support, particularly whenever Congress felt less inclined to provide the large sums of money needed to establish and operate government schools.

Summary

In the United States, the 1876–1920 era witnessed the evolution of five kinds of schools attended by Indians—reservation day schools, off-reservation boarding schools, on-reservation boarding schools, public schools, and long-established mission schools supported by Christian churches. A similar series of schools developed in Canada during those years, with the same aim as schools in the United States—to assimilate Indians into the dominant Euro-North-American culture.

A NEW DIRECTION IN THE UNITED STATES

By the mid-1920s, humanitarian reformers were aiming attacks at U.S. federal boarding schools' harsh discipline, overcrowding, widespread disease, unhealthy meals, and unyielding Euro-American immersion practices. Finally, the American public's growing dissatisfaction over the Indians' plight led Secretary of the Interior Hubert Work to commission a study titled *The Problem of Indian Administration,* also known as the *Meriam Report* after its main author, Lewis Meriam. The report caustically criticized the residential schools' relentless total immersion into Euro-American culture as a means of erasing Indians' traditional ways of life and assimilating them into the white man's world. The new education urged by the Meriam document would not abandon Euro-American content in the curriculum but would add important elements of Indian life, thereby transforming learning fare into a type of multiculturalism. Such an educational philosophy was heavily influenced by the burgeoning Progressive Education movement, with its child-centered focus as espoused by philosopher John Dewey and his followers.

The Meriam critique brought progressive-education leadership to the U.S. Bureau of Indian Affairs in the person of W. Carson Ryan, principal author of the Meriam Report's education section. He assumed the post of director of education in July 1930. In the report, Ryan had assailed the boarding schools' (a) restricted curriculum that ignored differences among tribal cultures and individual children, (b) requiring children to spend only a half day in studies and the remainder of the day working in fields and shops, and (c) enrolling pre-adolescent children rather than reserving residential schools for adolescents. It was during Ryan's five-year tenure as director that the government began to close down residential schools, replacing them with community day schools that prepared students with English-language facility and other basic academic skills plus training for vocations available in their communities. Subject matter relevant to the local tribe's culture was introduced, and courses unrelated to Indians' lives were gradually eliminated, such as English literary classics, algebra, geometry, and ancient history (Szasz 1999, 32). The entrenched Indian-Affairs bureaucracy, coupled with the economic depression, made changing the Indian education system slow and difficult. Nevertheless, a new direction had been charted that accorded greater recognition of Indians' needs and culture. When Ryan left the post of education director, the Bureau of Indian

Affairs was en route to better times for Amerindian students. During Ryan's years of service, President Herbert Hoover's administration—embarrassed at the Meriam reports' revelations—nearly doubled spending on Indian schools between 1928 and 1933.

When Franklin Delano Roosevelt became the U.S. president in 1933, he launched the New Deal, a massive government effort to save the nation from economic ruin. On April 21, 1933, John Collier became Commissioner of Indian Affairs, and in 1936 he appointed Willard Beatty as the bureau's director of education, a position Beatty would hold until 1952. Both Collier and Beatty were progressive-education enthusiasts and admirers of Indian culture. Both rejected the bureau's traditional strict assimilation policy. Both endorsed Ryan's concept of education for Amerindians, and they set about implementing that view with vigor and growing success. Collier's innovations included employing anthropologists to help plan progressive-education schooling for Indians by adjusting educational goals, teaching methods, and materials to tribal traditions as part of the Indian New Deal.

The campaign to open community schools and close boarding schools advanced gradually throughout the 1930s. The number of community schools doubled between 1933 and 1941—from 132 to 266 that enrolled 15,789 pupils. By 1941 there were still 49 boarding schools with 14,000 students, yet thousands of Indian children in remote regions lacked a school to attend (Szasz 1999, 61).

CONCLUSION

Over the period 1876 through 1949, the formal education of Indians in the United States progressed from the sole aim of assimilating Native Americans into Euro-American Christian culture to a multicultural goal after 1930 that combined European tradition with Indian tribal beliefs and practices. Across the decades, the role of public schools in Indian education expanded as the role of separate boarding and day schools for Indians declined.

The nature of Indian schooling in Canada during the same three-quarters of a century has been summarized by Brian Titley as follows:

> From Confederation (1867) until the end of the Second World War, Indian children were educated in isolation from other Canadians. The schooling provided aimed to 'Christianize' and 'civilize' them. In fact, the missionaries involved in this work favored boarding schools whenever possible as they avoided the "retarding and retrogressive influences of the home upon the pupils." Indian intellectual potential was regarded as quite limited and both church and state officials maintained a condescending attitude towards native cultural traditions. The Indians were treated as conquered people and the Indian Affairs Department was characterized by the indifference and arrogance associated with colonial administrations.
>
> (Titley 1980)

PART III

MODERN TIMES—1950–2007

Over the past half century, Native Americans in Canada and the United States have made significant progress toward winning deserved rights and obtaining reparations for at least a portion of the losses their peoples suffered after European settlers arrived in North America more than four centuries ago. Much of that progress has been due to increased political acumen and activism among present-day members of indigenous tribes. In addition, Indians' political awakening has been supported by a growing sense of guilt among non-native Canadians and U.S. Americans who believe steps should be taken to repair damage wrought by "white folks" in the past. Key events of that half century of progress are chronicled in Chapter 13: Political Triumphs. Included among those accomplishments is a cultural-renewal movement to restore and revitalize original religious beliefs and practices.

A second religious facet of the revival movement has been the attempt by Native North Americans to be compensated for physical, psychological, and cultural harm done to thousands of Indian children and youths who had been forced to attend the boarding schools conducted by Christian orders. The nature and success of that attempt in Canada, along with the potential for such an effort in the United States, are described in Chapter 14: Seeking Reparations.

Finally, the book closes with speculation about what the future may hold for North American Indians and their religions—Chapter 15: The Path Ahead.

· 13 ·

Political Triumphs

Before the mid-twentieth century, Native North Americans were ill equipped to successfully press for their rights when dealing with Euro-Americans and Euro-Canadians. During peaceful negotiations, the Indians had been disadvantaged by their insecure grasp of the English, Spanish, or French language, by their lack of written records, and by the absence of large intertribal political organizations that could represent their interests. During armed conflicts, the Indians' bows and arrows had been no match for the pistols, rifles, and cannons of the foreign invaders. Custer's last stand at the Little Bighorn was an exception to the typical battle outcome. Usually it was Euro-North-American armies and settlers that subdued and slaughtered the Indians rather than the other way around.

However, sociopolitical conditions changed as the twentieth century advanced. Particularly in the decades following World War II, native leaders acquired the education and political savvy needed to successfully navigate the channels of the U.S. and Canadian legal systems. They also developed mass political organizations to represent their cause, adopted effective publicity tactics, and engaged lobbyists to impress legislators with their grievances. The purpose of this chapter is to identify typical postwar Indian political organizations that adopted such strategies and to illustrate some of their noteworthy successes.

Readers are better prepared to understand the actions of Indian organizations as described throughout this chapter if they recognize the conception of power on which that description is based. Thus, the chapter opens with what is meant by *political power*, then continues with the development of Indian political groups and the results of their efforts.

A VIEW OF POLITICAL POWER

In this chapter, the expressions *politics* and *political* refer to the exercise of power, influence, and control among groups. Such power exists in *amount, form,* and *intent.*

The amount of a group's power is shown by how much a particular group's actions affect the behavior of another group. If Group A's behavior changes markedly because of Group B's acts, then Group B has great power over Group A. For example, Euro–North Americans' destruction of the buffalo herds in the middle and late nineteenth century had a devastating effect on the lives of Great Plains Indians. And the Spanish introduction of horses in the Southwest markedly changed the lives of Indians throughout the Great Plains and Plateau.

In contrast, if Group A's behavior does not change when Group B acts, then Group B has no power, influence, or control over Group A. For instance, the Spanish missions of the American Southwest apparently effected no change in the lifestyles of the Iroquois of the Great Lakes region.

Power can assume numerous forms—physical, psychological, legalistic, social. Warfare is a physical way to exercise power. Altering people's behavior by threatening them with excommunication from a religious order is a psychological version of power. Signing a treaty that transfers Indian lands into the hands of a Euro-North-American government is a legalistic form. Organizing a mass demonstration to influence legislators' votes on a bill that would recognize Indian belief systems as legitimate religions is a social type of power.

Attempts to exercise power are intended to achieve a group's desired outcome. Or the aim may be to achieve a goal of the group's leaders, but most members of the group are not aware of the leaders' true intent. Frequently a power strategy not only achieves a desired aim but also yields unexpected, unwelcome results in the form of collateral damage. For example, when the "civilized tribes" were ordered to leave their homeland in the Southeast and travel to the Oklahoma territory as part of President Andrew Jackson's removal policy in the 1830s, an estimated 3,500 Cherokees died in Alabama on what became known as the Trail of Tears. Those deaths were not what Euro-Americans with any compassion at all had intended for the Indians.

NATIVE-NORTH-AMERICAN POLITICAL ORGANIZATIONS

After the middle of the twentieth century, the number of North-American Indian associations expanded at an accelerating pace so that by 2007 there were hundreds across the continent. Their central goal was to promote the welfare of indigenous peoples through group action. The associations were of various types—general, scholastic, occupational, social-service, regional, and historical/cultural.

General Associations

The term *general associations* applies to organizations that enroll members from as many tribes and walks of life as possible in order to present a massive united front in nationwide political endeavors. The oldest and largest of those associations in the United States is the National Congress of American Indians (NCAI), founded in 1944 to take action against the U.S. Government's policies aimed at terminating Indians' treaty status in order to integrate native peoples into Euro-American society. From the original 100 individual NCAI members in 1944, the organization grew to a membership of 250 tribes by the early twenty-first century. The agenda of activities in 2007 included

- Protection of programs and services to benefit Indian families, specifically targeting Indian youth and elders.
- Promotion and support of Indian education, including Head Start, elementary, postsecondary, and adult education.
- Enhancement of Indian health care, including prevention of juvenile substance abuse, HIV-AIDS, and other major diseases.
- Support of environmental protection and natural resources management.
- Protection of Indian cultural resources and religious-freedom rights.
- Promotion of the rights of Indian economic opportunity both on and off reservations, including securing programs to provide incentives for economic development and the attraction of private capital to Indian country.
- Protection of the rights of all Indian people to decent, safe, and affordable housing. (Our history 2007)

The leading general association in Canada is the Assembly of First Nations, a nationwide coalition of 630 Indian communities. Originally the Assembly was named the National Indian Brotherhood when founded in 1968 to confront the federal government over its plan to assimilate Indians into mainstream Canadian society and remove First Nations from the Canadian Constitution. In 1982 the group's structure was improved and the name changed to Assembly of First Nations. By the twenty-first century, the Assembly's activities included efforts to protect aboriginals' rights and treaties, and to foster Native Peoples' economic development, education, languages and literacy, health, housing, social development, justice, taxation, land claims, environments, "and a whole array of issues that are of common concern which arise from time to time" (Assembly of First Nations 2007).

Scholastic Organizations

Amerindian students in many colleges, universities, and public schools have formed clubs or societies dedicated to Native Peoples' interests. A typical example of such groups is the Whitman College (Walla Walla, Washington) American Indian Association, composed of Indian and non-Indian students "dedicated to educating ourselves and others by utilizing our individual experiences and personal knowledge in order to preserve our Indian culture, both on this campus and abroad. We share the diverse traditions of our people and educate other interested members of the student body through informative native entertainment, speakers and educators" (Our mission statement 2007).

Some student organizations are nationwide bodies that have chapters in universities across the continent. An example of a typical chapter's purpose is reflected in the University of Maine's mission statement for its branch of the national Native American Law Students Association (NALSA). The Maine chapter's "native and non-native students [are] committed to education and reform with regard to issues affecting Native Americans. Working both locally and nationally, NALSA provides support for other native organizations and works with Maine Tribes to improve existing policies and legislation" (Mission statement 2007).

Occupational Groups

A host of Indian professional organizations have been founded to enhance the welfare of Native-American aircraft pilots, bankers, business operators, contractors, court judges, educators, engineers, finance officers, historic-tribal-information officers, law-enforcement officers, journalists, physicians, scientists, and more.

Occupational organizations typically offer three classes of membership, as illustrated by the Minnnesota American Indian Bar Association that enrolls American Indian attorneys, law students, and officers of tribal courts as well as non-Indian attorneys and law students who are interested in Indian law. The three membership categories are those of

> *Regular members*—persons enrolled in any Indian tribe, band, or persons who are recognized by their Indian community as being Indian. Regular members must also be members in good standing of a state bar.
>
> *Associate members*—persons enrolled in any Indian tribe, band, or persons who are recognized by their Indian community as being Indian. Associate members must also be law students or law school graduates not yet admitted to the bar or an officer of a tribal court.
>
> *Special members*—persons not enrolled members of any Indian tribe or band, and not recognized by an Indian community as being Indian. Special members must be members of a state bar, law school graduates not yet admitted to the bar, or law school students interested in Indian law (Membership Categories 2007).

Social-Service Organizations

Many Indian organizations are dedicated to improving the health and living conditions of Native Peoples of different age levels and health status. The following are examples of such groups: British Columbia Aboriginal Network on Disability Society, Canadian Aboriginal AIDS Network, Institute for Aboriginal Health (Canada), National Center for American Indian and Alaska Native Mental Health Research, National Indian Child Welfare Association, National Society for American Indian Elderly, and the Native American Reburial Restoration Committee.

Regional Bodies

Coalitions of tribes in a particular geographic setting include such organizations as Eastern Nations, Midwest Treaty Network, North Carolina Indian Tribal Organizations, Union of British Columbia Indian Chiefs, United South and Eastern Tribes, and Virginia Indian Tribal Alliance for Life.

Historical/Cultural Endeavors

Recent decades have witnessed an increase of groups dedicated primarily to recovering and maintaining Indian history and culture.

One such body is the Oklahoma-based Red Earth organization that began in 1978 as a museum (Center for the American Indian), then merged with the Red Earth Festival Association in 1992 to pursue the goal of disseminating information about Oklahoma's American Indian tribes, past and present.

Similar organizations in other parts of the continent include the Native American Cultural Center (Rochester, New York), Indian Arts and Crafts Association (Albuquerque, New Mexico), Lenni Lenape Historical Society and Museum of Indian Culture (Allentown, Pennsylvania), and the National Museum of the American Indian at the Smithsonian Institute (Washington, DC).

A highly specialized cultural association is the Keepers of the Sacred Tradition of Pipemakers, founded in 1996 for the purpose of "preserving the Sacred Tradition of the pipe, allowing free access to the great pipestone quarries [in Minnesota] for all Native Americans, [and supporting] the art of pipemaking" (Keepers 2006). Another specialized group is the California Indian Basketweavers Association whose mission is to perpetuate California Indian basketweaving traditions by providing opportunities for California Indians to study traditional basketry techniques and showcase their work.

Summary

Over the past six decades, modern-day descendents of North America's indigenous peoples developed the educational and organizational skills that equipped them to found hundreds of associations dedicated to the welfare of the continent's Indians and Inuits. The descendents have been joined by concerned non-Indians to mount political campaigns aimed at correcting what they consider unjust treatment of Native North Americans by European intruders since the early 1600s. Some results of those campaigns are described in the following pages.

INDIANS' POLITICAL ACCOMPLISHMENTS

Five channels through which Indians and Inuits were able to advance their welfare between the mid-twentieth century and 2007 have been those of (a) publicizing confrontations with oppressors, (b) recapturing indigenous culture, (c) revitalizing Amerindian religions, (d) promoting economic development, and (e) seeking the support of federal courts.

Publicizing Confrontations

One way Native North Americans have drawn public attention to their grievances is through public demonstrations widely publicized in the press. Here are three examples.

THE TRAIL OF BROKEN TREATIES

In October 1972, representatives of the American Indian Movement issued a detailed twenty-item manifesto demanding a "new relationship" between the U.S. government and the country's Indian nations. The issues on which the manifesto focused included (a) the Government's obligation to honor past treaties and create new ones, (b) the return of Indian lands that had unlawfully been confiscated in the past, (c) the consolidation of Indian land, water, and economic resources, (d) Indian nations' power to control their own people, (e) federal protection for offenses against Indians, (f) replacing the Office of Indian Affairs with an Office of Federal Indian Relations and Community Reconstruction, and (g) the protection of Indians' religions and cultural integrity. This final item was explained as follows:

> The Congress shall proclaim its insistence that the religious freedom and cultural integrity of Indian people shall be respected and protected throughout the United States, and provide that Indian religion and culture, even in regenerating or renaissance or developing stages, or when manifested in the personal character and treatment of one's own body, shall not be interfered with, disrespected, or denied. (No Indian shall be forced to cut their hair by any institution or public agency or official, including military authorities or prison regulation, for example.) It should be an insistence by Congress that implies strict penalty for its violation.
>
> (American Indian Movement 1972)

To publicize the manifesto, 800 Indians from 25 states formed a caravan that traveled from the West Coast by auto, bus, and van to arrive in Washington, DC, in November, one week before the presidential election. Upon their arrival, a group of the protestors commandeered the offices of the Bureau of Indian Affairs. Police surrounded the building and snipers took positions on nearby buildings as negotiations between federal officials and Indian representatives finally ended the siege.

> The occupation was reported on the front pages of the *New York Times* and many other newspapers. The publicity drew attention to Indian rights and provided a platform for the protesters to present their "20-Point Program" to increase the role of tribes in the formation of Indian programs. The "self-determination" federal legislation of the mid-1970s that shifted more local control to recognized tribes should be understood against the backdrop of the Red Power protest era, especially the Trail of Broken Treaties and the protests it inspired.
>
> (Trail of Broken Treaties 2007)

THE SIEGE AT WOUNDED KNEE

In February 1973, American Indian activists assembled at the village of Wounded Knee on the Sioux Indian Pine Ridge Reservation in South Dakota. Their purpose was to demand that the U.S. Government (a) enforce the 1868 Fort Laramie Treaty, which guaranteed the protection of the Sioux nation's territories and sovereignty, (b) investigate corruption within the Bureau of Indian Affairs, and (c) conduct honest elections on the local Pine Ridge Reservation (Means 1998).

The demonstrators selected Wounded Knee as the location for voicing their complaints because the site was famous as the place in which U.S. Army Seventh Cavalry troops had massacred 300 Lakota Sioux men, women, and children in 1890. The 1973 siege lasted 71 days as the Indians barricaded themselves in the town, surrounded by U.S. armed forces that exchanged intermittent rifle fire with the demonstrators. By the end of the siege, two Indians (one a Vietnam War veteran) had been killed and 15 wounded by government snipers. More than 600 protestors were arrested on federal charges but none was ever prosecuted.

One of the participants in the siege, an Oglala Lakota Sioux named Russell Means, later wrote that

> The media came from all over the globe to report on this armed insurrection by a group of people the U.S. government would have the world believe were safely pacified and out of sight, out of mind. All three major broadcast networks arrived, at times with three entire crews each, to cover the events outside and inside Wounded Knee. The added impact of the print media inside the "Knee" and the intense media coverage in general were some of the major reasons we did not suffer the same fate

as our ancestors. During the Seventies, Wounded Knee proved to be the third most photographed event of that era, surpassed only by the Vietnam War and Watergate. In a poll taken among Americans during the siege, 93 percent were aware of the events at Wounded Knee.

(Means 1998)

THE LEWIS AND CLARK BICENTENNIAL

In 2004, a key event among the celebrations commemorating Lewis and Clark's 1804 expedition through the U.S. Northwest was a reenactment of the trip. A group of celebrators retraced the Lewis and Clark route, stopping periodically along the way to conduct ceremonies at locations that were significant during the original journey. The trip was well publicized both nationally and in communities along the course. Groups of Indian activists accepted the commemorative journey as an opportunity to broadcast their distress over the ill treatment Native Americans had suffered ever since Lewis and Clark opened the West to exploitation by Euro-Americans. At the periodic ceremonies along the route, protesters challenged the right of the travelers to conduct such a trip, and they urged the celebrants to abandon the journey. The encounters were covered both locally and nationally by radio, television, and newspapers; and a United Nations periodical, *UN Observer and International Report,* published an article titled, "Lewis and Clark opened the door to the holocaust of the West."

Indians along the Lewis and Clark trail were not all of one mind. Some viewed the journey as a suitable way to recognize an influential historical event, while others considered it another Euro-American affront to Native Americans.

A surprise at the Ft. Pierre, SD Lewis and Clark Reenactment awaited the group of protesters when an elder of their own people came out dressed in traditional regalia and asked the men in the group if they came to shoot him. The elder said the protestors were not invited there and not wanted there. [The] lead organizer for the youth group responded that the protesters were not there to harm to anyone, they were there to engage in a peaceful protest and had a right to express themselves.

(White Plume 2004)

Recapturing Indigenous Culture

The question of how much of Indian culture—including culture's religious components—has been destroyed over the centuries cannot be answered with any precision. This is because individual Indians and Inuits have differed in the sorts of native cultural elements they have abandoned and in the aspects of Euro-American and Euro-Canadian life they have embraced. A large portion of Indian culture is related to indigenous religious beliefs and practices. Deities and supernatural forces are intimate elements of Amerindian celebrations, rituals, dances, chants, stories, societies, revered places, amulets, and art objects. In the confrontation between Indian and Christian worlds after 1600, many of those elements were discouraged, cast into disrepute, or distorted. During this cultural-exchange process, the extent to which Native North Americans adopted Christian culture ranged across the entire scale from Amerindians who became thoroughly doctrinaire Catholics and Protestants and cast off all vestiges of Indian belief systems to Amerindians who rejected all of Christianity and adhered solely to tribal traditions. In between those two extremes were many Indians who adopted certain features of Christianity while retaining preferred aspects of indigenous religions, a process that resulted in a diversity of syncretic belief systems.

From the mid-twentieth century to the present day, Indians have developed resources for recapturing their ancestral traditions, including such resources as powwows, Internet web sites, study centers, and cultural societies.

POWWOWS

A powwow is a celebration lasting several days in a temporary arena that is typically on a reservation campground. Events include Indian ceremonial dances and songs, sports contests, processions honoring deceased tribe members, and the distribution of food rations to families. Powwows are attended by local Indians, ones from other tribes who camp adjacent to the arena during the festivities, and non-Indian spectators.

The money—for prizes, preparing the camp, buying the rations, paying for the [master of ceremonies] and the "drums" (groups of singers around a large bass drum) who provide the music for the dances and honoring-songs—is taken from tribal funds or the proceeds from leases and spectators' fees....At the powwow, one is immersed in a crowd of Indians, hears the drumbeats and the distinctive Plains singing, and sees the brilliant Grass Dance costumes. For three days, one feels totally Indian through and through.

(Kehoe 1981, 329)

INTERNET WEB SITES

The richest present-day source of information about efforts to recapture, maintain, and develop Native American culture is the Internet. For example, entering the words *American Indian languages* into the search engine Google generates 40 million web sources. Entering *American Indian Art* identifies 26 million web sites, and *American Indian ceremonies* elicits 1.2 million. Entering *American Indian religions* reveals 23 million sources.

To discover the wealth of information available on just one of the language sites, searchers can open the page titled *Native Languages of the Americas* and find the following: (a) an alphabetical list and description of more than 1,000 American Indian tribes, (b) a chart of tribal names in both their original languages and their current versions, (c) an explanation of relationships among languages, and (d) vocabulary lists from various tribes. A similar site, labeled *Native American Languages,* lists a host of web links under the headings (a) language publications, (b) language statistics, (c) Indian language issues and institutions, (d) discussion sites, (e) maps and charts, and (f) Indian language endangerment and revitalization.

STUDY CENTERS

At an accelerating pace, institutions have been founded in recent decades to disseminate information about North-American Indians and their ways of life. Many such endeavors that are sponsored by universities and museums include research efforts aimed at discovering the history of Indian and Inuit bands and investigating current Native-North-American issues. The web page for the *Guide to Native American Studies Programs* lists more than 500 programs at higher education institutions in Canada and the United States.

Study centers' Internet web sites typically provide information about the groups' aims and activities. For example, the web page of the Alaska Native Language Center, founded in 1972 by state legislation, describes the program of documenting and cultivating the state's 20 Native languages. The organization is portrayed as

> the major center in the United States for the study of Eskimo and Northern Athabascan languages [and] publishes its research in story collections, dictionaries, grammars, and research papers. The center houses an archival collection of more than 10,000 items, virtually everything written in or about Alaska Native languages, including copies of most of the earliest linguistic documentation, along with significant collections about related languages outside Alaska. Staff members provide materials for bilingual teachers and other language workers throughout the state, assist social scientists and others who work with Native languages, and provide consulting and training services to teachers, school districts, and state agencies involved in bilingual education.
>
> (ANLC Mission 2007)

A highly specialized research facility is the First Nations Research Site sponsored jointly by the First Nations Child & Family Caring Society of Canada and the Centre of Excellence for Child Welfare, located in Winnipeg, Manitoba. Three of the site's goals are:

- To assist in building and strengthening research capacity among First Nations individuals, agencies, and organizations engaged in child welfare research, policy and/or practice;
- To build a pool of resources and networks from, within, and among academic and private First Nations researchers;

- To promote the development of techniques for evaluating the programs and services delivered to First Nations children, families, and communities (FNRS Activities 2007).

Among the scores of colleges and universities that offer Native-American studies, a typical program leading to a college degree is the bachelor of science specialization in American Indian affairs at Arizona State University, designed to furnish students "a broad knowledge of American Indian nations and peoples, with particular emphasis on Southwestern American Indian nations [including]...knowledge pertaining to American Indian culture, history, law, literature, language, art and government." Students choose their classes from among more than 30 Indian-studies courses, such as (a) Native American religious traditions, (b) American Indian languages and cultures, (c) crime in Indian country, (d) continuity and change in kinship systems, (e) women and literature, (f) Indian sovereignty and the courts, and (g) Native American art of the Southwest (American Indian studies 2007).

Arizona State also includes an administrative unit that focuses on schooling for Indians—the Center for Indian Education, established in 1959 as an interdisciplinary research and service organization to investigate American Indian and Alaska Native policies "that contribute to the quality of scholarship and effective practices in education, professional training, and tribal capacity-building." Since 1961, the center has published the *Journal of American Indian Education* (CIE mission 2007).

Some university programs emphasize research skills. An example is the Simon Fraser University (British Columbia) set of courses leading to a Certificate in First Nations Studies Research. Students "explore the history and pre-history, culture, language, and contemporary situation of Canadian native peoples, and [they] acquire basic research skills in Native issues. Particular emphasis is on the study of Native people in the interior of British Columbia. ...The certificate is especially suitable for Native individuals who wish to gain proficiency in studying Native issues and to acquire social research skills to use in their communities and nations" (Certificate in First Nations 2007).

Other opportunities for students to develop research proficiency are provided by short-term workshops or internships. For instance, the Smithsonian Institution in Washington, DC, offers 10-week internships for Native American college students to study Indian topics under the supervision of Smithsonian staff members.

In summary, opportunities for both Indians and non-Indians to learn about past and present Native North Americans' lifestyles and concerns have burgeoned over the past half century so that hundreds of places to study such matters are available today.

Revitalizing Amerindian Religions

In 1978, by dint of having successfully lobbied members of Congress, Indians in the United States achieved a goal that Native Americans had pursued for nearly four centuries—they won legal recognition of Indian belief systems as legitimate religions equal in public status to Christianity. The 1978 law, along with its later amendments, is known as the American Indian Religious Freedom Act. The legislation not only permitted Indians to continue traditional religious practices without government interference or censure, but it also stimulated interest in religious alternatives that had been popular in the distant past. Particularly in the nineteenth century, novel variants of Indian religions had occasionally emerged in Native-North-American communities, variants that often incorporated elements of Christian belief and practice. Three such belief systems were the Peyote Sect, the Ghost Dance, and the Shaker Church.

THE PEYOTE SECT

The substance *peyote* is derived from the tops of a small, spineless carrot-shaped cactus that contains mescaline, an alkaloid drug which creates hallucinations when ingested. Before the arrival of Europeans in North America, peyote served in Mexico as a medicine and a narcotic that induced supernatural visions. By the mid-nineteenth century, the use of peyote had moved north into the Great Plains where, around 1885, it assumed the form of a religion among the Kiowa and Comanche tribes in Oklahoma. During the 1890s, the religion spread as far north as Canada.

In its travel from Mexico into the Great Plains, peyotism morphed into various forms, with adherents' attempt to generate a vision taking precedence over medical treatment. Today, as in the past, the person sponsoring a peyote session

is responsible for the expense involved and for supplying the peyote; he selects the leader of the ceremony, who is assisted by a drummer and a fire tender. The leader's regalia include a staff, a gourd rattle, an eagle-bone whistle, a drum partly filled with water, and cedar incense....In some tribes even Christian elements entered, including Bible reading.
(Lowie 1954, 183)

Christian missionaries were appalled at peyotism. In the 1990s, John Jasper Methvin, superintendent of a Methodist Choctaw school in Oklahoma, wrote that peyote ceremonies were "a drug habit under the guise of religion....A dozen maniac asylums turned loose together would hardly be equal to the scenes enacted by these tribes...in their crazy, superstitious worship of the supposed Messiah as they dance day and night through heat and cold" (Milner & O'Neal 1985, 71).

The rite characteristically, but not always, takes place in a teepee around a crescent-shaped, earthen altar mound and a sacred fire. The all-night ceremony usually commences about 8 PM Saturday and is led by a peyote "chief." The services include prayer, singing, sacramental eating of peyote, water rites, and contemplation; they conclude with a communion breakfast on Sunday morning. The way of life is called the Peyote Road and enjoins brotherly love, family care, self-support through steady work, and avoidance of alcohol.

(Native American Church 1994)

Across the decades, peyote acquired the reputation—perhaps undeserved —of being a dangerous narcotic, so that frequent attempts were made to ban its use. In 1888 federal agents outlawed the use of peyote, as did 15 states over the following years. However, after the peyote movement assumed the organized form of an intertribal Native American Church in 1918, membership increased (an estimated 250,000 adherents by the late twentieth century) and the movement's political effectiveness solidified. Consequently, the U.S. Congress in 1994 amended the American Indian Religious Freedom Act to protect the ceremonial use of peyote.

[The] use, possession, or transportation of peyote by an Indian for bona fide traditional ceremonial purposes in connection with the practice of a traditional Indian religion is lawful, and shall not be prohibited by the United States or any state. No Indian shall be penalized or discriminated against on the basis of such use, possession, or transportation.

(Public law 103–344, 1994)

THE GHOST DANCE

Around 1870, a Paviotso Indian in Nevada envisioned the tribe's ancestors, in the form of ghosts, returning to the world to restore the old ways of life. From messages he received while in a trance state, he preached that once again there would be plenty of game to hunt and ancient rites to celebrate. Nearly two decades later, this theme was adopted and embellished by one of the seer's young kinsman, Wovoka (Cutter), a Piute [Great Basin] who acquired a reputation as a medicine man in 1888 when he fell seriously ill during an eclipse of the sun. While in a feverish state of delirium, Wovoka was directed by the Supreme Spirit to teach his tribesmen a dance that would reunite them with the dead. In addition to creating the Ghost Dance, Wovoka offered advice about ethical behavior that included rejecting violence and establishing peaceful relations with whites.

The Ghost Dance religion soon spread eastward to the warlike plains tribes who discarded the peace policy and, instead, changed the Ghost Dance into a stimulator of battles against Euro-Americans. Among innovations added by the Sioux was a Ghost Dance shirt that ostensibly rendered wearers invulnerable to physical harm. That assumption was tested during the 1890 massacre at Wounded Knee, when men in Ghost Dance shirts fared no better than the rest of the victims who were slain by U.S. cavalrymen. The tragedy of Wounded Knee spelled the end of the Ghost Dance as a cohesive religious movement, although vestiges of Wovoka's teachings were adopted by other sects, including by peyotism, and are still evident today. For example, the

Pawnee [Great Plains] chose a Ghost Dance form of painted teepee for peyote meetings and a variation of the drum and rattle that accompanied the Ghost Dance (Erowid & Trout 2002).

THE SHAKER CHURCH

Many individuals appear to meld Indian and Christian religious components to form a mingled belief system which, in North America's modern-day tolerant social climate, they can publicly pursue with little or no censure. An example is the Salish Shaker Church of the American Northwest, a religious movement that has no connection with the Shakers of New England but is so named because of its adherents' trembling during the sect's services. According to Shaker doctrine, in 1881 a Squaxin named Squsachtun (a.k.a. John Slocum) died at Sheldon, Washington.

> His relations went to Olympia in a canoe to buy a casket, and while they were gone he came back to life again. He told the people that he had died and gone to the gates of heaven, but could not get in because he had not lived the right kind of Christian life, so that he was sent back to be reborn. He was told to spend his life as a preacher among the Indians and found the Shaker Church.
>
> (Smith 1954, 119)

Christian elements among Salish Shaker practices include praying, reading from the Bible, saying grace at meals, and evoking Jesus's name in prayers, preaching, and testimonials. The style of Shaker wooden church buildings with a steeple at the front end is reminiscent of New England. "Ethics have a Puritan cast, and good Shakers refrain from drinking alcohol and smoking" (Smith 1954, 119). The Indian components of Shakerism came from traditional Salish shamanism—such features as the winter spirit dances and the ceremonies in which novices attempted to discover the song of the spirit that would become their lifelong protector. When Squsachtun introduced his novel religious faith, he replaced the Bible with his own revelation. This act and other "heresies" infuriated the local reservation's Christian missionary. Squsachtun and several of his converts were arrested until a friendly attorney "advised them that since they held land under the Dawes Act and voted and paid taxes, they were entitled to all rights of citizens, including freedom of religion" (Kehoe 1981, 440).

During the early decades of the twentieth century the Shaker Church spread north to Vancouver Island and south to California, where it continues today.

SUMMARY

In the twenty-first century, more than ever before, individuals who traced their spiritual heritage back to aboriginal America could openly engage in traditional religious practices. As one Canadian explained in a newspaper article,

Rather than going to church, I attend a sweat lodge; rather than accepting bread and toast [sic] from the Holy Priest, I smoke a ceremonial pipe to come into communion with the Great Spirit; and rather than kneeling with my hands placed together in prayer, I let sweetgrass be feathered over my entire being for spiritual cleansing and allow the smoke to carry my prayers into the heavens. I am a Mi'kmaq, and this is how we pray.

(Augustine 2000)

Promoting Economic Development

As described in Chapters 11 and 12, U.S. and Canadian government policies have shuttled back and forth between (a) relating to Indian tribes as sovereign nations and thereby permitting Indians to manage their own affairs, and (b) supervising Indians' and Inuits' lives and attempting to assimilate them into Euro-North-American society. It has long been apparent that these rather fumbling efforts left a large proportion of indigenous peoples in a condition of poverty, underemployment, and cultural confusion. However, in recent decades—principally since 1970 in the United States—significant steps have been taken toward treating Indian tribes as sovereign nations that are trusted to guide their own destinies. Thus, on more than 275 Indian reservations in the United States and on 600 reserves in Canada, leaders of indigenous bands have gained increasing freedom to manage their own affairs—governance, economic growth, and cultural renewal.

Tribes' efforts at economic development have varied greatly from one reservation to another, resulting in a mixture of successes and failures. Studies of Indians' projects by Stephen Cornell and Joseph Peggs Kalt led the authors to conclude that there is no single formula for guiding indigenous economic development because the conditions on one reservation that affect success can differ markedly from conditions on other reservations. However, from studying different tribes' ventures, Cornell and Kalt generated the following advice.

The first [...requirement for success] is sovereignty...the power [for Indian nations] to make decisions about their own futures. . . . As sovereignty rises, so do the chances of successful development. . . . The central determinant of political sovereignty is federal Indian policy among the executive branch, the Congress, the federal courts, and various public and private constituencies, of whom tribes are only one. These interactions can be influenced through lobbying, public relations, and litigation.
. . .

[A second requirement is that the development of formal institutions must be designed not only] to work in the abstract; they have to fit the informal institutions—the culturally derived norms and preferred way of doing things—of the tribal community.

The odds against successful economic development in Indian Country are high. On the basis of our research, however, we believe it is possible for Indian tribes to reload the dice, and significantly improve their chances in the development gamble.

(Cornell & Kalt 1992)

The most publicized reservation economic projects have been gambling casinos. The growth of casinos began after the U.S. Supreme Court in 1987 declared that, as nations with at least limited sovereignty, tribes could operate gaming casinos and bingo parlors free from states' regulations. The conditions under which casinos could operate were set by Congress in the 1988 Indian Gaming Regulatory Act. Over the following two decades, a growing number of tribes established casinos. The total annual income of $212 million at 70 casinos nationwide in 1988 grew to $14.5 billion at 330 facilities by 2003 (Rimlinger & Salisbury 2003).

The gaming operations provided an estimated 400,000 jobs. One quarter of the jobs were held by Native Americans and three-quarters by non-Indians. Casino income, in addition to furnishing employment for Indians, enabled sponsoring tribes to supply improved public services to members—school buildings, better infrastructure (roads, police and fire protection, communications), and the support of cultural traditions, including religious facilities, arts, and ceremonies. Thus, native religions profited slightly from some casino income.

Seeking the Support of Federal Courts

Federal courts in the United States and Canada have played a highly significant role in strengthening Indians' ability to direct their own affairs. The role was that of interpreting treaties that had been signed with Indian bands over nearly four centuries.

A nineteenth-century U.S. court ruling set the stage for the fair treatment of Indians in later legal disputes by the jurists contending that a treaty "must be construed, not according to the technical meaning of its words to learned lawyers, but in the sense in which they would naturally be understood by the Indians." A 1990 Canadian court adopted the same position in a case concerning a 1760 treaty with a Huron [Subarctic] band by stating that "treaties and statutes relating to Indians should be liberally construed and uncertainties resolved in favour of the Indians" (Indian treaties 2007). That decision was in keeping with section 35 of Canada's 1982 Constitution which affirmed "existing Aboriginal and treaty rights."

Throughout the decades, court cases have pitted Euro–North Americans (individuals, corporations, or state and provincial governments) against Indians over the ownership and use of resources. Even when pressured by powerful Euro-North-American political groups, U.S. and Canadian high courts have generally been staunch defenders of the Indians' rights in treaties. As Robert Miller has explained,

The United States treaties with many Pacific Northwest tribes are good examples of the operation of treaties as contracts and of the analysis that the Supreme Court applies to interpreting Indian treaties. The treaties that affect salmon and Columbia River fishing rights were negotiated in the mid-1850s. At that time, neither Oregon nor Washington was a state; instead, they were United States territories. The tribal populations in this region, however, outnumbered white trappers and settlers by more than 4 to 1 and the tribes possessed aboriginal title to the area. These tribal nations had not been defeated in war by the U.S. nor had they ceded their lands to the federal government. The tribes were independent sovereigns controlling, ruling, and living on their own lands....

There is good reason for judicial deference to the Indian side of treaty making and to closely scrutinize the negotiations of many Indian treaties. The United States and its negotiators often selected who was to be the "chief" of the tribe they would negotiate with; often the United States negotiators bribed and unduly influenced tribal negotiators with gifts and/or alcohol; the United States often was represented by attorneys while the tribes were obviously not so represented, and, of course, the treaties were written in English...which the Indians did not speak or read....

The promises contained in these treaties are still the supreme law of the land, guarantees the federal government must keep to fulfill its promises to Indian people. As one Supreme Court Justice stated in regard Indian treaties: "Great Nations, like great men, should keep their word."

(Miller 2006)

CONCLUSION

From the early seventeenth century until the mid-twentieth century, Native North Americans were usually losers in their confrontations with foreign invaders. Not only did the Indians lose most of their land, they died by the millions from imported diseases and warfare with the newcomers. As the immigrant Europeans imposed their rule and culture on the indigenous peoples, tribal languages, customs, and religions deteriorated and often disappeared. But as the twentieth century advanced—and especially after World War II—Native North Americans launched increasingly successful campaigns to better their lot. At the outset of the twenty-first century, Indians and Inuits were in the best position for controlling their destinies and meeting their needs than they had been since they began interacting with foreign settlers and governments more than four centuries ago.

· 14 ·

Seeking Reparations

Among the efforts Native North Americans have mounted in recent decades to repair damage from the past has been the attempt to extract reparations from institutions that Indians hold responsible for oppressing and exploiting their peoples across the centuries. Principal types of damage for which North American Indians have demanded compensation include (a) loss or ruin of property, (b) physical harm to individuals, (c) psychological harm to individuals, and (d) the destruction of culture.

Recompense for property loss or damage can consist of the return of the lost property, monetary payment for the property, or the substitution of other property of equal value. Compensation for physical harm to persons can be money and/or medical treatment. Reparations for psychological damage can be money and/or psychotherapy. Compensation for damage to a person's cultural heritage can include money and/or cultural reconstruction.

The purpose of this chapter is to describe the progress of a present-day case involving members of First Nations in Canada demanding compensation for alleged physical, psychological, and cultural damage to aboriginal children and youths who had been enrolled in boarding schools operated by Christian sects and financed by the Canadian government. Although the chapter's chief focus is on the Canadian case, the discussion has implications for tribes in the United States as well, because many U.S. Indians attended similar boarding schools and suffered the same sorts of mistreatment as those claimed by the Canadian litigants.

THE CANADIAN CASE

The following account opens with a brief description of how the Canadian lawsuits originally developed. Then the discussion addresses four questions that have been of keen interest to observers of reparation efforts: (a) What are the sources of reparation funds? (b) To whom does the reparation money go? (c) How do the recipients of reparations use the money? (d) How, and to what extent, can reparation money repair damage from the past?

Later in the discussion, a version of conflict theory is adopted as the vantage point from which to analyze the Canadian case.

The Background of the Reparations Issue

Although Christian missionaries had made desultory attempts as far back as the seventeenth century to educate Canada's indigenous peoples in a European mode, serious efforts to establish permanent residential schools for the native population did not appear until the middle of the nineteenth century. After 1840, the relatively few residential schools conducted by Christian churches increased to 54 by 1898, to 74 by 1920, and to a high point of 81 by 1946. During the mid-1940s, Roman Catholic orders conducted 46 of the schools, Anglican churches 20, the United Church of Canada 12, and Presbyterians 3 (*History of Residential Schools* 2001).

Before the mid-1800s, the churches were the sole sponsors of residential schools. However, the Bagot Commission Report of 1842 and the Gradual Civilization Act of 1857 opened the way for the Canadian government to fund schools that would teach English language and other features of European culture, including religion, to Indians and Inuits. In 1892 the government established regulations for operating the schools and agreed to give between $110 and $145 per student per year in support of residential schools as well as $72 per student in support of day schools. The residential-schools program was widely recognized as "an integral part of a national policy intended to assimilate First Nations people into the dominant Euro-Canadian culture" (Coleman & Thorpe 2001).

However, over the years some church authorities became increasingly disenchanted with the residential-schools program, disenchantment stimulated after the 1950s by human-rights activism in the broader Canadian society. As a consequence, most church-operated residential schools were closed during the 1960s. Seven remained open through the 1980s. The last one closed in Saskatchewan in 1996 (International Center 2006). Several schools were transferred to indigenous bands that subsequently managed them. Between 1840 and the 1980s, an estimated 125,000 Indian children had attended a residential school.

By the latter 1990s, a number of events had converged to set off the spate of litigation that would cost the churches and the government endless distress and millions of dollars. One event was the publication in 1972 of a policy statement entitled *Indian Control of Indian Education,* issued by the National Indian Brotherhood, the coalition of tribes subsequently known as the

Assembly of First Nations (AFN). The statement was a position paper emphasizing principles of local control of education, parental responsibility, and a culturally based curriculum. "We want education to provide the setting in which
our children can develop the fundamental attitudes and values which have an
honored place in Indian tradition and culture" (National Indian Brotherhood
1973, 2).

Another event was the 1996 report of a Royal Commission on Aboriginal
Peoples that found fault with the traditional aims and operations of residential
church schools.

Additional precipitating incidents were the public apologies offered by leaders of two Christian denominations to indigenous peoples who had attended
residential schools in the past. In 1993, at the second Anglican National Native
Convocation, Archbishop Michael Peers told a congregation of Aboriginal
Canadians,

> I have felt shame and humiliation as I have heard of suffering inflicted by
> my people, and as I think of the part our church played in that suffering.
> I accept and I confess before God and you, our failures in the residential
> schools. We failed you. We failed God. I am sorry, more than I can say,
> that we were part of a system which took you and your children from
> home and family...that we tried to remake you in our image...that in
> our schools so many were abused, physically, sexually, culturally and
> emotionally.
>
> (Peers 1983)

Peers' expression of contrition was matched in 1998 by a similar confession
of remorse by Bill Phipps, moderator of the United Church.

> On behalf of The United Church of Canada, I apologize for the pain and
> suffering that our church's involvement in the Indian Residential School
> system has caused. We are aware of some of the damage that this cruel
> and ill-conceived system of assimilation has perpetrated on Canada's
> First Nations peoples. For this we are truly and most humbly sorry.
>
> To those individuals who were physically, sexually, and mentally
> abused as students of the Indian Residential Schools in which The
> United Church of Canada was involved, I offer you our most sincere
> apology. You did nothing wrong. You were and are the victims of evil acts
> that cannot under any circumstances be justified or excused.
>
> (Phipps 1998)

These episodes led to a similar apology on the part of the Canadian
government.

In January 1998, the Government of Canada issued a "Statement of Reconciliation" acknowledging the failure of the residential school policy,

and admitting that residential schools were designed to assimilate Aboriginals. The Government acknowledged that attitudes of racial and cultural superiority led to a suppression of Aboriginal cultures and values that resulted in the weakening of Aboriginal identity, languages, and spiritual practices. It released a new public policy on respecting Aboriginal people, called "Gathering Strength, Canada's Aboriginal Action Plan". The Minister of Indian Affairs also announced the establishment of a $350 million healing fund to help victims of the residential schools.

(International Center 2006)

The government's announcement was promptly followed by a host of lawsuits. In the closing months of 2000, new suits were filed at an estimated rate of 40 a month, threatening to swamp the legal system (*Indian Suits* 2000).

Operators of the residential schools were charged with several sorts of offenses against students—mainly sexual abuse, physical abuse, and the destruction of students' indigenous cultures. Plaintiffs contended that the treatment students suffered in residential schools caused them extreme emotional anguish that lingered on for years, often resulting in confused personal identities, alcoholism, and the inability to engage in productive activities.

How all suits might eventually fare in court continued to be unclear. The charge of sexual abuse was the offense most readily verified and most obviously covered by existing law. But the claim of physical abuse was more difficult, since what was regarded as suitable disciplinary methods changed over the years. Corporal punishment of disobedient pupils in the form of spanking, whipping, and caning that was acceptable in 1900 or 1940 was no longer tolerated in 2000. The most controversial of the charges was the accusation that the schools destroyed the pupils' indigenous cultures, an offense that some of the schools' critics called "cultural genocide." A government offer in 2001 to furnish monetary reparations to former Indian-school residents was limited to physical and sexual abuse. By 2007, whether the claim of cultural destruction would be admissible as a cause for legal action had still not been settled in the courts. Officially, the few early cases that were completed over the 1999–2002 period focused solely on sexual and physical abuse, ostensibly ruling out consideration of cultural damage. However, as illustrated in the three-year Port-Alberni-School trial, which ended in July 2001, the matter of cultural harm continually arose during plaintiffs' testimony and perhaps affected jurists' decisions. For example, the official account of the Alberni trial includes such statements of former school attendees as:

I lost my Native language and Aboriginal culture and was removed from my family roots. The enormity of the loss of both my culture and my connection with my family feels overwhelming and the effects irreversible. I lost my identity as a Native person. I live with a sense of not knowing who I am and how I should be in the world. I lost the friendship and support of my friends and community. I suffered a loss of self-esteem.

(Brenner 2001)

In the Alberni case, the British Columbia Supreme Court determined that six claimants had been sexually abused by a member of the school staff at some point in the now-distant past. The more serious the mistreatment that a claimant apparently endured, the larger the amount of money awarded by the court.

Among non-indigenous Canadians, there apparently have been no objections to settling the sexual-and-physical-abuse charges in court, because such offenses were already covered by existing laws, no matter who the plaintiffs and defendants might be. However, there was marked opposition to the idea that claims of cultural destruction were legitimate legal issues, worthy of court action. Out of approximately 1,200 suits filed by 2001 against the Anglicans, 50 involved charges of sexual or physical abuse. The remaining 1,150 appeared to concern cultural damage (Csillag 2001). Likewise, of 500 suits faced by the United Church, by far the largest number focused on issues of students' cultural loss and separation from their families.

In summary, although church-operated residential schools for native peoples no longer existed, the rash of lawsuits engaged the nation in moral, legal, social-policy, and political controversies that probably were never before envisioned by most citizens.

By 2003, the clogging of the courts with lawsuits prompted the government to announce an *out-of-court dispute resolution* program to compensate survivors of the residential schools, offering them therapeutic services for sexual and physical abuse and wrongful confinement. By July 2005, 147 claims had been settled, another 1,992 applications had been filed and were awaiting hearing and/or adjudication. By September 2005, 12,455 tort claims had been filed and numbers of class actions were pending (International Center 2006).

However, an assessment of the dispute-resolution program by the Indians' Assembly of First Nations deemed the program unsatisfactory, thereby leading to new negotiations among the concerned parties, who included the AFN, legal representatives of former students of Indian residential schools, representatives of the churches involved in running those schools, and government officials. In November 2005, Canada's Deputy Prime Minister, Anne McLellen, announced that the four parties had reached an *Agreement in Principle* aimed at "a fair, just, and lasting resolution of the legacy of Indian residential schools" (News Release 2005).

The Agreement in Principle proposes a common-experience payment to be paid to all former students of Indian residential schools, an improved alternative dispute resolution process for claims of serious abuse, as well as measures to support healing, commemorative activities, and further investigation and education concerning past policies and their continuing impact on Aboriginal Canadians and their families.

(News Release 2005)

This new plan—referred to as a *Political Agreement*—obligated the government to "work and consult with the AFN to ensure the acceptability of the comprehensive solution, to develop truth and reconciliation processes, commemoration and healing elements, and to look at improvements to the Alternative Dispute Resolution process" (International Center 2006). In June 2006, the plan assumed a financial form that provided

> At least $1.9 billion available for "common experience" payments to former students who lived at one of the schools. Payments will be $10,000 for the first school year (or part of a school year [in which a student was enrolled]) plus $3,000 for each school year (or part of a school year) after that.
>
> A process to allow those who suffered sexual or serious physical abuses, or other abuses that caused serious psychological effects, to get between $5,000 and $275,000 each.
>
> Money for programmes for former students and their families for healing, truth, reconciliation, and commemoration of the residential schools and the abuses suffered: $125 million for healing, $60 million to research, document, and preserve the experiences of the survivors, and $20 million for national and community commemorative projects.
>
> (Settlement agreement 2006)

Thus, by 2007 a specific plan had been agreed upon by the main participants in the Canadian residential-schools dispute. The next two steps would be to collect former students' reactions during a series of court hearings and to work out the details of implementing the plan.

Now, with this brief background of the Canadian case in mind, we turn to the first of the three questions posed earlier: What are the sources of reparation funds?

SOURCES OF REPARATION MONEY

The principal, if not exclusive, origin of the funds to pay for the lawsuits has been the Canadian national government and the four church denominations that operated residential schools. Theoretically, the schools' staff members who had committed the abuses, and thus became the primary defendants in the trials, would pay at least part of the money awarded to plaintiffs by the courts. However, that was hardly possible, because most of the abusers were dead and the few remaining ones were in no position to come up with the money. For example, the direct defendant in the Alberni-School case, Arthur Plint, was already in jail at the time the Alberni civil suit came to trial in 1998. Plint, at age 77, had been sentenced to an 11-year jail term in 1995 on criminal charges of having sexually abused boys when he was an Alberni-School dormitory supervisor between 1948 and 1968. Like Plint, other perpetrators of sexual or physical abuse were unable to pay the court's monetary awards to plaintiffs. Consequently, the costs of the civil suits fell on the government and the churches that were charged as codefendants in the cases.

Two issues of dispute between the government and the churches were (a) how high the ultimate cost would be and (b) what proportion of the cost each of the responsible parties should pay.

The Ultimate Cost

The most decisive factor affecting the ultimate expense of the lawsuits would be a court ruling on whether cultural loss was an acceptable basis for legal action. Because cultural loss and separation from home were cited as the grounds for reimbursement in the great majority of the 12,000 lawsuits, financial liability became enormously greater if such grounds were honored by the courts than if they were not. This issue became a point of contention, not only between the defendants and the litigants, but also within the government and within the church denominations themselves. In July 2001, David Iverson, chairman of the United Church's Residential School Steering Committee, said his church insisted that the issue of cultural damage be included in determining reparations for harm done to the nation's indigenous inhabitants. He denounced the proposal of Canada's Deputy Prime Minister Herb Gray that the government must "protect taxpayers' interests" in reaching an agreement with the churches. Iverson contended that

> comments like this not only smack of political opportunism but also fail to acknowledge that [the national government in] Ottawa has an obligation to challenge each and every taxpayer to recognise that we all bear responsibility for this horrific chapter in Canadian history [so that] financial compensation for the legacy of residential schools, is a collective responsibility that all Canadians must share.
>
> (B. C. Court Decision 2001)

Although the question of cultural damage as a reason for reparations had not been definitively tested in court, in the Alberni-School trial the suit of one plaintiff was rejected because it was founded solely on a charge of cultural destruction, with the rejection based on a government proposal that such a charge was inadmissible.

In the 2006 *Political Agreement,* cultural loss was not directly addressed, but perhaps the amount awarded each former student on the basis of the number of years the student had attended a residential school was meant to include compensation for cultural damage and time away from home.

Share of Responsibility

When Iverson was conducting the United Church's negotiations with the Canadian government, he not only sought to expand the realm of financial liability to include reparations for cultural damage, but also to place the greatest portion of the expense of litigation on the government. In the Alberni case, the judge's apportionment of liability for the Canadian government was 75 percent and for the United Church 25 percent. Commenting on the percentage split, Iverson said,

> The decision is a step in the right direction. The church has always maintained that the major control and decision-making with regard to the schools lay with the federal government. Historians who have studied the system have concurred with this view. The judgment recognizes that reality.
>
> (B. C. Court Decision 2001)

The churches' efforts to shift the major part of the cost onto the government was motivated by their awareness that the magnitude of the expense they could incur had critical implications for their future viability. The problem was complicated by the administrative-structure differences among the four denominations. Whereas the United and Presbyterian churches were governed under a central headquarters, the Catholics and Anglicans were organized by independent dioceses that had very limited financial resources. By 2001, several Anglican dioceses were on the verge of bankruptcy. The central Anglican office offered relief to the local bodies by assuming a large part of the expense. By July 2001, the Anglicans had spent over $5 million in legal costs, leaving certain dioceses with few or no funds, while the central office's assets had been reduced to $3 million (Csillag 2001).

In 2001, the four church bodies formed an ecumenical committee to bargain with the government, but negotiations broke down near the close of the year, with each denomination thereafter parleying separately with government officials. The government's offer in October 2001 to bear 70 percent of the cost of reparations for physical and sexual abuse was criticized by church representatives as too low a percentage. At the close of 2002, the government reached an agreement with the Anglican Church under which the church would contribute up to $25 million to a settlement fund and would pay up to 30 percent of claims, with the government paying the rest ("Anglican Liability" 2002). By that date, no such agreement had been reached between the government and Catholic, Presbyterian, and United Church representatives, so that the government's settlement with those former sponsors of residential schools remained undetermined.

In summary, the costs of the lawsuits were borne jointly by the Canadian government and the churches, with disputes continuing over what proportion each would pay and whether claims of cultural damage would be accepted as grounds for litigation.

WHERE THE MONEY WENT

In the court settlements prior to the 2006 *Political Agreement*, all of the money expended by the government and churches went to pay lawyers, to compensate plaintiffs, to pay court costs, and to finance out-of-court settlements.

Most, if not all, of the 12,000 plaintiffs' cases were handled by lawyers on a contingency basis, so that the lawyers' fees were taken out of whatever money was awarded to plaintiffs. Of the $5 million spent by the Anglicans by mid-2001, barely 1 percent had reached plaintiffs in the form of settlements. The remaining 99 percent went to lawyers, the courts, and public-relations efforts. However, some of the money may have been used for grants to indigenous communities for "healing and reconciliation programs" (*Litigation and Alternative* 2001).

The size of payments to plaintiffs is suggested by the amounts awarded to six claimants in the Alberni-School sexual-abuse case. The first litigant received $145,000, the second $125,000, the third $95,000, the fourth $20,000, the fifth $15,000, and the sixth $10,000 (Brenner, 2001). In the latter months of 2002, claims were being settled out of court at a rate of about one a day, with the awarded amounts all below $100,000 ("Canada, Anglicans reach claims deal" 2002).

CAN MONEY REPAIR THE PAST?

Because the lawsuits were supposedly filed to rectify damage from the past, it seems reasonable to assume that a large part of the money spent on the trials should have been used in efforts to repair that damage—that is, to undo the past as far as possible. There are at least two methods for attempting such repair.

One method consists of providing counseling or psychotherapy for individuals whose present lives are in shambles, seemingly as the result of mistreatment they received in residential schools. And indeed, a portion of the money awarded to one plaintiff in the Alberni case was designated for counseling intended to render the victim's life more tolerable. However, the court made no apparent provision for monitoring the expenditure of the funds to ensure that the money would actually be used for psychotherapy.

The other effort at repair would involve using the money to finance culture-recovery activities, including additional (a) research into indigenous groups' customary ways of life, (b) the publication of such research, (c) the teaching of native languages, history, religion, arts, and crafts, and (d) the distribution of stage, motion-picture, radio, and television productions that focus on native traditions.

However, if the way the money was distributed in the completed cases was an indication of how it would be used in the future, then little, if any, would ever go toward repairing past damage. Most of the billions that the lawsuits might eventually cost would apparently enrich non-indigenous lawyers, pay court costs, and provide some personal spending money for plaintiffs.

A Conflict-Theory Perspective on the Canadian Case

From the vantage point of conflict theory, we need to ask who have been the contending parties in the Canadian case, what have their goals been, and what rationales have they offered in support of their actions?

As a way of understanding human behavior, conflict theory analyzes social events in terms of a power struggle among contending groups that hope to have affairs turn out the way they prefer. Otomar J. Bartos and Paul Wehr's version of the theory can prove useful for interpreting the Canadian residential-schools case, with the analysis guided by those authors' proposal that, within a society,

> incompatible goals are likely to lead to conflict behavior if conflict groups are formed. Among the conditions that favor groups' formation is not only incompatible goals but also high group solidarity and the availability of resources.
>
> (Bartos & Wehr 2002, 11)

Applying this conception of conflict theory to the Canadian example can lead to the following portrayal of the (a) goals of the conflicting groups, (b) the groups' rationales in support of their goals, (c) group solidarity, and (d) group resources.

GOALS OF CONFLICTING GROUPS

The competitors in the Canadian case can be divided into three major groups, each composed of two or more subgroups. The major groups are (A) the litigants, (B) the churches that operated the schools, and (C) the Canadian government. Group A consisted of former residential-school students and the lawyers they employed to file lawsuits. Group B included the four church denominations. Group C consisted of the Canadian federal government and provincial courts in which the lawsuits were tried.

The most widely publicized conflicts were among the three major groups. The plaintiffs (former students and their lawyers) blamed the residential schools for the plaintiffs' unsatisfactory present-day life conditions, so the plaintiffs sought payments from the churches and government. On the other side, the churches and government wished to avoid as much blame as possible for the indigenous people's plight and to incur as little expense as possible in settling the lawsuits. The conflict between the government and churches was over how much blame each deserved and how much of the cost of satisfying claims each should bear.

Controversies arose not only between the major groups but within each group as well. For example, the church denominations disagreed with each other on matters of compensating former residential-school students, and the federal government disagreed with provincial courts over how much of the responsibility for monetary payments to litigants should be borne by the government ("Anglican Liability" 2002; *B.C. Court Decision* 2001).

RATIONALES

In support of their goals, groups typically base their arguments on principles of justice. A *principle of justice* is a statement intended to convince others—

and perhaps to convince oneself—that a given action is reasonable. Such principles reflect values with which other people may or may not agree. Typical principles are those of *retribution* (exacting payment from wrongdoers for harm they have caused), *prevention* (deterring wrongdoers from committing future offenses), and *compensation* (reimbursing people who have been wronged). Each of these principles figured prominently in the rationales offered by plaintiffs in the Canadian lawsuits. The principle of *forgiveness* (absolving a wrongdoer of continued blame) was also cited by some indigenous people—ones especially devoted to Christianity—who hoped to mend the rift between the churches and the litigants (Larmondin 2001).

Another principle of justice, adopted by the courts in the Canadian case, is one that bore crucial financial consequences for plaintiffs, church members, and the taxpaying public. It is the principle of *vicarious liability*, sometimes referred to as *no-fault liability*. Vicarious liability is a tenet of civil law that results in one person or organization being held legally responsible for a wrongful act committed by someone else. Thus, the doctrine of vicarious liability obligates people who had nothing to do with causing an offense to share in the punishment meted out for the offense. Vicarious liability was the principle applied by British Columbia Supreme Court Justice J. R. Dillon in the 1999 trial of *Mowatt versus Clarke et al.*, which concerned accusations of sexual abuse committed years earlier at the Anglicans' St. George's residential school near Lytton, British Columbia (Dillon 1999). The *et al.* cited as codefendants along with Clarke (the former residential school staff member who had allegedly perpetrated the abuse) were the Canadian government and the Anglican Church. Justice Dillon declared, "The plaintiff is entitled to damages against all defendants" (Dillon 1999). Therefore, any money awarded by the court to the plaintiff would be paid by Canadian taxpayers and by Anglicans who had contributed money to their church. This doctrine of vicarious liability was also adopted in the Alberni trial that involved the United Church of Canada as a codefendant.

Apparently many Canadians objected to basing indemnity in the lawsuits on vicarious liability, particularly because that doctrine conflicts with the principle of *just deserts*, which holds that people should bear the consequences that their own behavior deserves. According to just deserts, it is solely the wrongdoer who should suffer punishment for the misconduct. Therefore, critics of the Canadian court rulings argued that because taxpayers and church members played no part in abusing students, they should not be expected to help pay damages. Thus, if taxpayers believed the plaintiffs were simply seeking a modicum of deserved compensation for past harm, then taxpayers would more likely support the plaintiffs' efforts than if they thought the plaintiffs were trying to "get in on a good thing" by "ripping off" the government and churches for as much spending money as they could get. Opposition to the native claimants' efforts could then assume the form of church members being unwilling to contribute money to the churches and of taxpayers pressuring government officials to resist accepting cultural-damage as a cause for legal action.

In summary, which moral principles should be applied in settling the claims of former residential-school students was a key issue of dispute in the Canadian case.

GROUP SOLIDARITY

In conflict theory, the greater the solidarity of a group, the more effective the group's efforts will be in pursuing the group's goals. One measure of solidarity is the number of group members who support a given policy or action. Applying this criterion to the indigenous-litigants group in the Canadian example suggests that the litigants' solidarity increased with the passing years. In 2000, the number of lawsuits filed was estimated at 7,000. In 2001 the figure reached 8,500, and by the end of 2002 it exceeded 12,000 (Boyles 2002; Brown 2001; *Litigation* 2001).

There appear to be no available reports of how many members of each of the four churches accepted or rejected particular ways of dealing with residential-school students' claims. However, occasional published statements have suggested that church members were not all of the same mind about what the indigenous claimants' deserved. For example, Bill Phipps, moderator of the United Church, acknowledged that there were members in his congregations who objected to paying reparations to former residential-school students.

> We know that many within our Church will still not understand why each of us must bear the scar, the blame for this horrendous period in Canadian history. But the truth is, we are the bearers of many blessings from our ancestors, and therefore, we must also bear their burdens.
>
> (Phipps 1998)

In effect, weaknesses in the internal solidarity of church denominations and divisions of opinion within the government could be expected to hamper efforts of the contending groups to negotiate a satisfactory settlement of their differences.

GROUP RESOURCES

The resources of the litigants grew rapidly in the form of greater numbers of former students filing lawsuits and more lawyers planning to receive their fees from reparation payments to plaintiffs. This growth greatly increased the threat to the financial resources of the churches. For example, the Anglicans were extremely hard pressed to generate the $25 million that its representatives in late 2002 agreed to provide toward settling former students' claims. Catholic dioceses were in even greater financial jeopardy, since they were cited as the defendants in 72 percent of the 12,000 lawsuits ("Canada, Anglicans reach claims deal" 2002). As for the Canadian government's financial resources, they shrank as a result of the worldwide economic recession of the late 1990s. However, an economic upturn in the first decade of the twenty-first century placed the government in a better position to bear the billions in reparations agreed upon in 2006.

Conclusion

By the closing years of the twentieth century, the earlier attempt of churches and the Canadian government to assimilate the nation's indigenous peoples into European culture was generally viewed as a morally reprehensible and failed venture. In an effort to make amends, Church leaders and government officials not only apologized for forcing Indian and Inuit youths into boarding schools but also agreed to furnish reparations via the courts or by means of a *Political Agreement* that promised (a) payments of various amounts (not to exceed $24,000) to 85,000 who had attended the residential schools, (b) payments to former students who had been physically or sexually abused, (c) financial aid to native peoples' education, and (d) money for the Aboriginal Healing Foundation that sought to assuage former students' lingering distress. By 2007, it was still unclear as to how the provisions of the agreement would be implemented, including how the agreement would fare in the courts. But it was clear that little could be done to truly cure wounds from the past. History could not be erased. The indigenous peoples were obliged to live with that fact.

REPARATIONS IN THE UNITED STATES

In contrast to the Canadian case, claims of harm wrought by church-operated boarding schools have not figured prominently in Native Americans' reparation negotiations. This does not mean that the matter has been overlooked. Indeed, present-day Indian activists and their non-Indian supporters continue to level strong charges against boarding-school personnel and against apologists for residential schools. The following typifies such critics' views.

The Indian boarding school era encompassed one of the most blatant expressions of racism in the history of North America—the wholesale taking of Indian children away from their large extended families and tribal nations and thrusting them into a foreign world, where they were abruptly, systematically and totally deprived of their Indianness. In the boarding schools, children's names, languages and clothing were taken away and their sacred objects destroyed. Their hair was cut to cut them off from their people. They were beaten and worse—even jailed within the schools—for minor infractions of rules they didn't understand. They were made to eat lye soap for trying to communicate with each other in their own languages. Many children died in the boarding schools, of disease, malnutrition, and broken hearts. For those who survived, brainwashing did not come easily, but when it did come, it was total. For the most part, the adults who came back to their tribal nations looked and acted like white people. They were no longer able to communicate with their families, they were rude to their elders, they did not know their place in the world. Neither brown nor white, they could not fit in any-where, and many succumbed to alcohol or suicide. This legacy of hope-lessness and despair still persists today, as whole Indian communities struggle to come to terms with—to heal from—the devastation of the Indian boarding school era.

(Slapin 2005)

In addition to alerting readers to damage from the past, some U.S. Indians have developed a network of groups that promote the healing of survivors of residential schools. The network operates on the belief that "We can't change the past, but we can change the future. Once you know about the boarding school system and the impact that it had on Indian families, the steps to undoing the shameful and painful legacy become clear." For teachers in America's schools today, Porterfield (2001) suggested that those steps can include:

Keeping the boarding-school experience in mind when you interact with American Indian parents. Understand that the wariness some parents feel toward schools and teachers is legitimate. Respect those feelings.

Examining how the policy of assimilating Indians is still imbedded in public school curriculum today. Might your school still be killing the Indian to save the man? What isn't being taught about American Indians that needs to be taught?

Remedying the gaps in your own education. American Indian technologies and ideas were excluded from public school classrooms, just as they were in boarding schools. We can't teach information that we never learned.

Understanding that the indigenous knowledge of American Indians is relevant to modern life. Try living without corn, peppers, tomatoes, potatoes, rubber, quinine, the number zero, and Interstate highways that were built over Indian trails.

Spreading the word about the accomplishments of American Indians in the areas of science, technology, agriculture, medicine, and political science. Acknowledging the rich heritage of American Indian inventiveness can be as simple as mentioning one American Indian accomplishment each day.

Thus, increased attention has been focused in recent years on the plight of Indians who attended residential schools. But how likely will the Canadian kind of reparation payments to former boarding-school students be repeated in the United States? Perhaps an answer can be inferred from three sorts of evidence: (a) Indian leaders' published grievances, (b) Indians' current interests reflected in news media, and (c) the U.S. Government's attitude toward reparations.

Published Grievances

As noted in Chapter 12, during 1972 the *Trail of Broken Treaties* manifesto issued by a coalition of U.S. Indian groups consisted of 20 proposals for changes in the way the U.S. Government dealt with the nation's original peoples. None of the proposals spoke about reparations for harm suffered by Indians in residential schools. The only proposal—very late in the list—that even mentioned religion said nothing about residential schools.

[Proposal 18] Protection of Indians' Religious Freedom and Cultural Integrity. The U.S. Congress shall proclaim its insistence that the religious freedom and cultural integrity of Indian people shall be respected and protected throughout the United States, and provide that Indian religion and culture, even in regenerating or renaissance or developing stages, or when manifested in the personal character and treatment of one's own body, shall not be interfered with, disrespected, or denied.

(Trail of broken treaties 1972)

Therefore, rather than expressing serious concern for victims of maltreatment in residential schools, most published grievances have involved such matters as the restoration of past treaty agreements, the return of tribal Indian lands that had been confiscated, and the recognition of Indian nations' sovereignty and rights of self-governance.

Interests Reflected in News Media

The most widely publicized news about Indians' recent interests and activities have concerned gambling casinos on Indian lands. The nature of those news articles is reflected in such headlines as:

Look Who's Cashing in at Indian Casinos

Casinos Now Called "The New Buffalo"

States Have no Power to Regulate Casinos

The Economics of Indian Casinos

Lobbyists Confirm Fees from Casinos

In frequency, a very distant second to Indian gaming news are stories about lawsuits filed by Indians to recover tribal lands, as in the dispute over former Shoshone lands in Nevada (Western Shoshone 2006).

If the amount of recent attention in the news media can be accepted as an accurate measure of tribal leaders' concerns, then it is apparent that leaders are far more interested in money-making ventures and achieving self-governance than in efforts to heal the emotional wounds of former residential-school students. And with the passing of time, the urgency of compensating former students continues to diminish as former students grow old and die off.

The U.S. Government's Attitude

The U.S. government has been reluctant to provide Indians reparations of any kind. A measure of self-governance has been awarded in partial recognition of tribal sovereignty, but the government has not supported moves to restore Indian lands to tribal control. And there appear to be few, if any, serious attempts to win government support for recompensing former students of boarding schools. Nor do scholars—who propose government policies that would provide justice for Indians—appear to include reparations for residential-school damage. For example, William Bradford (a Chiricahua Apache), in his *Beyond Reparations: An American Indian Theory of Justice* (2004), limits his attention to land restoration and Indians' legal rights. Consequently, advocates of government-funded efforts to alleviate the distress of Indians who attended residential schools seem to hold little hope that the measures adopted in Canada will be forthcoming in the United States. For example, Andrea Smith (a Cherokee) notes that

> While some Canadian churches have launched reconciliation programs, U.S. churches have been largely silent. Natives of this country have also been less aggressive in pursuing lawsuits. Attorney Tonya Gonnella-Frichner (Onondaga) says that the combination of statutes of limitations, lack of documentation, and the conservative makeup of the current U.S. Supreme Court make lawsuits a difficult and risky strategy.
>
> (Smith 2006)

CONCLUSION

The attempt in Canada to have former boarding-school students compensated for physical and psychological abuse has resulted in millions of dollars being awarded by the churches and the Canadian government to applicants for reparations, either by dint of court suits or a 2006 reconciliation agreement. And more millions will be spent in the future as the reconciliation plan moves ahead. However, most of the money in court settlements has not ended up in the hands of former boarding school students. Instead, it has gone to lawyers and courts. But the reconciliation agreement is supposed to ensure that most of the funds in the future will go directly to former students and to programs of cultural renewal.

In the United States, there appears little likelihood that reparations will be awarded to boarding-school attendees. Publicity about Indian tribes' wealth from their gambling casinos, coupled with churches' reluctance to admit and pay for harm wrought by their denominations' schools, suggests that U.S. Indians have little chance of being recompensed for physical or cultural damage to former students.

·

· 15 ·

·

The Path Ahead

In this final chapter, I speculate briefly about what might be expected in the future for (a) the religious faith adopted by North Americans of indigenous ancestry and (b) the discovery of more knowledge about Indian religions, past and present. The chapter's closing paragraphs suggest four kinds of unfinished business that confront present-day Indians and Inuits.

RELIGIOUS FAITH AMONG INDIGENOUS PEOPLES

As noted in Chapter 1, after the number of North Americans designated as Indians or Inuits had dropped significantly over the years 1600 to 1900, the number dramatically rose throughout the twentieth century. As a result, by the early twenty-first century more than 5 million people in the United States and Canada laid claim to Native-North-American heritage. There were several reasons for this recent growth, including improved medical care among Indians, higher birthrates, lower death rates, and a growing popularity of a person's having indigenous North-American ancestry. Such popularity was a relatively new phenomenon, because within the dominant Euro-North-American culture of past centuries, stigma had been attached to an individual's being all or part Indian. But at an increasing pace over the past half-century, the notion of having Indian stock in one's genetic background has acquired a romantic appeal. It allows North Americans who claim mixed European/Indian heritage to feel that they "really belong in this country" and are not undeserving, Indian-abusing interlopers.

Consequently, today there are more potential adherents of Indian religions than at any time since the early days of colonialism. So the question can be asked: How many of these claimants to Indian heritage can be expected to adopt indigenous religious practices in the future, and what might be the nature of those practices?

I imagine that only a small minority of the entire group will hold fast to a pure version of indigenous belief and practice, mainly because Christian missionaries over past decades were so successful at proselytizing among Indian tribes.

I believe the largest portion of the native population will adopt a mixture of Christianity and Indian tradition. A typical pattern of this blended religious faith may include such Christian components as:

- Honoring the Christian God as the supreme power over the universe, perhaps with such Indian names as Manitou, Glooskap, or Wakan Tanka also applied to that power,
- Viewing the Bible as the word of God,
- Accepting Jesus as the Savior who, in his death, washed away believers' sins,
- Praying to the Christian God, and
- Attending church on Sunday—or at least on Christmas, Easter, and such occasions as christenings, weddings, and funerals.

This syncretic belief system may incorporate such traditional Indian components as:

- Attending powwows to enjoy traditional dances, songs, and costumes,
- Revering nature—homelands, animal life, and sacred sites—
- Seeking visions so as to discover one's guardian spirit, which often will be an admired animal,
- Adopting an Indian name in addition to a Christian name,
- Studying Indian history,
- Wearing Native-North-American amulets and garments, and
- Collecting and/or producing Indian art and regalia.

The continuing rise in the number of people claiming mixed Indian/Euro-North-American lineage has apparently resulted not only from interethnic matings over past centuries but also from the increasingly multicultural composition of North America's population that has resulted in greater public acceptance of people of different ethnic backgrounds living together.

Finally, I estimate that a very small percentage of self-designated Indians will adopt worldviews that have little or nothing in common with either Indian religions or Christianity—such worldviews as atheism, agnosticism, secular humanism, Buddhism, Islam, Hinduism, and Wicca.

EXPANDING KNOWLEDGE OF INDIAN RELIGIONS

One of the great regrets of people who are interested in Indian lifeways is that most of the knowledge about how tribes lived in the past has been lost. Without written language, native peoples were obliged to depend on oral accounts for passing tribal lore from one generation to the next. When chroniclers of Indian life died, their knowledge died with them unless they had told their stories to the young. And that process of retelling tales and recounting events was always susceptible to revisions, deletions, and embellishments of the original versions of the accounts. Lacking written records, Indians were also confined to direct demonstration for teaching physical skills—carving sacred pipes, constructing a longhouse, hunting beaver and buffalo, fishing for salmon, weaving baskets, and more. As a result of those confining conditions, today's information about Indians' lives in the past is no more than a slim segment of the great bulk of knowledge about the many hundreds of bands that inhabited the continent, many of which are now entirely gone and forgotten.

Early Times

It is true that today there are some written descriptions of indigenous cultures from the colonial era and later. Nearly all of those accounts were composed by European and Euro-North-American white men, most of whom were adventurers, missionaries, government agents, and academics. The French explorer Samuel de Champlain (1567–1535) wrote about Indians of the Great Lakes region in his *Des Sauvages* (1603) and *Voyages* (1613, 1619) in which he included prayers and a Catholic catechism in two Indian languages. John Eliot (1604–1690), a Puritan missionary in the Massachusetts Bay Colony, helped preserve the Algonquin language by translating the Bible into Algonquin; his was the first Bible printed in America. Henry Rowe Schoolcraft (1793–1864) was a geographer, geologist, and ethnologist who served as a U.S. Government agent in Indian territories, where he recorded information about native lore and published traditional Indian stories in *Algic Researches* (1839). George Catlin (1796–1882) traveled among Indian bands to paint scenes of tribal life and write about his adventures; he compiled a collection of more than 500 paintings of Indians in their daily activities. Franz Boas (1858–1942)—often referred to as the Father of American Anthropology—wrote extensively about life among the Kwakiutl [Northwest Coast]; his collection of myths and folklore was published in 1910 as *Kwakiutl Tales*.

Therefore, by the twentieth century, readers had available a body of information about Indian life that was virtually all the product of Euro–North Americans who had reported their observations of, and interviews with, Indians and Inuits. Also available were sensationalized magazine articles and books for public consumption that portrayed the typical Native–North American as an unlettered, uncivilized, devious, pagan savage warrior who spoke no more than a few broken-English phrases.

Recent Times

During the twentieth century, and particularly after World War II, serious research into Indian life grew at a fast pace so that by the opening of the twenty-first century the prospects for future advances in knowledge of Indian religions were very bright, indeed. As described in Chapter 13, a host of pathways have opened for investigating Indian life, past and present. Particularly important are programs in colleges and universities that focus on the discovery and propagation of knowledge about Indian cultures, including Indian religions. Indigenous peoples themselves have become heavily engaged in the resurrection, preservation, and expansion of such knowledge, so that academic Indian studies are no longer the nearly exclusive province of Euro–North Americans.

Today the rapidly growing body of knowledge in this field is available in seven main forms: (a) printed documents, (b) elderly Indians' memories, (c) viewable artifacts, (d) photographic records, (e) audio recordings, (f) Internet web sites, and (g) scholarly conference presentations. The following paragraphs illustrate examples of resources about Indian religions over the decade 1997–2007.

PRINTED DOCUMENTS

Print materials include books, academic journals, newspapers, and academic theses.

Here is a brief sample of recent books:

Joel Martin's *Native American Religion* (1999)

Jack Schultz's *The Seminole Baptist Churches of Oklahoma: Maintaining a Traditional Community* (1999)

Flesche and Bailey's *The Osage and the Invisible World* (1999)

Kavasch and Baar's *American Indian Healing Arts: Herbs, Rituals, and Remedies for Every Season of Life* (1999)

John Major's *American Indian Religions* (2001)

Joel Martin's *The Land Looks After Us: A History of Native American Religion* (2001)

Kidwell, Noley, and Tinker's *A Native American Theology* (2001)

Gregory Ellis Smoak's *Ghost Dances and Identity: Prophetic Religion and American Indian Ethnogenesis in the Nineteenth Century Indians' memories* (2006)

Khyati Joshi's *New Roots in America's Sacred Ground: Religion, Race, and Ethnicity in Indian America* (2006)

The following are a few examples of academic journals that publish studies bearing on Indian religions:

Akwekon Journal

American Anthropologist

American Ethnologist

American Indian Culture and Research Journal

American Indian Quarterly

Canadian Journal of Native Education

Journal of Indigenous Nations Studies

Journal of American Indian Education

Native Studies Review

Plains Anthropologist

Tribal College Journal

Wicaso Sa Review

Theses and dissertations that students have completed during their pursuit of a master's degree or doctorate can be discovered either by finding their university or college library's web page on the Internet or searching the *Dissertation Abstracts Online* web site that contains précis of more than 2 million studies conducted by graduate students around the world. The following list illustrates a range of dissertation topics from the realm of Indian education.

They Called It Prairie Light: Oral Histories from Chilocco Indian Agricultural Boarding School

Cultural Genocide in the Classroom: A History of the Federal Boarding School Movement in American Indian Education

Indian and Pioneer Oral Narratives: An Examination of their Divergence from the Standard Written History of North Dakota

Constructing Meaning Through Multiple Sign Systems: Literacy in the Lives of Lakota and Dakota Young Adolescents

Presbyterians and "The People": A History of Presbyterian Missions and Ministries to the Navajos

Tribal Identity and Cultural Triumph in Traditional Anishinabe Indian Elders

Effects of U.S. Policy from 1819–1934 on American Indian Identity

Together as Family: Mètis Children's Response to Evangelical Protestants at the Macinaw Mission 1823–1837

Newspaper and magazine articles relating to Indian religions can be found on the publications' Internet web sites by entering descriptor words in a search engine—Google, Ask, Yahoo, or the like. If the desired articles were published in the somewhat distant past, then it may be necessary to enter the site's archives.

A newspaper dedicated entirely to information relating to Native Americans is *Indian Country Today* that maintains an Internet web site with daily news and opinion articles.

ELDERLY INDIANS' MEMORIES

As a contribution to the world's knowledge of Indian religions, researchers can profit from interviewing Native North Americans who grew up in traditional Indian or Inuit communities. Researchers can be of various kinds— academicians, students preparing theses or dissertations, college students writing term papers, or junior and senior high school students doing research projects. One of the best-known studies of this type was reported in two books— *The Sacred Pipe* by Joseph Epes Brown (1997) and *Black Elk Speaks* by John Neihardt. Black Elk (1863–1950) was an Oglala Lakota Sioux holy man who, at around age twelve, fought against Custer's army in the 1876 Battle of the Little Big Horn and later was injured during the massacre at Wounded Knee in 1890. The two books contain Black Elk's life story as he told it to Brown and Neihardt.

VIEWABLE ARTIFACTS

Indian artifacts of interest include traditional living quarters and ceremonial sites (teepees, hogans, kivas, longhouses, sweat lodges), garments (shirts, headdresses, moccasins), armaments (bows, arrows, spears, tomahawks, shields), amulets, kachina dolls, medicine bundles, musical instruments (drums, rattles, flutes, whistles), pottery, baskets, and more.

Artifacts also include skeletal remains from Indian burial grounds—remains which for decades have been of keen interest to paleontologists. In recent times, Indians have objected to people collecting the bones of their ancestors for scientific analysis or for the amusement of museum and curio-shop visitors. As Indian political activists have publicized their complaints and pressured legislators, they have managed to change the way excavations for highways and buildings are treated. It is now common practice for contractors to employ an anthropologist or tribal representative to monitor the handling of artifacts unearthed during the construction of roadways, buildings, or recreation facilities.

Artifacts relating to religion can be divided into two classes: (a) traditional objects from the past and (b) variants of artifacts that are created in the present. Items from the past are typically found in museums and individual collections. Ones from the present are creations of Indian artisans who produce traditional crafts for collectors or the tourist trade, often devising novel variants in style and material that advance Indian art into the future.

PHOTOGRAPHIC AND AUDIO RECORDINGS

The invention of photography in the nineteenth century and of motion pictures in the twentieth century provided invaluable tools for compiling Amerindian history. In the twenty-first century, progress in technology has equipped academicians, journalists, and students to produce high-quality still photographs and videos of Indians, sacred places, and the sights and sounds of religious celebrations. Audio-recording devices enable researchers to collect Indian music and interviews under even difficult environmental conditions.

INTERNET WEB SITES

The Internet's World Wide Web, with its billions of sites, has become the twenty-first century's most valuable resource for information about North-American Indian religions and Christianity. Not only do millions of web sites offer information about religions and their interactions that can be displayed instantaneously, but anyone can contribute to that body of knowledge by posting new information on web sites or, in the role of a blogger, by offering assessments of what others have posted.

SCHOLARLY CONFERENCES

Native-North-American organizations and university study centers conduct periodic conferences which feature individual speakers and panel discussions that often focus on topics related to Indian religions. The papers presented on those occasions are sometimes published as conference proceedings. The following are examples of conference presentations.

Oral Literature, Dance, and Music Among the Osage

Cultural Sovereignty and the Collective Future of Indian Nations

Tribal Wisdom and Science

Diabetes and Native American Ceremonies

An Indigenous Theory of Interreligious Dialogue

Living in Two Worlds: Balancing Success and Tradition

Skull Wars: Bridging the Chasm Between Archaeology and Indian Country

American Indian Children's Literature: Identifying and Celebrating the Good

In summary, by the early twenty-first century, the amount of knowledge about North-American Indian religions and about their interactions with Christian culture was growing at an accelerating rate, thus suggesting a very bright future for the study of such matters.

UNFINISHED BUSINESS

Chapter 13 and this final chapter have painted a cheerful picture of Indians' advances in recent decades, advances that might be accepted as harbingers of an optimistic future. Tribes and bands enjoy recently won freedom to manage their own affairs. Indians' religions have been accorded official honorable status, equal to that of Christianity. Legislators have passed laws protecting Indians' rights, sacred sites, and artifacts. Populations of Native Peoples, after centuries of decline, have been increasing in size. And in Canada the government and Christian churches have been compensating thousands of Indians who were exploited while attending Euro-Canadian boarding schools.

However, despite such marks of progress, all is not well with indigenous peoples. They continue to suffer more problems than do most non-Indians in health, personal identity, social status, and financial welfare.

Health

Heart disease is the number one cause of death for American Indians, with the incidence of heart disease among them double that of non-Indians. Furthermore, a higher percentage of Indians than Euro–North Americans die from tuberculosis, diabetes mellitus, alcoholism, pneumonia, influenza, suicide, and homicide.

Personal Identity

Many Indians have suffered from a confused sense of self. Their puzzlement over knowing "who I really am" has been fostered by Native North Americans being caught between two conflicting cultures—Indian and Euro-Christian. The result for many has been unhappiness, suppressed initiative, fear, shame, and guilt. And as John Reyner (2002) proposed, "Children need to develop the 'inner direction' to develop a strong identity to withstand the onslaughts of a negative hedonistic and materialistic popular TV and Hollywood culture, fears engendered by terrorism, and the pervasive culture of poverty that envelops many reservations and inner cities."

One way Indians may solve their identity problem has been proposed by a Choctaw/Cherokee from Oklahoma who had experienced a very painful adolescence, because he could not decide who he really was while growing up in a white suburban community.

> I could easily pass as white. [Finally, after years of research and soul searching] I have come to believe that faces such as mine, which I once questioned whether it could be called Indian at all, are the faces of tomorrow's Native America. As I was recently told in the course of sorting out my story, it is what is in my heart, not what pumps through it, that makes me Indian.
>
> (Benge 2004)

Social Status

Across the centuries, Native North Americans as a group have been held in low esteem by the majority of Euro-Americans and Euro-Canadians. Marge Bruchac (2001) recalled that

> Sadly, American Indian people in New England in the 20th century, especially northeastern Algonkian Indians, were faced by social issues that made it dangerous to identify [themselves] as Indian. Having persisted despite centuries of colonial settlement, plagues, wars, and prejudice, they often faced the scorn and disapproval of white neighbors who expected all Indians to have been removed to reservations. White schoolchildren grew up hearing tales of frontier savagery, "last of the Indians," and similar motifs, and failed to recognize there were Native people still in New England. In the 1910s, the federal government, the Ku Klux Klan, white vigilantes, and eugenicists were actively hunting Indians in order to forcibly remove them to reservations, or, if that failed, to sterilize or kill them.

Over the past century—and particularly during recent decades—the social position of Native North Americans has remarkably improved. However, in numerous communities Indians as a group are still not accorded the same level of respect given people of some other ethnic backgrounds.

Financial Welfare

The U.S. Census Bureau's economic survey for 2003–2005 reported that 24 percent of the nation's Indians and Inuits were living in poverty, a proportion essentially the same as among Blacks and Hispanics but higher than that of Whites. Amerindians' median annual family income of $33,132 was substantially below the national average of $44,389. More than 29 percent of Native Peoples had no health insurance. Although 60 percent of Native American families owned homes, that was 10 percent lower than among the general population. Seventy-six percent of Indians age 25 and older had a high school diploma, but only 14 percent had a college degree. Native entrepreneurship continued to rise, bringing the total to 206,000 Native-owned businesses, but the great majority of Indian firms (181,000) had only one employee—the proprietor (Fogarty 2005).

The financial status and social welfare of Indians in Canada have been similar to conditions in the United States. By 2006, 25 percent of First Nations children lived in poverty, compared to 17 percent of Canadian children in general. Nearly 12 percent of people in First Nations communities had to boil their drinking water, and 6 percent of the homes were without sewage services. Life expectancy for Indian men was 7.4 years shorter than for Euro-Canadians and for Indian women 5.2 years shorter ("Aboriginal peoples" 2006).

Thus, it is apparent that North America's Native Peoples as a group are not as well equipped financially as their non-Indian neighbors for living above the poverty level and enjoying the amenities of modern life.

So it was that Native–North Americans had made remarkable progress toward equity in rights and welfare by 2007. However, the struggle was not over. There was still the need to improve life conditions in the years ahead.

Coda

From the vantage point of this book's focus, a closing question can be posed as a challenge for the future: How might Indian religions—or a blending of Indian and Christian cultures—contribute toward solving native peoples' problems of health, personal identity, social status, and financial welfare?

REFERENCES

"Aboriginal Peoples, 10 Years after the Royal Commission." 2006, November 21. *CBC News.* Available online: http://www.cbc.ca/news/background/aboriginals/status-report2006.html.

"About Young Life." 2006. *Young Life.* Available online: http://www.younglife.org/pages/AboutYL.htm.

Adams, D.W. 1995. *Education for extinction: American Indians and the Boarding School Experience 1875–1928.* Lawrence: University Press of Kansas.

Adherents. 2005. *Largest Religious Groups in the United States of America.* Available online: http://www.adherents.com/rel_USA.html.

Age of Enlightenment. 2005. *Wikipedia.* Available online: http://en.wikipedia.org/wiki/The_Enlightenment.

All about Saints. 2006. Available online: http://www.catholic.org/saints/faq.php.

American Indian Movement. 1872, October. *Trail of Broken Treaties.* Available online: http://www.aimovement.org/ggc/trailofbrokentreaties.html.

American Indian Studies. 2007. *Arizona State University.* Available online: http://www.asu.edu/clas/americanindian/POS.htm.

American Knights of the Ku Klux Klan. 2006. *Our Creed.* Available online: www.texasamericanknights.org.

"Anglican Liability in Abuse Cases Capped at $25M." 2002, November 19. *Toronto Star.* Available online: www.thestar.com/.

ANLC Mission and Goal. 2007. *Alaskan Native Language Center.* Available online: http://www.uaf.edu/anlc/mission.html.

Anti-Defamation League. 2005. *Ku Klux Klan.* Available online: http://www.adl.org/learn/ext_us/KKK.asp?xpicked=4&item=18.

Assembly of First Nations—The story. 2007. *Assembly of First Nations.* Available online: http://www.afn.ca/article.asp?id=59.

Atlas of Canada. 2001. *Religious Affiliation 2001.* Available online: http://atlas.nrcan.gc.ca/site/english/maps/peopleandsociety/religion/religion01/1.

Augustine, N. 2000, August 9. "Grandfather was a Knowing Christian." *Toronto Star.*

Backgrounder Historic Indian Treaties. 2001, July 5. *Indian Northern Affairs Canada.* Available online: http://www.thepeoplespaths.net/history/INAC010705Historic Treaties.htm.

Baird, W.D. 1985. "Cyrus Byington and the Presbyterian Choctaw Mission." In *Churchmen and the Western Indians 1820–1920.* Edited by C.A. Milner II & F.A. O'Niel. Norman: University of Oklahoma Press.

Bajema, S. 2005, December. "Are you Sure?" *Christian Reformed Churches of Australia.* Available online: http://crca.org.au/content/view/226/ 47/.

Baker, D. 2007. "What Happened to the Indians in the Years after Lewis and Clark?" *PBS: Living History—The Journey of the Corps of Discovery.* Available online: http://www.pbs.org/lewisandclark/living/idx_9.html.

Bartos, O.J., and P. Wehr. 2002. *Using conflict theory.* New York: Cambridge University Press.

B.C. Court Decision Rules Canada 75% Liable in Alberni Indian Residential School Trial. 2001, July 10. Available online: United Church of Canada web site: http://www.united-church.ca/aboriginal/schools/archive.

Benge, G. 2004, May 3. "Determining American Indian Identity." *Gannett News Service.* Available online: http://www.spokesmanreview.com/ breaking/story.asp?ID=2119.

Berlandier, J.L. 1969. *The Indians of Texas in 1830.* Washington, DC: Smithsonian Institution Press.

Big Turnip, A. 1975. In *Plains Indian Mythology* Edited by A. Marriott and C.K. Rachlin. New York: Thomas Y. Crowell, pp. 72–74.

Blair, E.H., ed. 1911. *The Indian Tribes of the Upper Mississippi and the Great Lakes.* Cleveland, Ohio: Arthur H. Clark Company.

Blowsnake, S. 1912. "Bluehorn's Nephews." *Hotcake Encyclopedia.* Available online: http://www.hotcakencyclopedia.com/ho.BluehornsNephews.html.

Boyles, J. 2002. *Residential Schools Update #15.* Available online: www.anglican.ca/ministry/rs/.

Bradford, W.D. 2004. *Beyond Reparations: An American Indian Theory of Justice.* Available online: law.bepress.com/cgi/viewcontent.cgi?article =1411&context=expresso.

Brenner, D. 2001, July 10. *Blackwater v. Plint et al.* Vancouver: Supreme Court of British Columbia.

Brians, P. 2000, May 18. *The Enlightenment.* Available online: http://www.wsu.edu:8080/~brians/hum_303/enlightenment.html.

Brief History of the YMCA Movement. 2006. Available online: http://www.ymca.net/about_the_ymca/history_of_the_ymca.html.

Bright, W. 1993. *A Coyote Reader.* Berkeley: University of California Press.

Brown, D.L. 2001, December 9. "Suing Church and State." *Washington Post,* p. A18..

Brown, S. 1953. "The Spirituals." *Phylon.* Available online: http://www.english.uiuc.edu/maps/poets/a_f/brown/folkexpression.htm.

Bruchac, M. 2001, May. "Musings on Northeastern Indian Identity." *Ne-Do-Ba.* Available online: http://www.avcnet.org/ne-do-ba/menu_who.shtml.

Buffalo-Bison. 2007. *Lewis and Clark Trail.* Available online: http://lewisandclarktrail.com/buffalo.htm.

Can you tell me...What is a Christian? 2007. Available online: http://www.abideinchrist.com/messages/canutel.html.

"Canada, Anglicans Reach Claims Deal." 2002, November 20. *United Press International.* Online. Available: www.upi.com.

Canadian Charter of Rights and Freedoms. 1982. Available online: http://laws.justice.gc.ca/en/Charter/index.html.

Certificate in First Nations studies research. 2007. *Simon Fraser University.* Available online: http://www.sfu.ca/fns/fnrc.htm.

Chalice. 2006. *New Advent: The Catholic Encyclopedia.* Available online: http://www.newadvent.org/cathen/03561a.htm.

Cherokee bear legend. 2007. *Native American Tales.* Available online: http://www.fortunecity.com/skyscraper/temple/1451/na/page16.html.

Christian Research Institute. 1994, August 31. "Baptist Battle over Freemasonry Erupts Anew." *News Watch.* Available online: http://www.iclnet.org/pub/resources/text/cri/cri-jrnl/web/crj0162a.html.

Christian symbols. 2006. *Gocek.* Available online: http://www.gocek.org/christiansymbols/?search=cross.

CIE mission statement. 2007. *Center for Indian Education.* Available online: http://coe.asu.edu/cie/index.html.

Clark Historical Library. 2007. *Federal Education Policy & Off-Reservation Schools 1870–1933.* Available online: http://clarke.cmich.edu/indian/treatyeducation.htm#gnp.

Clements, W. M. 1986. *Native American Folklore in Nineteenth-Century Periodicals.* Athens, Ohio: Swallow Press.

Coleman, V., and B. Thorpe. 2001, March 22. "Researcher Defends Residential Schools." *The National Post.* Available online: http://www.uccan.org/airs/010323.htm (accessed June 4, 2001).

Colonial Period Indian Land Cessions in the American Southeast. 2006. Available online: http://www.tngenweb.org/cessions/colonial.html# george3.

Constitution of Canada. 2007. Available online: http://en.wikipedia.org/wiki/Constitution_of_Canada.

Cornell, S., and J. P. Kalt. 1992. "Reloading the Dice: Economic Development on American Indian Reservations." In *What can tribes do? Strategies and Institutions in American Indian Economic Development.* Edited by S. Cornell & J. P. Galt. Los Angeles: American Indian Studies Center, University of California.

"Coyote Kills a Giant." 2007. *Indigenous Peoples' Literature.* Available online: http://www.indians.org/welker/coyokill.htm.

Cremation Association of North America. 2006. *Cremation Statistics.* Available online: http://www.cremationassociation.org/html/statistics.html.

Cremin, L. A. 1970. *American Education: The Colonial Experience.* New York: Harper & Row.

———. 1980. *American Education: The National Experience.* New York: Harper & Row.

Crisp, T. 2006. *Extracts from Dream Dictionary.* Available online: http://www.dreamhawk.com/d-amer.htm.

Csillag, Ron. 2001, July 10. "Anglicans Face Bankruptcy over Residential Schools." *Toronto Star.* Available online: http://www.Thestar.com/.

Curtis, E. S. 1912. *Hopi Rain (Snake) Dance.* Available online: http://www.curtis-collection.com/hopiraindance.html.

Darwin, C. 1859. *The Origin of Species.* London: John Murray.

Dawes Act. 1887, February 8. *Archives of the West—1887–1914.* Available online: http://www.pbs.org/weta/thewest/resources/archives/eight/dawes.htm.

Deer Dance of the Navahos. 2007. Available online: http://www.inquiry.net/outdoor/native/dance/deer_navahos.htm.

DeJong, D. H. 1993. *Promises of the Past: A History of Indian Education in the United States.* Golden, Colorado: North American Press.

Department of Indian Affairs and Northern Development. 2000, March. *Treaties with Aboriginal People in Canada.* Available online: http://www.ainc-inac.gc.ca/pr/info/is30_e.html.

Devil's Tower National Monument. 2006. Available online: http://www.geocities.com/wyfriendsworld/tower.html.

Dieterle, R. L. 2006. "How the Hills and Valleys Were Formed." *Hotcake Encyclopedia.* Available online: http://hotcakencyclopedia.com/ho.HowHills%26 ValleysFormed.html.

———. 2007. "Hare, or Rabbit (Wacdijigéga)." *Hotcake Encyclopedia.* Available online: http://hotcakencyclopedia.com/ho.Hare.html.

Dillon, J. R. 1999. *Mowatt v. Clarke et al.* Vancouver: Supreme Court of British Columbia.

Divine Comedy. 2006. *Wikipedia.* Available online: http://en.wikipedia.org/wiki/The_Divine_Comedy.

Eagle Dance of Tesuque. 2007. Available online: http://www.inquiry.net/outdoor/native/dance/eagle_tesuque.htm.

Eastman, C. A. 1986. "The Sioux Mythology." In *Native American Folklore in Nineteenth-Century Periodicals.* Edited by W. M. Clements. Athens, Ohio: Swallow Press, pp. 211–216.

Eggan, F. 1950. *Social Organization of the Western Pueblos.* Chicago: The University of Chicago Press.

Encomienda. 2006. *Wikipedia.* Available online: http://en.wikipedia.org/wiki/Encomienda.

Erowid, N. C., and K. Trout. 2002, May. "A Brief Summary of the Relationship between Peyote Use and the Ghost Dance." *The Vaults of Erowid.* Available online: http://www.erowid.org/plants/peyote/peyote_history1.shtml.

Figueira, A., L. Williams, and O. Trujillo. 1998, March. *Selected Dissertations in Indian Education 1987–1997.* Available online: http://coe.asu.edu/cie/diss.html#lan.

Fire leggings. 2007. *Children's Native American Stories.* Available online: http://www.apples4theteacher.com/native-american/short-stories/fire-leggings.html.

Fire race. 2007. *Indigenous Peoples' Literature.* Available online: http://www.indians.org/welker/coyofire.htm.

Fixico, D. L. 1986. *Termination and Relocation: Federal Indian Policy—1945–1960.* Albuquerque: University of New Mexico Press.

FNRS activities. 2007. *First Nations Child and Family Caring Society of Canada.* Available online: http://www.fncfcs.com/projects/FNRS.html.

Fogarty, M. 2005, November 23. "Census Bureau Releases Annual Snapshot." *Indian Country Today.* Available online: http://www.indiancountry.com/content.cfm?id=1096411975.

Garman, G. 1998. *Indian Treaties and Affairs.* Available online: http://www.sunnetworks.net/~ggarman/indian.html.

Giese, P. 1997, April 5. *U.S. Federally Non-Recognized Indian Tribes.* Available online: http://www.kstrom.net/isk/maps/tribesnonrec.html.

Gorham, N. 1823. *Senekas.* Available online: http://digital.library.okstate.edu/kappler/Vol2/treaties/sen1033.htm.

Gray, S. E. 1995. Methodist Indian Day Schools and Indian Communities in Northern Manitoba, 1890–1925. *Manitoba History* (30). Available online: http://www.mhs.mb.ca/docs/mb_history/30/methodistdayschools.shtml.

Greaves, T. 2002. *Endangered Peoples of North America.* Westport, Connecticut: Greenwood.

Greene, J. 1962. *Epitaphs to Remember.* Chambersburg, Pennsylvania: Allen C. Hood.

Hanson, H. 2006. "Albany Mounds, Old Indian Burial Site is Preserved for the Future." *Community Courier.* Available online: http://www.communitycourier.com/albany_mounds.htm.

Harrold, H.L. 1996. Death. In *Encyclopedia of North American Indians.* Edited by F.E. Hoxie. Boston: Houghton Mifflin.

Hassrick, R.B. 1964. *The Sioux.* Norman: University of Oklahoma Press.

Heaven. 2006. *New Advent: Catholic Encyclopedia.* Available online: http://www.newadvent.org/cathen/07170a.htm.

Heizer, R.F. 1978. *California.* Washington, DC: Smithsonian Institution.

Henderson, B. 1996. *The Indian Act, R.S.C. 1985, c. I-5 (Annotated).* Available online: http://www.bloorstreet.com/200block/sindact.htm.

"Historical Legend of Spokane." 2007. *Native American Myths and Legends.* Available online: http://www.wellpinit.wednet.edu/sal-myths/myth.php?iinclude=../sal-myths/si_myt04.txt.

History of Canada. 2006. Available online: http://www.cybernorth.com/canada/history.html.

History of Residential Schools in Canada. 2001. Available online: http:www.sd83.bc.ca/stu/9801/mrl3his.html (accessed January 6, 2002).

Hoebel, E.A. 1960. *The Cheyennes.* New York: Hold, Rinehart, & Win-ston.

Holy Bible—King James Authorized Version. 1611. New York: American Bible Society, 1929 edition.

Howard, L.H. 1996. "Death." In *Encyclopedia of North American Indians.* Edited by F.E. Hoxie. Boston: Houghton Mifflin.

Howell, L.M. 1662/2006. *The Book of Common Prayer.* Available online: http://www.eskimo.com/~lhowell/bcp1662/index.html.

Hummon, S.F. 2006. *American Indians, Missions, and the United Church of Christ.* Available online: http://www.ucc.org/aboutus/histories/chap1.htm.

"Hungry Fox and the Boastful Suitor." 2007. *Native American Tales.* Available online: http://www.fortunecity.com/skyscraper/temple/1451/na/page21.html.

Immigration to the United States. 2006. *Wikipedia.* Available online: http://en.wikipedia.org/wiki/Immigration_to_the_United_States#American_Dream.

Indian education. 2007. *Encyclopedia of American History.* Available online: http://www.answers.com/topic/education-indian.

Indian Face Painting. 2007. Available online: http://www.craftsinindia.com/arts-and-crafts/indian-face-painting.html.

Indian Perceptions of Crater Lake. 2006. Available online: http://www.nps.gov/archive/crla/hrs/hrs4.htm.

Indian Residential Schools in Canada—Historical Chronology. 2007. Available online: http://www.irsr-rqpi.gc.ca/english/historical_events.html.

Indian treaties. 2007. *Canadian Encyclopedia.* Available online: http://www.thecanadianencyclopedia.com/index.cfm?PgNm=TCE&Params=A1ARTA0003983.

Inipi lodge. 2006. Available online: http://www.bluecloud.org/inipilodge.html.

International Center for Transitional Justice. 2006, May. *Canada.* Available online: http://www.ictj.org/en/where/region2/513.html.

Introduction to the Navajo Culture. 1997. Available online: http://waltonfeed.com/peoples/navajo/culture.html.

Inuit. 2001. *Aboriginal People of Canada.* Available online: http://www12.statcan.ca/english/census01/products/analytic/companion/abor/groups3.cfm.

Irwin L. 1996. "Dreams." In *Encyclopedia of North American Indians.* Edited by F.E. Hoxie. Boston: Houghton Mifflin.

Jackson, A. 1830, December 8. *First Annual Message to Congress.* Available online: http://www.mtholyoke.edu/acad/intrel/andrew.htm.

Kapplar, C.J. 1904. *Indian Affairs: Laws and Treaties—Vol. II.* Washington, DC: Government Printing Office. Available online: http://digital.library.okstate.edu/kappler/Vol2/Toc.htm.

Keepers of the Sacred Tradition of Pipemakers. 2006. Available online: http://www.pipekeepers.org/.

Kehoe, A.B. 1981. *North American Indians.* Englewood Cliffs, New Jersey: Prentice-Hall.

Knights of Columbus—History. (2006). Available online: http://www.kofc.org/about/history/index.cfm.

Lake-Thom, B. 1997. *Spirits of the Earth.* New York: Plume.

Lapham, I.A. 1855. *The Antiquities of Wisconsin.* Washington, DC: Smithsonian Institution Press.

Larmondin, L. 2001, July 10. *Native Bishop Forgives Church, Primate.* Available online: http://www.anglican.ca/.

Lawton, I. 2006, November 26. "If the Earth Billed us for its Services, Could we Pay?" *Christ Community Church.* Available online: http://www.christ-community.net/sermonarchive.htm.

Leland, C.G. 1884. *The Algonquin Legends of New England.* Boston: Houghton, Mifflin.

"Lewis and Clark Expedition Discoveries and Tribes Encountered." 2007. *National Geographic.* Available online: http://www.nationalgeographic.com/lewisandclark/resources_discoveries_animal.html.

Lewis and Clark Reenactment Protests. 2004. *Dakota-Lakota-Nakota Human Rights Advocacy Coalition.* Available online: http://www.dlncoalition.org/dln_coalition/2004landc.htm.

Litigation and Alternative Dispute Resolution (ADR). (2001). Anglican Church of Canada web site. Available online: http://anglican.ca/ministry/rs/litigation/html.

Loeb, E.M. 1933. The Eastern Kkuksu cult. *University of California Publications in American Archaeology and Ethnology* 33(2), 139–232.

Lopez, B.H. 1977. *Giving Birth to Thunder, Sleeping with his Daughter.* Kansas City, Missouri: Sheed Andrews & McMeel.

Lord, L. 1997, August 18. "How Many People Were Here before Columbus?" *U.S. News.* Available online: http://www.usna.edu/Users/ history/kolp/HH345/PRE1492.HTM.

Lowie, R.H. 1954. *Indians of the Plains.* New York: McGraw Hill.

Mails, T.E. 2002. *Mystic Warriors of the Plains.* New York: Marlowe.

Mann, C.C. 2005. *1491.* New York: Knopf.

Marriott, A., and C.K. Rachlin. 1975. *Plains Indian Mythology.* New York: Thomas Y. Crowell.

Masonic Foundations of the United States, The. 2006. Available online: http://www.watch.pair.com/mason.html.

McGregor, E. 2006. *Registered Indian Population by Sex and Residence, 2005.* Ottawa: Department of Indian Affairs and Northern Development.

Means, R. 1998. "Russell Means on the Siege at Wounded Knee." *Rolling Stones in the '70s.* New York: Little, Brown. Available online: http://www.russellmeans.com/read_02.html.

Membership Categories. 2007. *Minnesota American Indian Bar Association.* Available online: http://www.maiba.org/about.html.

"Mexico's History: The Colonial Era." 2006. *Mexperience*. Available online: http://www.mexperience.com/history/colonial.htm.

Miller, B.W. 1988. *Chumash*. Los Osos, California: Sand River Press.

Miller, P. 1963. *The New England Mind: The Seventeenth Century*. Cambridge, Massachusetts: Harvard University Press.

Miller, R.J. 2006. "Indian Treaties as Sovereign Contracts." *Flash Point Magazine*. Available online: http://www.flashpointmag.com/indtreat.htm.

Milner, C.A., and F.A. O'Neal. 1985. *Churchmen and the Western Indians*. Norman: University of Oklahoma Press.

Mission statement. 2007. *NALSA University of Main School of Law*. Available online: http://www.geocities.com/CapitolHill/9118/nalsa2.html.

Mizrach, S. 2007. *Thunderbird and Trickster*. Available online: http://www.fiu.edu/~mizrachs/thunderbird-and-trickster.html.

Morison, S.E. 1936. *The Puritan Pronaos*. New York: New York University Press.

Museum of the Native American Resource Center. 2006. *Indians Rout the Klan*. Available online: http://www.uncp.edu/nativemuseum/collections/victory/index.htm.

Musinsky, G. 1997. Manitou. *Encyclopedia Mythica*. Available online: http://www.pantheon.org/articles/m/manitou.html.

Nagel, J. 1996. *American Indian Ethnic Renewal*. New York: Oxford University Press.

National Indian Brotherhood. 1973, July. "Indian Control of Indian Education." *The Indian News* 16(3).

Native American Church. 1994. *Encyclopaedia Britannica* (vol. 8, pp. 553–554). Chicago: Encyclopaedia Britannica.

Native American Designs. 2007. Available online: http://www.buckagram.com/buck/symbols/.

Native American Flute. 2007. Available online: http://www.nativelanguages.org/composition/native-american-flute.html.

Native Traditions in Boston. 2006. Available online: http://www.fas.harvard.edu/~pluralsm/98wrb/nati_itr.htm.

Nerburn, K., ed. 1999. *The Wisdom of Native Americans*. Novato, California: New World Library.

New England Primer: Or an Easy and Pleasant Guide to the Art of Reading. 1836. Boston: Massachusetts Sabbath School Society.

Newcomb, W.W. Jr. 1961. *The Indians of Texas*. Austin: University of Texas Press.

Newhouse, E. 1999, August 22. "Bane of the Blackfeet." *Great Falls Tribune*. Available online: http://www.gannett.com/go/difference/greatfalls/pages/part8/blackfeet.html

News release. 2005, November 23. Indian Residential Schools Resolution Canada. Available online: www.irsr-rqpi.gc.ca/english/news_23_11_05.html.

Nichols, K.L. 2002. *Native American Trickster Tales*. Available online: http://members.cox.net/academia/coyote.html.

Niehardt, J.G. 1932/1979. *Black Elk Speaks*. Lincoln: University of Nebraska Press.

O'Bryan, A. 1956. *The Diné: Origin Myths of the Navajo Indians*. Available online: http://www.sacred-texts.com/nam/nav/omni/index.htm.

Ogunwole, S.U. 2002, February. *The American Indian and Alaska Native population, 2000*. Washington, DC: U.S. Census Bureau.

"Origin of the Winds." 2007. *Native American Tales*. Available online: http://www.fortunecity.com/skyscraper/temple/1451/na/page32.html.

Our History. 2007. *National Congress of American Indians*. Available online: http://www.ncai.org/About.8.0.html.

Our Mission Statement. 2007. *Whitman American Indian Association*. Available online: http://www.whitman.edu/aia/.

Paine, T. 1776. *Common Sense*. Philadelphia: W. & T. Bradford. Available online: http://www.bartleby.com/133/.

———. 1794. *Age of Reason*. Available online: http://libertyonline.hypermall.com/Paine/AOR-Frame.html.

Palfrey, D.H. 1998a. *The Economy of New Spain*. Available online: http://www.mexconnect.com/mex_/travel/dpalfrey/dpcolonial3.html.

———. 1998b. *The Settlement of New Spain*. Available online: http://www.mexconnect.com/mex_/travel/dpalfrey/dpcolonial1.html.

Peace Policy. 2007. Available online: http://www.accessgenealogy.com/native/sioux/story/peace_policy.htm.

Peers, M. 1993. *Anglican Leader Apologizes to Aboriginal People for Residential Schools*. Available online: http://www.anglican.ca/Residental-Schools/reports/pr8.htm.

Philips, K. 1999, September. *YWCA History Highlights*. Available online: http://www.geocities.com/ywca_berkeley/historyhl.html.

Phipps, B. 1998. *To Former Students of United Church Indian Residential Schools, and to their Families and Communities*. Available online: http://www.united-church.ca/beliefs/policies/1998/a623.

Population History of American Indigenous Peoples. 2006. *Wikipedia*. Available online: http://en.wikipedia.org/wiki/Population_history_ of_American_ indigenous_peoples.

Porterfield, K.M. 2001. Brain Washing and Boarding Schools. In *The Encyclopedia of American Indian Contributions to the World*. Edited by E.D. Keoke and K.M. Porterfield. Available online: http://www.kporterfield.com/aicttw/articles/boardingschool.html.

———. 2006. *Timeline of European Disease Epidemics among American Indians*. Available online: http://www.kporterfield.com/aicttw/articles/disease.html.

Powers, W.K. 1973. *Indians of the Northern Plains*. New York: G.P. Putnam Sons.

Prucha, F.P. 1979. *The Churches and the Indian Schools 1888–1912*. Lincoln: University of Nebraska Press.

Public Broadcasting System. 2001. *Francisco Vázquez de Coronado*. Available online: http://www.pbs.org/weta/thewest/people/a_c/coronado.htm.

———. 2007. *Indian Removal 1814–1838*. Available online: http://www.pbs.org/wgbh/aia/part4/4p2959.html.

Public law 103-344. 1994. *American Religious Freedom Act Amendments of 1994*. Available online: http://www.nativeamericanchurch.com/law.Html.

Rain Dance of Zuñi. 2007. Available online: http://www.inquiry.net/outdoor/native/dance/rain_zuni.htm.

Rain Song. 2007. *First People*. Available online: http://www.firstpeople.us/FP-Html-Legends/RainSong-Sia.html.

Reader's Digest. 1978. *America's Fascinating Indian Heritage*. Pleasantville, New York: Reader's Digest.

Rice, J. 1998. *Before the Great Spirit*. Albuquerque: University of New Mexico Press.

Rimlinger, C., and I. Salisbury. 2003, September 3. "Indian Casinos Generate $14.5B a Year." *Patriot Ledger*. Available online: http://www.southofboston.net/specialreports/casinos/pages/casinos-folo1-090303.html.

Robinson, B.A. 2003, April 18. The Federal Equal Access Act. *Religious Tolerance*. Available online: http://www.religioustolerance.org/equ_acce.htm.

———. 2005.*The History of the Christian Fish Symbol*. Available online: http://www.religioustolerance.org/chr_symb.htm.

————. 2006. *The Afterlife*. Available online: http://www.religioustolerance.org/heav_-hel2.htm.

Records of the American Home Missionary Society. 2001. Available online: http://www.wheaton.edu/bgc/archives/GUIDES/142.htm#3.

Reff, D.T., 1987, September. "The Introduction of Smallpox in the Greater Southwest." *American Anthropologist* 89(3), 704–708.

Relics in Christianity. 2006. *Religion Facts*. Available online: http://www.religionfacts.com/christianity/things/relics.htm#locations.

Rice, J. 1998. *Before the Great Spirit*. Albuquerque, New Mexico: University of New Mexico Press.

Richter, D.K. 2001. *Facing East from Indian Country*. Cambridge, Massachusetts: Harvard University Press.

San Francisco Peak. 2006. Available online: http://www.lapahie.com/San_Francisco_Peak.cfm.

Schugurensky, Daniel, and Renee Shilling. 1972. *National Indian Brotherhood Releases Indian Control of Indian Education*. Available online: http://www.wier.ca/~daniel_-schugurens/assignment1/1972nib.html.

Selma, G. 2007. *Face Paint Practices*. Available online: http://www.manataka.org/page1901.html.

Settlement Agreement. 2006, June 25. Available online: http://www.turtleisland.org/discussion/viewtopic.php?p=7132#7132.

Shawnee Indian Mission. 2006. Available online: http://www.kshs.org/places/shawnee/history.htm.

Shelton, L.R., Sr. 2006. "How and Why God Saved a Baptist Preacher." *Radio Missions*. Available online: http://www.radiomissions.org/sermons/bapprch.html.

Shifflett, C. 1998. *Virtual Jamestown*. Available online: http://www.virtualjamestown.org/rlaws.html.

Shrines of Italy: Journeys of Devotion to Holy Sites. 2006. Available online: http://www.mycatholictradition.com/italy.html.

Slapin, B. 2005. Review of Cooper's "Indian School: Teaching the White Man's Way." *Oyate*. Available online: http://www.oyate.org/books-to-avoid/indianSchool.html.

Smith, A. 2006. *Soul Wound: The Legacy of Native American Schools*. Available online: http://www.amnestyusa.org/amnestynow/soulwound.html.

Smith, M. 1954, August. Shamanism in the Shaker Religion of Northwest America. *Man*, Nos. 180–181, pp. 119–120.

South Shore YMCA. 2006. *What is YMCA Character Development?* Available online: http://www.ssymca.org/camps/Character_Development.asp.

Sparks, K., ed. 2006. *Encyclopaedia Britannica Book of the Year*. Chicago: Encyclopaedia Britannica, pp. 541, 644, 723.

Spurgeon, C.H. 2006. *Enduring to the End*. Available online: http://www.abideinchrist.com/spurgeon/spurgeon-enduringtotheend.html.

Stine, M. 2006. How to Live in a Rotten World. *Spreading Light*. Available online. http://www.spreadinglight.com/sermons/m-r/rotten.html.

Szasz, M.C. 1999. *Education and the American Indian*. Albuquerque: University of New Mexico Press.

————. 2006. Education. *Encyclopedia of North American Indians*. Available online: http://college.hmco.com/history/readerscomp/naind/html/na_010900_education.htm.

Terrell, J.U. 1979. *The Arrow and the Cross*. Santa Barbara, California: Capra Press.

Thomas, R.M. 2007. *God in the Classroom—Religion and America's Public Schools*. Westport, Connecticut: Praeger.

Trail of Broken Treaties. 2007. *Answers.com.* Available online: http://www.answers.com/topic/trail-of-broken-treaties.

Trail of Broken Treaties: 20-Point Position Paper. 1972, October 1972. Available online: http://www.aimovement.org/ggc/trailofbrokentreaties.html.

Trivedi, T.P. 2004, April 9. "Jesus' Shroud? Recent Findings Renew Authenticity Debate." *National Geographic Channel.* Available online: http://news.nationalgeographic.com/news/2004/04/0409_040409_TVJesusshroud.html.

U.S. Geological Survey. 2006. *Klamath Indian Legend.* Available online: http://craterlake.wr.usgs.gov/history.html.

Utley, R.M. 1984. *The Indian Frontier of the American West 1846–1890.* Albuquerque: University of New Mexico Press.

Vaughn, A.T. 1972. *The Puritan Tradition in America, 1620–1730.* Columbia, South Carolina: University of South Carolina.

Waldman, C. 1999. *Encyclopedia of Native American Tribes.* New York: Checkmark Books.

Warren, B.S.W. 2007. "The Legend of the Cherokee Rose."*Native American Culture.* Available online: http://www.powersource.com/cocinc/articles/rose.htm.

Waters, F. 1950. *Masked Gods: Navaho and Pueblo Ceremonialism.* Albuquerque: University of New Mexico Press.

Western Shoshone File Lawsuit against Mining Companies. 2006, January 10. Available online: http://www.minesandcommunities.org/Action/press 871.htm.

What is Free Masonry? 2006. Available online: http://www.gotquestions.org/audio/Free-Masonry.mp3.

White, C.P. 2006. "Coyote and the Another One." *Indigenous Peoples' Literature.* Available online: http://www.indians.org/welker/coyoanon.htm.

White Face, C. 2006. *Sacred Bear Butte Threatened.* Available online: http://www.manataka.org/page278.html.

White Plume, D. 2005, September 18. Should we Celebrate Lewis and Clark or Stop Them? *Stop Lewis and Clark Reenactments.* Available online: http://www.stoplewisandclark.org/protest_bad_river.html.

"Wicked and Righteous Comingled." 2007. *Gospel Chapel Ministries.* Available online: http://www.gospelchapel.com/Devotion/Genesis/28.htm.

Wilkins, D.E. 2002. *American Indian Politics and the American Political System.* Lanham, Maryland: Rowman & Littlefield.

Williams, M.L. 1956. *Schoolcraft's Indian Legends.* East Lansing: Michigan State University Press.

"Wolf Clan and the Salmon." 2007. *Stories from Alaska and the Northwest Coast.* Available online: http://www.northwest-art.com/NorthwestArt/WebPages/StoriesWolfClanandSalmon.htm.

Wright, R.E. 2001, June 2. Spanish missions. *Handbook of Texas.* Available online: http://www.tsha.utexas.edu/handbook/online/articles/SS/its2.html.

"Yaqui and Mayo Indian Easter Ceremonies." 2007. *Rim Journal.* Available online: http://www.rimjournal.com/arizyson/easter.htm.

Yazzie, E.P. 2002. *Missionaries and American Indian Languages.* Available online: www.eric.ed.gov/ERICWebPortal/recordDetail?accno=ED482043.

YMCA Membership Tops 20 Million across America. 2005. Available online: http://www.ymca.net/about_the_ymca/press_release_20050926_ymca_membership.html.

Youth for Christ. 2006. Available online: http://www.yfc.net/Brix?pageID=6552.

Yupanqui, T. 1998. *The Iroquois Dream Experience and Spirituality.* Available online: http://www.webwinds.com/yupanqui/iroquoisdreams.htm.

INDEX

ABOUT THE AUTHOR

R. Murray Thomas is Professor Emeritus, University of California, Santa Barbara, and the author of several books, including *Religion in Schools— Controversies Around the World* (Praeger, 2006), *Violence in America's Schools* (Praeger, 2006), and *God in the Classroom* (Praeger, 2007).